# The Theatrical Event

STUDIES IN

THEATRE HISTORY

*&* CULTURE

Edited by Thomas Postlewait

# The Theatrical Event

Dynamics of
Performance and
Perception

*Willmar Sauter*

UNIVERSITY OF IOWA PRESS

Ψ Iowa City

University of Iowa Press,
Iowa City 52242
Copyright © 2000 by the
University of Iowa Press
All rights reserved
Printed in the United States of America
Design by Richard Hendel
http://www.uiowa.edu/~uipress

Printed on acid-free paper

Library of Congress
Cataloging-in-Publication Data
Sauter, Willmar, 1947–
    The theatrical event: dynamics of
performance and perception / by Willmar Sauter.
        p.        cm.—(Studies in theatre history and
culture)
    Includes bibliographical references and index.
ISBN 0-87745-731-X (cloth)
    1. Theater—Europe—History—
20th century.   2. Theater—Political
aspects—Europe—History—
20th century.   3. European drama—20th
century—History and criticism.   4. Theater
audiences—Europe—History—20th
century.   I. Title.   II. Series.
PN2570.S29   2000
792'.094—dc21                                00-034366

00 01 02 03 04 C 5 4 3 2 1

The following essays have previously appeared:
"Approaching the Theatrical Event: The
Influence of Semiotics and Hermeneutics in
European Theatre Studies," *Theatre Research
International*, 22/1 (1997): 3–14. Also published
in Chinese in *Theatre Arts* 2 (1998, Special
Issue: Foreign Theatre, Shanghai Theatre
Academy): 68–77. "Theatre or Performance
or Untitled Event(s)? Some Comments on the
Conceptualization of Our Studies,"
*GESTOS, Teoría y Práctica del Teatro Hispánico*,
12/24 (November 1997): 27–40. Also published
in Swedish in *Visslingar och rop* 7 (1999): 74–95.
"Theatrical Events Revisited: Playing Culture
and the Historiography of Early Nordic
Theatre," *Nordic Theatre Studies* 12 (1999): 8–22.
"Reflections on *Miss Julie* 1992: Sensualism and
Memory," *Nordic Theatre Studies* 6/1–2 (1993):
3–10. "Museum-Stage—The Frames Move into
the Exhibition Hall," in *Interarts Poetics: Essays
on the Interrelation of the Arts and Media*, ed.
U.-B. Lagerroth et al. (Amsterdam and Atlanta:
Rodopi, 1997), pp. 85–92. "Theatre Talks,
Or: How to Find Out What the Spectators
Think," *Nordic Theatre Studies* 2–3 (1990): 9–22.
"Strindberg's Words versus the Actor's Actions:
The Success of the Actresses of the Intimate
Theatre in Stockholm (1907–1910)," in
*Strindberg—The Moscow Papers*, ed. Michael
Robinson (Stockholm: Strindbergssällskapet,
1998), pp. 187–192. A more extensive version
was published in German under the title "Die
verschrumpfte Avantgarde," in *Theater Avantgarde:
Wahrnehmung—Körper—Sprache*, ed. Erika
Fischer-Lichte (Tübingen and Basel: A. Francke
Verlag, 1995), pp. 291–323; and in Polish in *Mity
teatru XX wieku: od Stanilawskiego do Kantora*,
ed. Dorota Heliasz (Krakow: Nakladem
Uniwersytetu Jagiellonskiego, 1995), pp. 53–66.
"Beyond the Director's Images: Reviews and
Views on Robert Lepage's Production of
*A Dream Play* at the Royal Dramatic Theatre,"
in *Lepage*, ed. Joe Donohoe (Chicago: University
of Chicago Press, 2000).

FOR DAVID

# Contents

# Acknowledgments

When the well-known Shakespeare scholar John Crawford Adams was promoted to the position of dean at Hofstra University in the 1940s, one of his colleagues deeply deplored his move: he assumed that it meant the end of Adams' scholarly ambitions. Many academics have experienced similar situations when "advancing" to department head, dean, or president of an academic association. During the last decade I have shared this experience to a certain degree, but my friends and colleagues have continued to invite me to conferences and to ask for a contribution to a colloquium or an essay for a journal. One feels flattered by such invitations and agrees too easily to present a paper or to write an article. Usually the deadline for such assignments seems far away at the moment when one is asked. Sooner or later the paper has to be ready, no matter what administrative tasks have to be accomplished in the meantime. This is how most of the chapters in this book have been written.

I want to thank all those who have helped me to keep my scholarly ambitions awake. The first four chapters are the result of invitations from Mitsuya Mori (Tokyo), Domingo Adame (Puebla), Josette Féral (Montreal), and Pirkko Koski (Helsinki). Some chapters in the second part of the book were initiated by Ulla-Britta Lagerroth (Lund), Henri Schoenmakers (Amsterdam), Michael Robinson (Norwich), Freddie Rokem (Tel Aviv), Joseph Gómez (Barcelona), and Kela Kvam (Copenhagen). To all of them I extend my gratitude for demanding and promoting my contributions on various occasions.

Attending conferences and international board meetings also meant being absent from my department in Stockholm. My colleagues and students have continuously supported my extensive traveling not only through tacit consent, but also through active discussions. I am very grateful for their support, and I especially want to thank my patient colleagues Sven Åke Heed, Lena Hammergren, Karin Helander, and Tiina Rosenberg. They represent a wonderful team with a wide international orientation.

My scattered writings would never have been brought together into a readable book without the determination and collaboration of Thomas Postlewait, the editor of this series. He encouraged me from the first time I mentioned the possibility of conceiving of the theatrical event as an overall perspective for the articles I had been writing during the last ten years. He read all the material very carefully, suggested additions and omissions, corrected my English, and asked uncomfortable questions. His instructions were easy to follow, but he had to spend many more hours reviewing the chapters for this book. Once more, his commentaries were an indispensable guideline for the completion of the texts. I feel privileged to have been supported by such an eminent and caring scholar, advisor, and friend. I owe him a lot more gratitude than I can express.

Holly Carver of the University of Iowa Press has been a most understanding director of this project. I am particularly grateful for her willingness to accept the sometimes unorthodox illustrations I suggested for this book. I also want to thank Charlotte Wright and her colleagues for their editorial work, especially Kathy Lewis, who has made the best possible English out of the text I handed over to her.

My thanks go to the Drottningholm Theatre Museum, the Strindberg Museum, and the Modern Museum in Stockholm for contributing illustrative material. I also want to thank all the editors of journals and anthologies who have allowed me to reprint and rework previously published material.

# The
# Theatrical
# Event

# New Beginnings

How many attempts to define theatre have we heard of? Peter Brook's man in an empty space, Eric Bentley's A impersonating B while C looks on, Ingmar Bergman's trinity of play, actor, and spectator, Aristotle's six parts of the drama, Tadeusz Kowzan's thirteen semiotic elements of the performance, etc. There is not one definition which has not been seriously questioned or argued against. The idea of theatre is too wide to be caught in a single statement or in some recipe-like descriptions, especially when theatre is thought of as a phenomenon including all kinds of performative activities.

This book does not provide yet another definition or description of the essence of theatre; instead, it attempts to present a theoretical reconsideration of the object of theatre and performance studies. To see theatre as an event means to emphasize a certain view of theatre rather than inventing a new theory which supposedly would solve all the problems. On the contrary, I hope that this book demonstrates that the concept of the theatrical event raises more questions than I am able to answer.

## Theorizing Experiences

The term "theatrical event" appears in various writings, but I have devoted a number of years to elaborating the theatrical event as a concept. The first engagements go back to the 1970s, when I was studying the impact of European politics on the Swedish theatre of the 1930s and 1940s. There was of course a political theatre in Sweden during these politically difficult decades, but it was not immediately recognizable as such; it did not have a particular look; it did not have a special name; there were no obvious dividing lines between political and nonpolitical performances. What then made certain theatre performances political?

The two aspects which I found to be of specific importance in discussing not only political theatre in history but also theatre in other forms and during other periods were the nature of communication, what is going on between stage and auditorium, and the circumstances in which this communication is taking place. These aspects could be called the (internal) communication and the (external) context. Putting internal and external in parentheses is meant to indicate that such a distinction is very relative: the communication is heavily dependent on the context, and the context itself interacts with theatrical communication on many levels. It is important to underline from the very beginning that the context is equally decisive for the players and for the observers, who both live in the same artistic and social framework of conditions. In my survey of the political theatre during the time when Nazism and fascism dominated political systems in Europe, it became obvious that the message of a performance relied as much on the audience's way of perceiving and interpreting the stage actions as on the images and political references presented on the stage itself. An artificially enlarged nose was no longer funny, but became the stereotyped stigma of a persecuted "race." And it was not simply a question of the length of the nose—a number of circumstances influenced its significance. I examine these particular circumstances in chapter 13. Here it is important to keep in mind that in the theatre the "message" is not something which is neatly packed and distributed to an anonymous consumer; instead, the meaning of a performance is created by the performers and the spectators together, in a joint act of understanding.

What I learned from historical research was confirmed during the 1980s, when I devoted most of my time to the study of the spectator from a sociological and psychological perspective as well as from an aesthetic point of view. It was obvious that not every spectator experienced the same theatrical performance in the same way, but what created the differences? I assumed that varying demographic backgrounds had a major impact on the perception of performances. Different psychological dispositions and the specific circumstances of a particular theatre visit also caused a wide range of interpretations, and there were certainly other factors or combinations of factors which could have recognizable effects on theatre audiences. What do different groups of spectators experience when confronted with various types of theatrical performances? This question became the point of departure for a number of reception studies which I carried out between 1980 and 1988. The original question needed more precision. What are the different groups of spectators? And in what respect do they differ? Pierre Bourdieu's book *La distinction*, published in 1979, was a great help in defining the "economic and cultural capital" and the "habitus" of different social groups. In this way theatregoing also could be seen as an integrated part of people's social behavior. This behavior was largely responsible for the spectators' taste and their preferences in theatrical genres, but was it responsible for the way in which a performance was actually enjoyed and understood?

While there are numerous theories on the sociology of groups and on human behavior in general, it was much more difficult to find a theoretical ground for the actual experience a spectator had during a performance. The field of semiotics, which was in vogue at the time, was not very useful in empirical reception studies: spectators do not perceive "signs" which they describe and interpret for a scholar; they perceive "meaning"—and they have fun! Semiotics had no way of accounting for the pleasure and the enjoyment which spectators experience in the theatre. Furthermore, the spectators judge what they see and hear, and this judgment proved to be highly important for their understanding of the performance. Although my collaborators and I managed to develop methods for registering the spectators' interpretations, emotions, and evaluations of the performances they saw, it remained difficult to find an adequate theoretical frame to cover all these varying reactions.

One of the results of these reception studies became the cornerstone for the further development of the theoretical aspects of theatrical communication. Trying to find out on what grounds a performance is appreciated or not, we tested all judgments of the various details of a performance against the overall judgment a person had expressed. This showed that the evaluation of the performance as such always correlates with the appreciation of the acting, even if other aspects of the show (the drama, the directing, the set, the costumes, etc.) were estimated higher or lower. This close relationship between the appreciation of the acting and the overall evaluation of the performance proved to be independent of the social background of the spectator and also independent of the type of performance. Furthermore, we observed that a lack of appreciation for the acting almost automatically prevented the spectator from engaging in the content of the performance. In other words, if a spectator does not like the actors, the performance becomes "meaningless." More details and some exceptions to these rules are described in chapter 10.

The problem I faced was to construct a theory, or rather a concept of theatrical communication, which allowed for the inclusion of all aspects of the relationship between the performer and the spectator: the creation of meaning, the enjoyment of artistry and skills, and the personal evaluation of the performer. I must admit that this problem was not solved within the framework of my reception studies, but I think that these studies made me a more observant spectator.

During these research periods, I had the privilege to teach courses in performance analysis. The idea of these courses was not primarily to analyze the making or the composition of a performance, but to equip the students with tools to express their own understanding of what they had experienced as spectators. How can the students argue for reasonable interpretations of live performances? For years, my colleagues and I in the theatre department at Stockholm University had been using hermeneutics as a basic theory of interpretation. The process of interpretation could be structured and the results of the process could be made visible not only through the hermeneutic circle, but also through the basic requirements such as the relationship between the parts and the whole of the performance, the coherence between the description and the object of description, and the comprehensibility and the logic of the arguments.

Returning in the early 1990s to the work of Hans-Georg Gadamer, the key figure of modern hermeneutics, I found more aspects of a theory of theatre and performance. First, Gadamer's concept of "horizons" of understanding explains that every interpretation of an object to a large degree is a personal one. At the same time, the "fusion of horizons" supports the empirical observation that interpretations made by different people nevertheless have a great deal of resemblance. Although Gadamer reserves the "fusion of horizons" for a scholar's encounter with historical objects, it seems fully reasonable to me to apply this idea to both past and present experiences. Another aspect of the process of understanding is the importance of the observer's own view, which Gadamer calls "Vorurteil." Literally this German word means prejudice, but he breaks the word into its two parts, "Vor-Urteil," meaning pre-judgment (i.e., the set of norms and values a person is equipped with at the moment of the encounter with an object). A third term is "playing," the basis for all art, which Gadamer describes in a special chapter of his book *Truth and Method.*

He presents an elaborate and convincing argument that the basic experience of art is playing. Playing has its own rules, and those who participate subordinate their will to the rules of the game. The game is playing the players, as Gadamer puts it: *something* is being played. In the case of art, this playing is also a playing for *someone,* an observer, a spectator. The player and the observer participate in the playing, both usually knowing the rules. In the performative arts, the creation and the experience of it are simultaneous processes, which take place in the form of an event. Unlike traditional communication theories, Gadamer does not split the process into a sender, who neatly packs the message in some suitable form, and a receiver, who decodes it; the processes of creating and experiencing theatre are united through the act of playing, through the mutual contact between performer and spectator. Some aspects of this theory are discussed further in chapter 4. Through the concept of playing as a basis of the theatrical event, I saw the possibility of integrating those aspects of theatrical communication which I had seen so clearly in my empirical studies, but which I could not find in theoretical treatments on theatre and performance.

My studies of Gadamer and the phenomenological tradition from which he emanated convinced me to use the term "perception" in the subtitle of this book. Having worked with reception studies for so many years, the choice between these two terms was not an easy one. Both terms are frequently used in the following chapters. The difference between perception and reception can be described in various ways. To a certain degree, they belong to different traditions: "perception" carries connotations that tie it to phenomenology, while "reception" refers to cultural studies and the analysis of social values and mental worlds. Another distinction would be to understand perception as an aspect of the communicative interaction—therefore I pair perception with presentation—while reception describes the process taking place after a performance (i.e., it is a consequence rather than an integral part of the theatrical event). While perception focuses on the communicative process, reception describes the result of communication. Although these nuances are important, it is my intention to include both terms and both perspectives in the concept of the theatrical event.

## Modeling Events

In 1995 my colleague Jacqueline Martin and I published a book called *Understanding Theatre*, in which I tried to combine my practical studies of reception research and my teaching and writing experiences of performance analysis with Gadamer's concept of playing. I was looking for the intersection between the stage performance—prepared perhaps during a long period of rehearsals, but finally created in front of the audience—and the audience, which consists of a collective of individual spectators. Theatre does not exist as physical reality unless it is an event including both performer and spectator. We can, of course, speak of theatre, remember it or plan it, make it part of the ongoing discourse; but as actual experience I think it is useful to conceive of it as a theatrical event. In *Understanding Theatre* I made the attempt to describe both the communicative features of the performer-spectator relationship and the structure of some of the essential contexts in which this communication is taking place. Since this concept became the basis of the texts collected in this volume, I will very briefly summarize its principles by pointing out the key terms.

The stage actions are called "presentation," because this is the basic mode of performance: actions are presented, no matter what the purpose of this presentation is. They are presented for someone, a spectator, who perceives them. Therefore, the perception is closely tied to the presentation. The communicative field between presentation and perception is thought of as being constituted by three levels or aspects, the sensory, artistic, and symbolic modes of communication. In the book *Understanding Theatre* I still used the term "fictional" instead of symbolic. Today the concept of fiction seems to me too limited, since the transformation of actions into various meanings does not always produce fiction in the traditional sense of the word. I think that a symbolic level of communication is also more appropriate when we want to leave the traditional theatre world in order to consider private or public ceremonies, the rhetoric of political speeches, theatrical aspects of sports, etc.

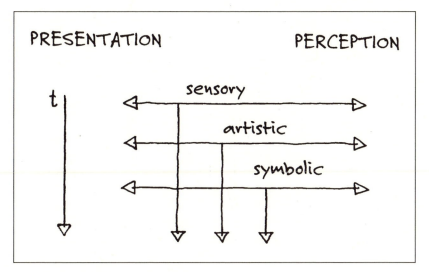

*1. A simple model of theatrical communication.*

The *sensory* level describes the interaction between performer(s) and spectator(s) as a personal relationship. The spectator perceives the physical and mental presence of the actor and reacts to it more or less spontaneously, just as the actor senses the presence of an audience, its size as well as its mood. The *artistic* level makes the theatrical event different from everyday life. What happens on stage is not real life; it is a presentation with some kind of artistic merits which can be appreciated by the audience or not. The *symbolic* mode of communication, finally, is a consequence of the artistic otherness of the event: meaning can be attributed to the artistic actions. At this point I want to underline the importance of the interaction between presentation and perception: nothing is symbolic in itself unless it is perceived as such by the observer.

Any attempt to specify the performer's actions and the spectator's reactions creates terminological turmoil. Not only is the conceptualization of these functions difficult, but the words used to describe those functions might easily be misunderstood. I am well aware that even a long explanation cannot amend the risk of connotations leading into the "wrong" direction. I see these terms as suggestions, pointing out the possibilities of the concept rather than exposing its shortcomings.

In addition to the three levels of communication, the model contains the adjective "communicative" to indicate the purpose of all theatrical actions and reactions: to communicate with each other. The word is

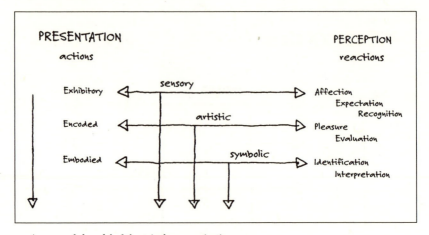

*2. An expanded model of theatrical communication.*

used here in the sense that Jürgen Habermas attaches to it when he speaks about communicative actions (i.e., seeking consensus). The actor and the spectator carry out their actions in the consensus of the theatrical situation.

The performer enters the space designated as stage to present him/herself to the spectator. These are willfully exhibitory actions, including the performer's physical appearance as well as a number of mental qualities and moods. The spectator, in turn, reacts to these exhibitory actions both emotionally and cognitively. Affection, expectation, and recognition are just a few of the possible reactions. Other possibilities could be added, such as curiosity, attention, excitement, or, in negative terms, repulsion, disregard, and fatigue. I find it necessary to stress the sensory communication again and again, because it is of utmost importance for all other communicative processes. Without an interest in the person one wants to communicate with, there will not be enough attention to make the other levels of communication work sufficiently.

The artistic level includes the encoded actions presented in a performance, which are mainly characterized by genre, style, and skills. Every theatrical genre has its own codes of communication—in opera the performers sing, in ballet they dance, etc. Within each genre there exist a number of more or less distinct styles, depending on historical, geographical, and personal traditions. Furthermore, these features of genre and style can be presented with the varying skills and personal manners of the individual performer. This latter aspect, in particular, is closely correlated with the sensory level: a fat dancer needs special skills to make a favorable impression on the audience. Also, the spectator has to have a certain competence concerning the encoded actions to be able to react to them. Even on this level I distinguish between intuitive and cognitive reactions. It is also on this level that I place the aesthetic pleasure a spectator receives from the presentation and the judgment made about the performer.

The symbolic level is the one which is most easily understood, because it has always been the focus of theatre studies, often the only one. What I want to point out here is the difficulty of distinguishing between encoded actions, which have a performative function and thereby become embodied actions, and those which do not. Embodied actions designate the activities of the performer which aim at the presentation of fictional images. Nevertheless, I want to underline the fact that the fictional character is created by the performer and the spectator together. There is no Hamlet on stage: he is only in the mind of the spectator, aided through the images presented by the performer. Even on this level the spectator reacts emotionally (for instance, through identification or empathy with a fictional figure) and intellectually by interpreting the actions on stage.

The most important feature of this figure is the significance of the contexts for both the presentation and the perception of a performance. This is, in part, indicated by the time arrow, which in figure 3 as in the preceding figures goes from the top to the bottom of the sketch. Time is always a factor in communication; what I want to point out through this simple sketch is that the contexts not only are the background of the performance but are constantly present for performer and spectator alike, during the preparations for the event as well as after the event, when it has inscribed itself into the context.

A short comment on contexts might be in place. The three contexts depicted closest to the event (but not necessarily the most relevant ones for a particular event) are those which in a way belong to the theatrical sphere: the *conventional* context, indicating the traditions and features of a theatre world in a certain place and a certain time; the *structural* context, describing the organization of theatre in a society (subsidies, locations, legal frames, etc.); and the *conceptual* context, reflecting the ideology which society expresses in relation to theatre, such as the functions of theatre as a means of entertainment, propaganda, or education and the

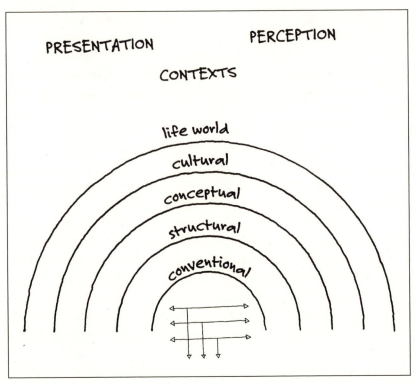

*3. A model of performance in context.*

political consequences emanating from the ideological positions, attitudes, and values of journalists, politicians, theatre practitioners, and theatre scholars.

The *cultural* context marks the interdependence of theatre and other art forms. What happens in the theatre, artistically and economically, often also happens in museums, galleries, cinemas—and sometimes theatre even happens in these places. The cultural field is nevertheless wider than the various art forms. It includes education, history, religion, and also cultural aspects of any other area of society, such as the culturally patterned behavior of businesspeople, food and drinking habits, weddings and other private ceremonies, and proxemic norms when people speak to each other. These general aspects of culture almost become synonymous with the context of the *life world*, a word describing a vast range of things that we might consider important for a theatrical event.

I see the theatre researcher as part of the cultural context and thus as an inhabitant of the life world. Every scholar is integrated into the sociocultural frames which constitute the basis of ideologies, historical patterns, research attitudes, and scholarly preferences. I can see a dialectical relationship between these ideologies, attitudes, and preferences on the one hand and the characteristics of the theatrical event itself on the other. A theatrical event might suggest certain reasonable perspectives as fruitful and interesting, such as gender, sexuality, ethnicity, nationality, postcolonialism, religion, class, demography, or postmodernism. In the end it is up to the scholar to decide which approaches seem to be the most promising.

## Conceptualizing Attitudes

A theatrical event is not defined exclusively by the communication relationship between performer and spectator; nor is it sufficiently distinguished from the surrounding contexts, of which the event itself is part. What status does the theatrical event occupy—is it a theory, a concept, a model? What does it mean to describe theatre as a communicative event within certain contexts, seen from a perspective of a playing culture?

When I speak about the theatrical event I think of it foremost in terms of a concept. I conceptualize theatre and other performative activities as events, not in the sense that they have to be major or important events, but because all theatre takes place as events. In the following chapters I sometimes use the non-English word "event-ness" to emphasize that theatre always materializes in the form of an event. As a concept this is in strict opposition to theatre as a "work of art," something which is produced, distributed, consumed, etc. In my eyes, theatre manifests itself as an event which includes both the presentation of actions and the reactions of the spectators, who are present at the very moment of the creation. Together the actions and reactions constitute the theatrical event.

I call the idea of theatre as event a "concept" and as such it can be compared with other concepts, not in order to argue against them but for the sake of clarity. Many scholars have described theatre as a "composite work of art," meaning that it consists of literary texts, art like set designs and costumes, sound and music, and also more specifically the art of acting (maybe the only element which might be considered genuinely theatrical). All these elements are coordinated by a director or by someone else with similar responsibilities, who thereby is assumed to create the "work," and could be equated with an author of a piece of literature. This rather simplistic concept was questioned and revised by the semioticians in the 1960s, who saw theatre as a "system of signs." There were many ways of dividing the theatrical signs into various classes and groups to investigate their interrelationships, to see how they produced meaning. For a long time semioticians believed that it was possible to find *the* meaning of a performance, provided the right model of sign relations could be applied. Meanwhile most semioticians agreed that meaning is not only produced, but also perceived. Theatre understood as event is a comparable concept, but it builds on the communicative functions of theatre, on a perspective of playing culture and a framework of contexts. The historical significances of these and other concepts of theatre within the discipline are discussed further in chapters 1 and 14, on theatre, performance, and theatrical events.

Whereas the "composite work of art" was built on positivist theory that believed in the possibility of reconstructing "facts," theatre as a "system of signs" was considered a subdivision of the overall approach to all human sciences, which could be understood as a study of the production, distribution, and consumption of signs (although normally only the production seemed interesting to researchers). In this sense, theatre as a "communicative event" could be traced to hermeneutic theories, both as a philosophical approach and as an empirical system.

The central focus is of course on the event itself, the presentation and perception of actions (in the widest sense). As in all communication theory, this model assumes that the partners understand each other. The act of understanding continues during the entire event. It seems reasonable that such processes of perception, understanding, and interpretation can be studied from a hermeneutic perspective, attending to both how the subject understands and how the object can be described. A theatrical presentation is prepared for in various ways—translated, repeated, learned, rehearsed, tried out—in other words, a chain of interpretations has already taken place before the presentation reaches the spectator. In a conventional production of spoken drama this means that a number of artists participate in the process (dramatist, translator, director, designers, actors, technicians, etc.). All of these processes can be equated to a constant flow of hermeneutic processes of understanding. This flow of interpretations also continues after the event has ended in terms of the direct physical encounter. Of course, many of the spectators go home thinking of the performance they just have seen, and we know that this process can go on for years. Modern hermeneutic philosophers like Gianni Vattimo have given special considerations to the problems of the "actuality of the event."

So far I have not distinguished between past and present events. I am, however, very well aware of the problems such negligence might raise. The basic problem for the theatre historian, as is commonly assumed, consists of the absence of the object. The theatre historian cannot engage aesthetically with past performances in the way literary historians read poems or art historians study paintings. The aesthetic experience is possible when we deal with theatre performances of the present. After all, there is a difference between past and present events, but how problematic is this difference? In my view, it is primarily a question of the available material, whereas the theoretical problems remain the same. For the conceptualization of the object of theatre studies the same assumptions have to be considered, no matter when the event took place. The model of theatrical communication is equally valid for past and present performances. We tend to exaggerate these differences anyway. What does it mean to deal with performances of today? The performance is only present while we see it, as long as we are active spectators. When the scholar starts writing about it, the performance is already "historical." We are writing from our memory, and memory is, as we know, a tricky medium. Of course, it makes a difference if we have seen what we are describing instead of depending on other material. This difference is, in my view, one of degree, and not one of theoretical significance. It is more important to discuss "what" we are describing and analyzing than "how" we collect information about it. In other words, the differences between past and present theatrical events concern the methodological approaches, but not the theoretical foundation. This problematic issue exceeds the format of this introduction, but I hope that the way in which I apply the idea of the theatrical event to historical as well as contemporary performances in the following essays will further illustrate the topic.

Seen as a concept, the theatrical event still needs to be equipped with some practical tools to make it applicable to practical research. I have developed such tools in the models presented in *Understanding Theatre*. Some of my colleagues and students have made use of these models and have also modified them, opening up interesting new perspectives, which I have followed with great curiosity. What I think is important concerning these models is not that they are used in exactly the way in which I have presented them here—my own applications show certain variations in terminology and emphasis—but that they underline the most important features of the concept, which, once more, can be summed up as the communicative mutuality of performer and spectator, the elements of play, and their dependence on the surrounding contexts.

## Presenting Practices

During the last decade I have written some fifteen essays which use the concept of the theatrical event. Some of them are more openly hermeneutically inspired; others relate to sociological and psychological theories. Some deal with contemporary theatre; others take up historical topics. Some have their main interest in the stage performance; others consider the audiences more closely. For this book I have chosen to present these articles—slightly updated and revised—in two sections.

Part I contains five chapters which discuss some important theoretical aspects of the theatrical event. I think these perspectives are essential for the understanding of the concept. In these essays I trace research on the theatrical event in European theatre studies, as well as the discussions about drama, theatre, and performance, which have emanated from the United States since the early 1990s. The "Untitled Event," the title of chapter 2, refers, of course, to the event performed at the Black Mountain College in 1952 by John Cage, Merce Cunningham, Robert Rauschenberg, and others. These artists also play a prominent part in chapter 9, on the Happenings at the Modern Museum in Stockholm. The key term "theatricality" is examined in the third essay, and the implications of the concept for historiography are brought into the discussion in chapter 4. Finally, I attempt to apply the concept of the event to the wider field of culture, as a principle of all cultural encounters. All these theoretical essays are illustrated with practical experiences: the female opera singer entering the stage, a scholar jumping on a table to perform the *Turkish Tailor*, my encounter with the rock carvings from the Bronze Age in western Sweden, and last but not least some issues of cultural politics. When these fundamentals have been established, the reader might want to choose some of the following chapters which seem most promising. The following brief outlines of these chapters may serve as guidelines.

Part II contains ten chapters in which the theoretical groundwork is applied to a variety of topics. The first three chapters focus mainly on actors and acting in relationship to the spectator. In chapter 6, on Sarah Bernhardt, the actress and the spectators are located in theatre history. In this essay I try to illustrate not only how the concept of the theatrical event can be applied to historical material, but also how the "event-ness" of Bernhardt's acting does not confine the study to one single "event." It is rather seen as a specific quality, and as such I see my approach as a model for the study of historical acting.

Chapters 7 and 8 look at two contemporary performances which I have seen during recent years. The essay on Dario Fo's *Mistero Buffo* in Stockholm features a Swedish actor and raises questions about how certain effects are accomplished by the performer and through the dramaturgy of the performance. August Strindberg's *Miss Julie* was presented in a fascinating staging by a young Swedish director in Copenhagen, but my interest is mainly focused on the actress who gave such a memorable performance. The essay deals more with my reactions as a spectator than with the technique of the acting itself.

Chapter 9 represents a little excursion into the world of Happenings in the 1960s. The question I try to pursue in this essay is the transformation of seemingly meaningless Happenings into ideas of order and meaning that the spectator attributes to these events.

In chapters 10 and 11 my main interest is the perspective of the spectator. Theatre Talks were a method I developed and applied during the 1980s, and this essay tries to summarize the sometimes surprising results from ten years of research. The essay on "Fiction, Mainly Fiction" represents one of the first applications of both reception research and the model of theatrical communication. The puppet performance *A Lonely Ear* for very small children illustrates this approach very clearly, since every step is taken openly and is fully comprehensible to the observer.

The remaining chapters of this part can be described as meta-texts, since they all deal with writings of artists, critics, and scholars. Chapter 12 focuses on Strindberg's ideas about a "chamber style" of acting and its application in his own Intimate Theatre. I have investigated to what degree he was right in his assumptions about the acting profession as expressed in his *Memorandum* to the actors.

Chapter 13 brings up the problem of the length of a Jewish nose on stage. This is not meant to be a joke; on the contrary, the ethnic image was a highly political issue at a time when debates on immigration of Jewish refugees were cutting through Swedish society in the 1930s. Chapter 14 deals with political issues in the seventeenth century. Methodologically, this essay tries to demonstrate that the concept of the theatrical event can successfully be applied to fresh readings of old texts.

Chapter 15 discusses two kinds of texts about contemporary performances: reviews from daily newspapers and essays written by scholars. In what way are these texts different, and what are the reasons for these differences? All the texts surveyed deal with Robert Lepage's impressive staging of Strindberg's *A Dream Play* in Stockholm in 1994.

The title of the concluding essay, "To Be Continued," indicates that the concept of the theatrical event can be useful in a number of studies. I give a few examples, which also, in my view, represent certain extensions of both the concept itself and the scope of possible applications. I hope that there is more to come in a few years, as more scholars take up the investigation of the theatrical event.

# Part I

## Theatrical Event
### *Foundations*

# I

## Approaching the Theatrical Event
### The Influence of Semiotics and Hermeneutics on European Theatre Studies

In the introduction to his posthumous book on acting, Max Herrmann, a pioneer of European theatre studies, addresses the problems of exhibiting stage models, costume sketches, and blueprints of theatre buildings in theatre museums and points out the difficulties for a visitor in relating to past theatrical events: "How telling are the words of a lady on leaving such an exhibition! Asked by her husband about her impressions, she replied: 'Very nice, indeed, but you know, it's like fishbowls and no fish in them.'"[1] While ordinary people are interested in seeing the fish, it seems theatre scholars are destined to study fishbowls. Put another way, the fundamental concern of all theatre researchers is with the very "object" of theatre itself.

### The Phenomenon

Many analysts offer minimal descriptions of the necessary elements of theatre, the most famous being Eric Bentley's formula "A impersonates B while C looks on."[2] Shorthand definitions of this kind always provoke debate, though not always very fruitful, and most scholars agree today that the pursuit of a definition is not the greatest priority. A more recent concern is how "theatre" can be distinguished from almost synonymous terms like "drama" and "performance." Marvin Carlson makes reference to this in his *Theories of the Theatre*.[3] His distinction between "drama" as the written text and "theatre" as the process of performance certainly is a simplification, but seems acceptable as such. His use of the term "performance" follows an anthropological path, including "dance and opera, not to speak of happenings, circus, ritual, festival and ultimately the performance elements of everyday life."[4] It reduces the term "theatre" to a description of certain genres, the foremost being spoken drama, which seems a less productive limitation, since opera and dance, at the very least, have always been considered part of theatre history. This has been the case in Europe; and, as far as I know, such a distinction between spoken, sung, and danced performances is irrelevant outside the Western world.

I do not wish to investigate such definitions and distinctions any further, but rather to survey the research which has been carried out by European scholars in the twentieth century. This discussion does not include any statistics on the frequency of certain genres or periods, dramatists, or theatre buildings; my concern lies with the concept of theatre at various times and places in Europe. The "object" of theatre studies is considered an essentially phenomenological problem: is it a question of materiality, people, relationship; is it an idea or a condition; is it permanent or transitory? How do scholars conceptualize theatre, and how does it affect their writing about theatre?

## A Paradigm Shift

An overview of European theatre studies in the twentieth century allows me to observe a transition in the conceptualizing of theatre: a shift from the idea of theatre as a "work of stage art" (or simply "a piece of art") toward an understanding of theatre as a "communicative event." This shift signifies to me a paradigmatic change of emphasis, which has not gained full recognition by theatre scholars worldwide. It is the purpose of this essay to demonstrate the motivations and consequences of historical traditions as well as their gradual replacement by new concepts. This is not an exercise in the historiography of theatrical scholarship, but a necessary reflection on the basic role of scholars in the world of theatre. My point of departure is the fact that in today's world an abundance of electronic media compete for the attention of "customers." Electronic games, electronic mail, mobile telephones, the internet, databases, hyperspace, and virtual reality are becoming etched in our lives. This explosion of new communicative devices calls into question

the function of theatre, as the new technologies easily could replace theatre's outmoded means of production and distribute the results to an
unlimited number of purchasers. Through computer games, our desire
for influence on the dramaturgical structure of our entertainment can be
satisfied easily. Film and television have already raised serious questions
about theatre's place in society. These media have had a direct effect on
both theatre and theatre scholarship. At the start of a new millennium,
it might be time to reconsider the meaning and the future possibilities
of the art of theatre.[5] With this in mind, let us retrace our steps.

## Reconstructions

In his history of the German theatre during the medieval and Renaissance periods, Max Herrmann emphatically proclaimed the necessity
of reconstructions. Since the theatrical productions of the past are
gone, this must be the first task of the theatre historian, according to
Herrmann. Reconstructions included all theatrical elements: the space
in which a production was performed, the stage design, the costumes,
the acting style, the playscripts, the auditorium, performance times, and
so on. To carry out such reconstructions all kinds of documents had to
be discovered and interpreted. It is still amazing how much material was
gathered and collected in theatre museums and archives during those
early years. Herrmann himself focused on Hans Sachs' Carnival Stage in
Nuremberg. Scholars such as John C. Adams and Walter Hodges devoted their lives to the reconstruction of Shakespeare's Globe Theatre.
Other scholars, such as Wilma Deierkauf-Holseboer, Donald Roy, and
Graham Barlow, have calculated of the measurements of the Théâtre
du Marais from carpenters' bills. The list of examples is endless, but here
we must focus on the purpose behind these reconstructions.

Therein lies the specific problem of the then young discipline of theatre studies which our older colleagues had to solve. The neighboring
aesthetic disciplines all had their objects at hand: literary historians read
poems and novels; art historians studied paintings, sculptures, and buildings; archaeologists excavated cities and palaces; and even musicologists
had access to scores and period instruments. In a sense they could all
communicate with their aesthetic object in a direct manner. Theatre historians, however, first had to re-create the objects of their studies and

then convince other disciplines that theatre studies as an academic activity was built on scientific principles. In their struggle, two issues were at stake: first, they had to prove that there was a solid object — although reconstructed — and, second, they had to convince their colleagues that this object was theatre and not drama.

Theatre scholars held differing positions as regards drama, and a distinction between a central European and an Anglo-American tradition can be made. In the Germanic-speaking countries of central and northern Europe in particular, a strong defense of theatre as theatre, as opposed to theatre as the performance of drama, was launched quite early. Once more Max Herrmann provides a convincing example:

> Drama as poetic creation does not concern us as theatre historians at all or only insofar as the dramatist, while writing his play, also considered the conditions of the stage, or insofar as the play provides information about past theatrical conditions. . . . Specific poetic qualities remain outside our considerations; an artistically worthless playlet, under certain circumstances, might be more important than the greatest masterworks in world literature.[6]

The English-speaking world seemed more attached to drama than were Continental scholars. There are a number of reasons for this, not least the overwhelming dominance of Shakespeare, which certainly no English scholar can escape. The discipline, as taught in English and American drama schools, usually combined theoretical studies and the practical education of actors, directors, designers, and so on, thus emphasizing the production process, the page-to-stage approach, always taking the written text as the point of departure.

A third aspect of British and American theatrical life during the first half of this century which might have contributed to the dominance of drama was that no director achieved fame to equal that of, for example, Max Reinhardt, Leopold Jessner, and Erwin Piscator in Austria and Germany, the Cartel des Quatre in France, August and Per Lindberg in Sweden, or Vsevolod Meyerhold, Nikolai Evreinov, and Aleksandr Tairov in Russia. These great directors had a dual effect on the development of the discipline. First, they proved the absolute autonomy of theatre as an art form, including its independence from the dramatic text. (It is against the background of Reinhardt's spectacular productions that we have to understand Herrmann's statement on the importance of "in-artistic" texts within the framework of theatrical performances.) Second, these highly creative directors functioned as "auteurs" comparable to novelists, poets, painters, and composers.

Early theatre historians, of course, were all informed by a positivist attitude to scholarship. It was quite natural, therefore, that they believed in theories of evolution, by which specific periods were held up as ideal fixed points in the history of aesthetics; they developed solid instruments for the criticism of sources, thus assuming that documents provided "true" facts; they hesitated to judge past productions in aesthetic terms. These well-known consequences of positivism should not blur our view of other useful ideas, which survived positivism, including the concept of theatre as a work of stage art and the focus on its creator, the director.

This scholarly attitude toward theatre has prevailed for many years. Professor Gösta M. Bergman, Stockholm University, published a handbook on theatre studies in 1973, in which he wrote about the necessity of what were then called "attempts at reconstruction" as the basic skills of theatre researchers. Reconstructions remained the nucleus of theatre scholarship. Furthermore, most publications in theatre as opposed to drama are devoted to directors and critics, who are primarily concerned with the dramatic text and its interpretation by the director. This same view, I contend, affected structuralist and semiotic theories when a new generation of scholars entered the arena in the 1960s.

## Semiotics — The Production of Meaning

Under this heading I include all brands of structuralism and semiology: the Russian Formalists at the time of the First World War, the contributions of the Prague School in the 1930s, the rediscovery of Ferdinand de Saussure's and Charles Peirce's linguistics and their transformation of theatre theory mainly carried out by French and Italian scholars during the 1960s, the broad interest in semiotics in the 1970s, and the definitive inclusion of communicative aspects in the science of the sign in the 1980s. The history of the semiotic movement is quite well known and needs no introduction.[7]

Three major contributions by semiotics to European theatre studies deserve mention. First, semiotics instigated an awareness of the importance of theory in theatre studies. The theoretical frames of the positivist tradition rarely were discussed openly — even Marxists accepted them, albeit on their own terms. Semiotics shifted the debate within the discipline from methodologies and research strategies to a level of profound theoretical thinking. For some time it seemed as if semiotics not only provided a most interesting theoretical approach, but represented the only possible theory of theatre. A second achievement of semiotics has already been mentioned indirectly: a radical break from theatre scholars' fetishization of historical documents. The finding, describing, and evaluating of sources — mainly pictorial and written documents — had become their main occupation, impairing a discussion on the nature of the object which they were so desperate to reconstruct. A third aspect I would like to emphasize is that semiotics put the theatrical performance right back in the center of the debate. Instead of depicting possible frames and references, through which the (lost but "reconstructed") past performance should be considered, semioticians asked themselves in what theoretical terms such past and present performances could be described. The whole field of performance analysis, which today should be well established in all theatre departments, received its basic impulses from semiotics, although many scholars subsequently moved on to alternative approaches.

Semiotics, however, was not the savior of the discipline, as I have made it out to be. One of its main failings was that many of the most prominent semioticians were not theatre scholars, and they used the complex structure of theatre to illustrate general theses without attempting to present a coherent semiotic theory of theatrical performance. Those who were concerned with constructing such a semiotics of theatre restricted most of their writing to "pure" theory — often having a most conventional theatre in mind — and never even attempted to relate theory to live performance.

Another failing, which concerns my specific perspective in this essay, was one-sided concentration on the production itself: the making of meaning through the structures, signs, and codes of the stage. At its most introverted, semiotics sought for a "grammar of theatre," thus revealing its linguistic roots and the fallibility of its concept of theatre as a product. Other semioticians were well aware that the theatrical sign is part of a communicative process and that someone must interpret the signs. There was also an insight into the complicated patterns of interpretation, as Erika Fischer-Lichte points out in *The Semiotics of Theater*:

> Even though these processes [of producing and interpreting signs] occur parallel to each other, one cannot conclude, that they are analogous to each other: The actor and the spectator may not at all attribute the same meaning to the signs, which the actor has produced. Very often there is a discrepancy between the meaning, which the actor thought to constitute, and the meaning, which the spectator constitutes during the process of reception.[8]

It is significant that this quote appeared in a footnote when published in German in 1983. Even if there was an awareness of the communicative aspects of theatre, they were rarely included in the semiotic systems. A very good example is offered by one of the early theatre semioticians, Tadeusz Kowzan, whose 1968 article "Le signe au théâtre" became most influential.[9] Kowzan divides a theatrical performance into thirteen elements then regroups them into visual and auditive signs and signs unrelated and related to the actor. He does not include the rhythm of a performance or other dynamic categories; nor does he make mention of the space in which a performance takes place. His focus is solely the spectacle on stage and the way in which meaning is produced. The spectator and the process of reception are completely ignored, as was the case in many books on theatre semiotics.[10]

Semiotics tended to "over-sign" everything that happened on stage. By attributing signifying functions to every detail, semioticians risk missing communicative elements which are not connected to the fictional world — since everything on stage is simply not a fiction. It is true that semioticians have brought the actor back onto the stage, and there is very little mention of directors. Has the above-mentioned focus on the director as "auteur" of the theatrical art work disappeared? It is obvious that the art work was more important to semioticians than its creator, at least as long as they were occupied with theory. As soon as performance analysis entered the field, the question of there being a "true" or a "near truthful" interpretation of a production was raised. At this point, the director reappeared in theatre studies: a valid interpretation would be one which gets close to the intentions of a director. In practical work it was difficult to describe the intentions of directors other than through interviews, while semiotic analysis hardly could offer valid answers. Nevertheless, theatre scholars with a semiotic approach continue to focus their energies on the work of directors rather than that of actors, stage designers, musicians, and so on.

In 1982, a conference in Amsterdam brought together semioticians and reception researchers under the heading of "Performance Theory." At that time, I was engaged in constructing theoretical frames and methodological approaches which attempted to combine performance analysis with the analysis of spectator response. Because I was no semiotician, I found myself quickly labeled an "empiricist," like everyone else who had engaged in any practical experiment. Since that conference, I believe some considerable changes have to be taken into account.[11]

## *Enter the Spectator*

In theatre studies, the spectator has had a marginal existence. Although acknowledged as an integral part of theatre, audiences have mainly been treated in social categories: age, gender, social background, and postperformance activities. Scholars have long lamented the lack of material concerning audiences through history, but authors like Alfred Harbage, John Lough, and Roger Herzel have been able to make considerable contributions to our knowledge of Elizabethan and French audiences of the neo-classical period. Their books deal very little with actual performances, concentrating on the social composition of the audiences. Most typical is Heinz Kindermann, who, after a series of ten weighty tomes on the history of European theatre, started anew with a series of books on the audiences of antiquity and the Middle Ages.

Since the 1940s, empirical audience surveys — built on sociological methodology — have been carried out on a regular basis in many countries. These surveys, very often commissioned by state authorities or by the theatres themselves, provide a wealth of information on all aspects of the public's attitude to theatre: expectations, preferences, customs, and attendance figures, how theatre interest is generated, and what obstacles prevent potential visitors coming to performances. These surveys are very valuable for our general knowledge of contemporary theatre as well as for the marketing and funding of theatre. But traditional audience research does not follow the spectator into the theatre.

Other research strategies had to be found; as often happens, theatre scholars looked to neighboring academic disciplines. In the 1970s, reception theory had already been popularized within a wider field of scholars through the work of the so-called Konstanz group, including Robert Jauss and Wolfgang Iser. Although none of them studied theatre, their idea of an "implicit reader" was easily transferred to an implicit or ideal spectator. The obvious question is for whom such a spectator was implicit. The answer is: for the director, as the closest equivalent to the author or the "author in the text." It also showed that the ideal spectator rarely was to be found in a theatre auditorium.

Speculative theories of that kind will not answer the question which the Russian critic Michail Zagorsky formulated in 1925: "Who is experiencing what in the theatre and why?" To be able to gain an understanding of the spectator's experiences during and after theatrical performances, radically different research strategies have to be applied.[12] This is not the place to assess various methodological approaches; let me simply mention some of the most relevant insights which this research has generated. The components of the theatrical experience have been differentiated. The physical experience, which includes not only the sight lines and the acoustics of a theatre building and the particular seat one occupies, but also the notion of sharing a space with other spectators as well as with the performer. On an emotional level, the spectator experiences identification, empathy, and sympathy — and their opposites — in relation to both character and performer. (The importance of this is discussed later.) The intellectual reactions of the spectator likewise are directed toward both the fictional content, its interpretation and evaluation, and the act of presentation, including the acting skills, the beauty of the sets, the rhythm of the performance, and so on.

It is extremely important that these characteristics of spectatorship are related to actual presentations on stage, since they also affect and change our concept of theatrical norms. Henri Schoenmakers has pointed out one such possible complication:

> By focusing on the relation between stage images and the background of spectators, a theoretical approach in fact states that a performance in itself is not innovative, nor has it immanent qualities; it

is only innovative against a background the spectator has brought with him into the theatre. This relation between stage images and the background of the spectator is decisive to the function theatre may have. . . . A highly subsidized performance of *Don Giovanni* for a cultured elite might fulfill the same function as a commercial popular musical for spectators with another background.[13]

Since scholars writing a performance analysis can only refer to their own experiences, they can no longer be considered objective observers; instead they are just members of the audience, as prejudiced and intolerant as everyone else. Therefore, a more elaborate theory became necessary, which would account for the interaction between the actions on stage and the reactions in the auditorium.

### Hermeneutics — The Understanding of Meaning

The messenger and demigod Hermes lent his name to hermeneutics, the science of interpretation. Hermes not only brought the news from the gods, but also made it intelligible to humans. Likewise, it has been necessary to interpret the texts of the Bible as well as statutes of law books — the areas in which hermeneutics was developed as a methodology of interpretation. In the nineteenth century, hermeneutics was transformed into a more general theory of understanding in the sense of interpretation and translation. Under the influence of Edmund Husserl's philosophical phenomenology, a hermeneutic concept of life was developed, considering understanding as the basis of human existence. This philosophy was summarized in 1960 by Hans-Georg Gadamer in his book *Truth and Method*,[14] in which he also examines the specificities of play and the play characteristics of art. Play includes mimetic activities and is, according to Gadamer, always a playing for someone who is able to understand it. He shows very clearly how the player/performer is connected with the observer/spectator. He assumes that performers experience a greater reality than they realize, and it is one which only the spectators are able to recognize. The artists' intention is beyond their control, and the performance becomes open to interpretation. The process of understanding brings together the horizon of the understanding subject and the position of the object. Interpretation, therefore, is always historic in the sense that it is related to a specific time, a specific place, and a specific mode of understanding (for more about this topic, see chapter 4).

It is surprising that so few theatre scholars reacted to Gadamer's suggestions at the time. Of course, these were the heydays of structuralism and semiotics, which might explain why it took almost two decades for hermeneutics to make its appearance in theatre research (and elsewhere). It was in the field of performance analysis that Kirsten Gram Holmström in Sweden and Erika Fischer-Lichte in Germany independently applied hermeneutic theories to their work. Two experiences assumed fundamental importance. First, hermeneutic methodology most appropriately reflected the common experience of theatregoing and allowed the researchers to recapture their own responses in a dynamic and performancelike account. Second, the philosophy of hermeneutics served as a frame of understanding, even when other methodologies, such as semiotics, were used. Although hermeneutics presents certain methodological tools such as the hermeneutic circle and criteria concerning coherence and comprehension, it seems reasonable to consider hermeneutics a basic ontological and epistemological approach. Rather than answering questions, hermeneutics broadens the range of questions we might ask: What do we want to understand, and what is the process of understanding?

Meanwhile, semiotic hermeneutics has been tested successfully with hundreds of students and in many articles on performance analysis.[15] But the significance of hermeneutics for theatre studies might be much more far-reaching. Hermeneutic theory points out that theatre primarily can be understood as a communicative process in which neither the stage image nor the spectator is privileged, but where their mutual interaction marks the nucleus of scholarly interest. In that sense, hermeneutics is far from being restricted to a strategy of performance analysis, but is capable of informing all areas of theatre studies.

## After Reconstruction, Deconstruction

Toward the end of the 1980s, theatre studies experienced a veritable crisis. Semiotics as a dominant force lost ground as it began to focus on the communicative elements of the sign-receiver relationship. Hermeneutics was hardly recognized in academe. Instead, new passwords were given out and on the scholarly horizon appeared the more fashionable recruits of Postmodernism, Deconstructionism, New Historicism, Interculturalism, Ekphrasis, and Body Politics. Ronald Vince summarized the situation at the Eleventh World Congress of the International Federation for Theatre Research in Stockholm in 1989: "As theatre historians we are in the midst of a paradigm shift, in which we question existing assumptions, categories and definitions, without, at the same time, being able to replace them with anything other than not always clearly articulated notions of indeterminedness, infinality and discontinuity." [16]

It was easy to agree with Ronald Vince then, but have theatre scholars managed to become more concrete in formulating the new paradigm? Erika Fischer-Lichte thinks that this plurality of theoretical approaches has been fruitful and declares particularity a virtue: "The new orientation in historical sciences has not so much caused rivalry between different schools, but rather enhanced the acknowledgment of a basic plurality of theories and methods. Particularity as a principle became the condition for a possible historiography. Every theory explains a different kind of microhistory; every method relates to another level." [17]

These statements on theatre history are fully applicable to the current situation in performance analysis.[18] But we must ask if historical and analytical approaches differ, or if a fusion of theories finally can be achieved. Reconstructions were solely devoted to historical problems; semiotics and reception theory, in practice though not explicitly, were related to contemporary theatre. In more recent discussions, the division between the history and the analysis of theatre has been seriously questioned. Why not analyze history; why not historicize analysis? [19] One possible key to reconciling these two fields within the discipline would be to describe theatre as a communicative event. In my opinion, the "event-ness" of theatre is crucial for the understanding of theatre as an art form as well as for theatre scholarship.

The theatrical event always takes place at a certain place, at a certain time, and in a certain context. The theatrical event also presupposes two partners: those who make a presentation and those who perceive it. Such commonplace statements are applicable to every performance, past and present. No matter how much we know about the event itself or the contexts of the event, theatre and theatre history consist of such events and are defined by them. In this sense, the notion of the theatrical event might bridge the gap between theatre history and performance analysis, on the one hand, and stage direction and spectator reading, on the other. I have characterized such a concept as a major shift in theatre studies of paradigmatic significance.

## The Theatrical Event

What characterizes a theatrical event? A few ingredients have already been mentioned, such as the simultaneous activities of the performer and the spectator, their unification in a certain place and time, and their mutual interaction. Such a description is neither surprising nor new. What is still necessary is the description of the interaction between performer and spectator, the nature and mutuality of this interaction and its relation to various contexts within the life of the theatre and outside it.[20]

Following a phenomenological path,[21] I have divided theatrical communication into three levels or aspects, distinguishable by their nature, but dynamically interconnected during a performance: the sensory, the artistic, and the symbolic. All three are characterized by the mutuality of the performer's actions and the spectator's reactions. Performer and spectator are here presented in the singular, which is a simplification of the whole ensemble on stage and the variety of many individual spectators, assembled in the auditorium. I also must emphasize that the levels of communication undergo changes of meaning in the course of a performance. Time is a crucial and dynamic part of this model.

To explain these three aspects in a more concrete fashion I invite the reader to an imagined performance in a huge European opera house. I shall pretend to represent the spectator and sit in the auditorium close to the stage. I also assume that the action starts with a female singer appearing on stage. From empirical reception studies it is a well-established fact that gender relation is an important factor in the theatrical experience. My choice of a female singer should not be taken as a sexist notion, but rather as an attempt to avoid the predominant "he" in most texts of this kind.

What happens on the *sensory* level of theatrical communication the moment the singer became visible to me? At first glance, I react very much as I would in an everyday situation. I look at her. I watch her moving. I observe her appearance and complexion. I register the beauty of her costume and so on. By doing so, I automatically react in at least two different modes. There are emotional reactions such as feeling her presence, my concentration, perhaps a touch of physical attraction, or maybe a sigh of recognition. Intellectually I would be able to determine her age, guess her ethnic origin, compare her to the woman I saw on this stage last time and other more or less relevant — and involuntary? — reflections. The woman on stage knows that I am watching her, along with a thousand other pairs of eyes. Our watching is the very reason for her being there, so she deliberately shows herself to us. Of course, she wants to be seen in a certain way, so she puts herself across as powerfully as she can. Perhaps stage fright prevents her from looking directly at the audience. Perhaps she tries to hide these feelings from us. In other words, even the singer is experiencing both emotional and intellectual processes, but they are not the same as the spectator's, although they are related to each other through the situation. Whether her entrance takes only a few seconds or whether she has been standing on stage for a while before she starts singing, the sensory communication continues throughout the performance. It is the fundamental basis of my attention in the theatre; once I lose interest in her, she will notice and work hard to recapture it by intensifying her exhibitory actions. The sensory communication continues, while her first notes add another level of communication.

The *artistic* aspect of communication is built on encoded actions, and each theatrical genre has a specific set of expressive strategies. In opera, I am prepared to hear the performer sing: if I were at a ballet performance, I would be quite perplexed if a dancer sang an aria. Every artist presents these encoded actions with certain skills, partly personal, partly traditional, and belonging to a certain time and place. The spectator, too, is part of the tradition, which becomes more evident in foreign theatre traditions. In my case, I would say that I am quite familiar with opera, although far from being an expert. My reaction to the woman's singing therefore is mainly emotional: I do enjoy it. My appreciation is very important for her, and for me it is a pleasure to listen. Intellectually, I only realize that she sounds the way sopranos usually do, maybe a little softer — or is this last notion the result of my liking her on the sensory level? If I was an opera critic and more knowledgeable in singing techniques, I might be able to discern her intonation, classify her tone production, criticize the accuracy of her phrasing, her cooperation with the conductor, and so on. But even the critic takes pleasure in listening and lets emotions affect the experience. Naturally a lot of other expressive means are at work while she is singing: facial, gestural, kinetic and proxemic movements, the display of her costume, the sound of the orchestra, the set, and so on. But I have still not yet understood any symbolic meaning of her encoded actions. What I see and hear is a sympathetic woman who is engaged in singing while moving on the stage. From these impulses I accumulate information concerning a possible role.

The *symbolic* level is affected by both the sensory and artistic aspects of communication, but also — and especially in opera — by my prior knowledge of the fictional story presented. It might be easy for me to recognize Tosca through the diva's actions. These consist of real actions, such as her moving toward another singer, and pretended actions, such as her look of surprise. Of course, she is not surprised to find the other singer in position, but she wants us to believe that the character Tosca is surprised. I observe her expression of surprise; and while I store this information about Tosca on the fictional level, I also admire her well-crafted facial expression, which belongs to the artistic level. Even a sensory reaction is possible: for instance, when I think that this expression of surprise lights up her face. This interplay of the communicative levels on behalf of both the performer and the spectator is an important feature of my model and accounts for the dynamic of the performance. There are also different degrees of awareness as regards these levels or aspects. At times I might be really involved in the construction of the fictional actions; at other times I might mainly enjoy the pleasure of excellent singing, no matter what it signifies.

I have applied this model in a comparative analysis of a number of different productions of *The Phantom of the Opera*.[22] Since the staging — set, movements, costumes — is identical all around the world and controlled by Andrew Lloyd Webber's London-based company, it was possible to compare the eminent importance of the performers. By taking into account their exhibitory, encoded, and embodied actions, I could point out how and why they were telling different stories, to such a degree that audience reactions were noticeably different: while people were sighing with relief in Stockholm, sobs and tears were characteristic of the reception in Los Angeles, due to the differences in acting.

I have also applied the model in my study of Sarah Bernhardt, the celebrated French actress who died in 1923 (see part II, chapter 6).[23] In this case I have been working with documents, mainly written accounts — including her own — but also photographs and an ancient sound recording. I found that the reviews of her performances could be analyzed in the way I have proposed here: emotional and intellectual reactions on the levels of sensory, artistic, and fictional communication. Much praise was lavished on Sarah Bernhardt's stage presence despite her legendary emaciated appearance, as well as on her "Golden Voice," her fabulous diction, and so on, but very little is to be found in those reviews about her actions on stage. Even the comments on the fictional characters she played are dominated by emotional responses, whereas a thorough interpretation of her portrayal of say, Phèdre, is rare. The impression is that Sarah Bernhardt's fame was strongly built on her ability to provoke emotional responses, appealing to the spectators' intuition, rather than on cognitive reflection.

### Events in Context

Neither Sarah Bernhardt's performances nor my pretended opera performance take place in a theatrical vacuum. Every production goes through a process of rehearsals, and all the preceding performances of the same production are included in the collective experience of the performer and all the other members of the production team. As for the spectator, reactions do not stop when the curtain comes down, but the performance continues in the mind and eventually will become part of theatrical memory. These pre- and post-performance elements take place within the framework of theatrical and nontheatrical contexts. Let me simply mention some of the most relevant contexts within the theatre world: the conventional or aesthetic context, the structural context, and the conceptual or ideological context.

Attitudes toward genre, the traditions of performance in a specific country at a given period, the artistic coding of a performance, and the spectator's competence in understanding these codes all make up the conventions of theatre. Of course, simultaneously there are different conventions in theatre life, as well as different genres and styles and even preferences and tastes. The conventional context is in turn closely related to the structural context, which describes the organizational patterns of theatrical life in a certain area. All of this relates to the conceptual context and creates the framework in which theatre operates. These concepts include everything from governmental subsidies to the notion of the collective benefits of theatre to society.

Even given the uniqueness of each performance, theatrical contexts change, some swiftly, some noticeable only over centuries. As theatre historians, we are mostly interested in these contexts rather than in the individual performance; performance analysis, in contrast, treats the contextual frames reductively. I trust that the model I have presented can make visible the communicative levels and theatrical contexts, unite them, and remind us of the "event-ness" of all theatre, past and present. It is my aim to rediscover the sensory qualities of theatre and to acknowledge the pleasure we experience as an essential part of theatrical communication. I think it is necessary to rediscover theatre as event.

# 2 | *Theatre or Performance or Untitled Event?*
Some Comments on the Conceptualization of the Object of Our Studies

There has been an ongoing argument at U.S. conferences as well as in drama journals, theatre journals, and performing arts journals as to whether we are engaged in drama studies, theatre studies, or performance studies. This debate can be seen as a scholarly discussion about the "real" object of our studies or perhaps about the supposed object or even the recommended object of our research and our teaching.

My perspective on this controversy is European. For a European (and I am just one European, not the European), this whole upheaval about drama, theatre, and performance looks bewildering, strange, almost exotic. But the implications of this hot issue are quite complex and highly relevant from a global view of our common field.

The whole controversy can also be understood as an institutional power struggle, as William B. Worthen has suggested in an article in the *Drama Review* (*TDR*), where he writes: "Stage vs. page, literature vs. theatre, text vs. performance: these simple oppositions have less to do with the relationship between writing and enactment than with power, with the ways in which we authorize performance, ground its significance."[1]

Pierre Bourdieu would probably describe the situation in terms of a struggle for a dominant position in the academic field — by expanding the borders of the field, old positions have to be redefined and new power relations are established. Bourdieu might also say that this is the habitus of academics: to cover their ambitions to gain influence and power with scholarly arguments instead of an open political rhetoric.[2]

My engagement in this struggle is not focused primarily on the power play and only to some degree on U.S. educational politics. I am interested in the various descriptions of the field itself: the objects of our studies, scattered about both in the center of the field and along its periphery — along the fences, so to speak.

In this sense, the issue at stake is far from being an American issue. First of all, a look at the lists of subscribers to any of the more prominent U.S. journals in our field — such as *Performing Arts Journal, Drama Review,* and *Theatre Journal* — will easily expose the fact that these journals are spread all over the world. They are read and discussed at many universities outside the United States and therefore widely influential. U.S. conferences are likewise attended by many scholars from all parts of the world, and most of them are very impressed by the standard of the discussions.

This is my second point: I readily want to admit that North American scholarship is vital, expansive, and, most of the time, interesting. The level of theorizing studies is impressive and based on solid scholarly work. We meet refreshing new attitudes toward academic writing as well as a dedication and enthusiasm which are contagious. Furthermore — and this is especially interesting from a European point of view — it is noteworthy that the main sources of this revitalizing theoretical thinking come from European philosophy, once its central texts have been translated into English. The larger part of the poststructuralist canon originates from European languages, like French (Derrida, Lacan, Foucault, Bourdieu, Kristeva, Cixous); or German (Gadamer, Adorno, Habermas, Wittgenstein); or East European (Ingarden, Bahktin, etc.). It is true that U.S. scholars have appropriated these philosophical ideas more openly than many of my European colleagues. In that sense, we Europeans have to blame ourselves when we were less attentive to these sources of inspiration, although some of us might have written about these issues in "small" languages, which are rarely read outside the borders of our own countries.

There are, in other words, good reasons to observe the U.S. scholarly scene closely. My point of view in the theatre/performance controversy concentrates on the arguments used in the debate. I would like to comment on how these terms (i.e., theatre and performance) are conceptualized, used, and understood by Americans and how these concepts compare to the situation in those parts of Europe with which I am most familiar, namely northern Europe, Scandinavia, the German- and Dutch-speaking countries, and, to a lesser extent, France and Italy.

The fact that many of us use the English language as a means of scholarly communication easily creates confusion about the meaning of the same words. We all know that words as well the concepts they are meant to express are highly dependent on the context in which they occur.

The word "performance" is just one example of how confusing the English language is. For me — and probably for many of my European colleagues — the word "performance" is thought of as equivalent to the German *Aufführung*, the Scandinavian *föreställning*, the French *représentation*, or the Italian *rappresentazione*. All these terms relate to a theatrical presentation in front of an audience, an event defined in time and space. A performance should be distinguished from a "mise-en-scène" or a "production," which could be described as the result of a rehearsal process, a collective competence, so to speak, which can only materialize in a number of performances. In this sense we also understand the term "performance analysis" as a scholarly approach to a (mostly live) theatrical presentation, starting from and consciously using the scholar's own experience of that performance. Performance analysis is, of course, not limited to spoken drama, but can be applied to any kind of theatrical event, be it opera or musical, dance or pantomime, puppet theatre or Happenings. Performance analysis can also be applied to performance art.

"Performance art" is not the art of performance, however. Rather, it constitutes a specific genre, emanating from the 1960s as a follow-up to the Happenings. I am using this term according to such handbooks as RoseLee Goldberg's *Performance Art* or Marvin Carlson's *Performance*. Carlson's title indicates a new tendency in the use of this term. By omitting the word "art," the term "performance" has assumed a new significance, meaning both a specific genre, formerly called performance art, and a unique theatrical event, as in the case of performance analysis. Etymologically, the word "performance" originates from the Latin *per formam*, meaning "through form" — something is expressed through a certain form. In English dictionaries, performance is related not only to a performance on stage, but also to the performance of a car or an athlete, the playing of musical instruments, and other accomplishments. The linguistic aspects of performance will not solve our problems of mutual understanding. Some of these meanings might be interesting for our discussion later on, but more directly influential in our context is the notion of performance as a description of certain aspects of culture in the anthropological sense.

A concept of "cultural performance" was introduced in the 1950s by Milton Singer and later popularized by Victor Turner and Richard Schechner.[3] Singer's idea of cultural performance was developed in opposition to the prevailing notion that cultural expressions consist of artifacts, namely, documents and monuments. For Singer, celebrations such as holidays, weddings, mourning processions, festivals, and temple dances were as much articulations of a culture as the "dead" artifacts. Erika Fischer-Lichte also points out the fact that Singer's pioneering view was historically paralleled by Roland Barthes' distinction between the process of writing and the written text and John Austin's speech-act theory. When Victor Turner discussed Milton Singer's theory — among other things — we can also observe an interesting shift of terminology between two collections of Turner's articles, published in 1982 and 1987, respectively. The one from the beginning of the 1980s was entitled *From Ritual to Theatre: The Human Seriousness of Play.* The one from the second half of the 1980s is called *The Anthropology of Performance.* The broad perspective which Victor Turner offered in these books is best summarized by the title of one of the articles: "Images and Reflections: Ritual, Drama, Carnival, Film and Spectacle in Cultural Performance."[4] We also note that the word "theatre" is not included in this list.

While Turner had difficulties in defining the play elements in human behavior, Schechner has tried to locate play and playing not within the system of theatre, but within the framework of performance. Contrary to Jerzy Grotowski's search for universal modes of expressions or Eugenio Barba's notion of pre-expressiveness, Schechner is well aware of the significance of the cultural context. For Schechner, interculturalism, not universalism, became the basis of performance studies, which in his view implies a paradigmatic shift away from theatre studies. Interculturalism became for him the bridge to a much wider understanding of that which is performative in human behavior.

## *The Controversy*

Schechner presented his concept at a conference of the Association for Theatre in Higher Education (ATHE) in Atlanta in 1992. "The new paradigm is 'performance,' not theatre," Schechner proclaimed, because "theatre as we have known and practiced it — the staging of written dramas — will be the string quartet of the 21st century: a beloved but extremely limited genre, a subdivision of performance."[5] Schechner's criticism of the existing theatre departments is very harsh, since these schools produce "graduates who are neither professionally trained nor academically educated" (p. 8). Therefore, he says, "'Theatre departments should become 'Performance departments.' Performance is about more than the enactment of Eurocentric drama" (p. 9). The four main areas of performance studies are entertainment, education, ritual, and healing. Performance can be observed in "politics, medicine, sports, religion and everyday life." Schechner offers a catalogue of activities which should be included in performance studies; under the heading of popular entertainment, for example, he suggests: "rock concerts, discos, electioneering, wrestling, con games and stings, college and professional sports, vogueing, street theatre, parades, demonstrations, and a panoply of religious rituals ranging from staid old church services to hot gospel sings, to the rituals of Asian and African religions, to the practices of New Age Shamanism" (pp. 9f). In all of these human activities there are a great variety of performative elements worthy of study. Some scholars might, nevertheless, call these elements theatrical, depending on what implications they give the term "theatricality."

Schechner's speech in Atlanta, the formation of a performance studies "focus group" within ATHE, and the printed version of his speech in the winter issue of *TDR* were indeed a revelation for some and a provocation for others. Small wonder that Schechner's attack on theatre studies was followed by a great number of comments, not only at the ATHE conference, but also in writing. I have already mentioned Bill Worthen, former editor of *Theatre Journal*, who pointed out the political dimensions of the controversy: "Like many negotiations, boundary wars are as much a contest of authority and power as of 'truth' or 'method'"(*TDR*, 39). At the same time, Worthen was also questioning the novelty of the performance paradigm, since Schechner is "largely multiplying 'objects' of study (that is, merely expanding the turf [Bourdieu's field!]) under the banner of 'intercultural' performance, rather than articulating the conceptual paradigm that would offer new modes of analysis and explanation, a new sense of what counts and of how it counts in the identification, analysis, and explanation of performance" (p. 21).

Worthen's main argument is that a text — not least a drama text — is as fragile and undetermined as a performance. Therefore, texts constitute an object of studies as much as any kind of performance. Worthen does not want to abandon drama studies, especially since Schechner does not offer any real conceptual alternatives. In his conclusion he states: "New paradigms are often ghosted by their history in ways that are difficult to recognize, acknowledge and transform; to understand 'performance studies' through a simple opposition between text and performance is to remain captive to the spectral disciplines of the past" (p. 23).

Worthen's article — originally presented at the American Society for Theatre Research (ASTR) conference in New Orleans — in turn provoked a number of reactions. Some voices, such as those of Joseph Roach and Phillip B. Zarrilli, were very polemic, questioning Worthen's — in their view — text-performance binary, defending interculturalism, and denying the "stabilities" of any kind of paradigms. In the ensuing issue of *TDR*,[6] Jonathan Warman, on the other hand, presented what could be called an apology for "live, European-style theatre" (p. 7). By this he means "that form of performance which lives in the shadow of Aeschylus, Shakespeare, Racine, Calderón, and their peers and executors, or which is created in direct reaction to, or against, such performances" (p. 8). He advocates new forms of theatre, but still emphasizes theatre, because, as the title of his article says, "Theatre Not Dead."

Jill Dolan, who had already taken up this issue in an article in *Theatre Journal* in 1993, held a more conciliatory position in the controversy.[7] She admits that "a focus on 'performance' per se, at conferences and in academic departments or programs, might not ensure radical contents and considerations, politically, methodologically, or disciplinarily" (p. 31). Instead of competing with each other or trying to replace each other, Dolan suggests that theatre studies and performance studies should be "seen as mutually empowering each other" (p. 32). If I understand her correctly, she still can see links between theatre and performance studies which her own feminist studies have established for her work.

## *Theatre: The Terminology*

What kind of theatre does Schechner have in mind when he speaks about the Eurocentric string quartet of the twenty-first century? Let me

quickly draw a sketch of the impressions I have gathered from my reading about the controversy.

Speaking about theatre at U.S. universities seems to be equivalent to
speaking about the production of spoken drama. Theatre is understood
as text-based in the sense that the starting point for theatre is a drama
text. Drama texts are almost exclusively texts for spoken drama. Opera
libretti or dance scenarios are scarcely part of the curriculum. Dance is
studied at special departments, and musical theatre is hardly taught any-
where. Dramatic texts for spoken drama are supposed to contain characters, which means that theatre also is character-based. Student actors
are trained nearly exclusively to impersonate characters. They tend to
treat characters almost as living human beings with a personal history,
an individual psychology, and a distinguishable personality.

I call this description typical, meaning that this is a normal and wide-
spread concept of theatre at U.S. universities. There are certainly colleges where such a narrow idea of theatre is not prevailing, but I think
my picture of theatre as it is referred to in the theatre/performance debate is fairly accurate. Even from a European perspective this is a recognizable species of theatre. One will find it in almost every European
city with a municipal or national theatre institution. Quite a few of the
productions at these places are conservative and undynamic presentations, while others are very interesting. It is the kind of theatre in which
directors such as Peter Zadek, Antoine Vitez, Robert Wilson, Heiner
Müller, and Ingmar Bergman are or have been working. These were the
home environments of actors like Greta Garbo and Ingrid Bergman,
Laurence Olivier, Jean Vilar, Gérard Depardieu, and Jutta Lampe. The
European notion of theatre as part of the nationally endowed culture — including music theatre and to some extent dance — is indeed
different from America's concept of theatre. Furthermore, the same European authorities also subsidize music theatre and dance, which, especially in Germany, are often located in the same theatre building. U.S.
theatre, in contrast, as we see it from the other side of the ocean, is not
just a well-acted version of BBC domestic television dramas or Hollywood family series. We think of musicals — which are an original genre
from the United States — and of Happenings and Performance Art,
off-off Broadway experiments, stand-up comedies, Shakespeare-in-the-
park and other open air events, and similar things. U.S. theatre is cer-

tainly not restricted to spoken drama, but the theatre described as "legitimate theatre" has, roughly speaking, the same limitations as university theatres: the more or less realistic (re)production of written dramas with decent characters engaged in an understandable plot. I think it is such a reductionist view of theatre which Schechner accuses theatre departments of employing.

The theatrical work of directors like Peter Stein, Ariane Mnouchkine, or Ingmar Bergman could probably be labeled "Eurocentric string quartets," or maybe we would prefer to see them as symphonies of European theatre. But the European notion of theatre — among politicians, spectators, or scholars — is, on the contrary, far from being restricted to the symphonic or chamber format.

At least for northern European scholars the term "theatre" does not designate any given genre of artistic activities. There are at least five major types of theatrical expressions which are conventionally looked upon as theatre: spoken drama, music theatre, dance theatre, mime/pantomime, and puppet theatre. These types of theatre are not mutually exclusive (spoken drama can very well be presented as puppet theatre, and many operas contain sections for ballet, etc.) — nor is the list complete. Circus, cabarets, parades, and radio theatre are just a few examples that could be added. This broad understanding of theatre is of course a culturally conditioned concept. Not only does the picture of European theatre history include all these variations of theatrical activities, but it has also deeply influenced the scholarly approach to theatre, especially concerning the role of drama. The following two historical references might illustrate the significant difference between drama-oriented and performance-oriented approaches to early theatre studies.

Kenneth Macgowan and William Melnitz explicitly state in their book, *The Living Stage: A History of World Theatre* (1955) that "for almost two thousand years the theatre of Europe lay dead. Between 400 BC and close to 1600, no dramatist wrote a single great play. From Euripides to Lope de Vega, Marlowe, and Shakespeare, the stage was barren — when there was a stage."[8] The pioneer of German theatre studies, Max Herrmann (referred to in the previous chapter), has expressed his attitude toward drama in an often quoted passage in which he dismisses drama studies altogether, except for the use of drama texts as historical sources.[9] Herrmann's position, expressed already in 1914, is typical of the attitude of much central European theatre research throughout this century, and I see it as a strong opposition to the Anglo-Saxon tradition of drama studies.

## Theatre: Three Concepts

So far I think I have distinguished at least three major categories of theatrical concepts: the American type of legitimate theatre, text- and character-based drama, quite influential within the educational system of colleges and universities; the European view of theatre, much wider than the American one, including a multitude of theatrical and semitheatrical genres; and last but not least performance, a category embracing "politics, medicine, sports, religion and everyday life," in Schechner's already quoted terms. Each of them most likely has virtues as well as defects.

The type of legitimate theatre (i.e., the spoken drama) reflects a common American understanding of theatre as an art form as opposed to the U.S. entertainment industry. In this sense, legitimate theatre qualifies (sometimes) for subsidies from the National Endowment for the Arts. Although a narrow concept, it is very clear, with a certain canon of plays, a historical approach to the text, a specific — mostly Stanislavskian — style of acting, a director at the center of critical attention, and an emphasis on content and interpretation. It is also obvious that the type of spoken drama discussed here has its origin in a specific period of European theatre history, roughly speaking, the postromantic era, from the second half of the nineteenth century onward. What is less frequently observed is that this period includes the most expansive years in European history — in economical, political, and cultural terms. This is the period during which the bourgeoisie gained power, formulated its ideology, and exported its ideas as eternal values to the rest of the world. During this age of increasing industrialization and deepening cultural colonization, especially around the turn of the century, the realist, drama-based theatre was exported to colonies as well as free countries outside Europe. It created such (hybrid) forms as the Shin Geki in Japan, the Huaju in China, the English-language drama in India and large parts of Africa (and also its French, Spanish, and Portuguese equivalents), and the Teatro Independiente movement of the 1930s in Argentina. There is, in other words, a colonial stench to legitimate theatre, which should not be neglected. It should also be clear that this type of theatre has been and still is a self-representation of the (white, Christian, educated) middle class.

The European concept of theatre is — I maintain — much wider, but also includes the American concept of legitimate theatre. In Europe we do not use such a line of demarcation between serious theatre and entertainment theatre — we have all read Bertolt Brecht and we know that serious thoughts need to be entertaining. Opera is serious, mostly, and so is modern dance, and many European theatre artists are even taking children's theatre seriously. Among scholars, the scope of theatrical activities has been considered very broad, and a number of topics — like Renaissance parades, Dadaist cabarets, or cross-dressing during any period of theatre history — might even qualify as performance studies. The main field of scholarly interest is, nevertheless, focused on a great variety of activities, which, in a broad sense, can be looked upon as theatrical modes of expression, but with limitations which are regularly debated.

Performance studies as a discipline does not seem to set any limits to what could be interesting as a field of inquiry. There are performative aspects to all kinds of human behavior. Some recent research has shown that such an approach can be fruitful in many areas. Just one example is the collection of articles published under the title *Cruising the Performative*, edited by Sue-Ellen Case, Philip Brett, and Susan L. Foster. In this volume transvestism, tango, eighteenth-century elephants and Sea World whales, queer performativity, religious lyrics of devotion, and even the hyphen are points of departures for inspiring adventures in reading. This extremely open attitude has its risks as far as theatre studies is concerned, however. Schechner himself has noted a drop in the number of subscribers to *TDR* by 80 percent during the last twenty-five years. Richard Hornby, in a letter to the editor, found the reason obvious: "While hundreds of thousands of Americans are seriously interested in theatre, only specialists are interested in shamanism and the semiotics of figure skating."[10] Is this comment to be taken seriously? I don't know, but the theatre/performance controversy seems to have many kinds of implications. There is, however, an overshadowing problem implicit in all of these concepts: all these categories are based on the exclusion or inclusion of certain genres. "What counts?" as Bill Worthen asked in his article. What can still be considered as "theatre" and what not? How many genres can a European concept of theatre account for? Is there anything which might be excluded from performance studies?

For me, these are not very fruitful questions. The whole discussion becomes a quantitative enumeration of study areas, although everybody intended to bring up qualitative arguments. To avoid a power struggle about who is authorized to make distinctions — to put up fences in Bourdieu's field — we should rather reconsider the theoretical principles and the epistemologies of our studies.

## Theoretical Reorientation

One thing is for sure: on both sides of the ocean — and probably along other shores, too — there is an enormous emphasis on the production side of theatre and performance. How are performances produced? What intentions were articulated or implicit, what aesthetic concepts did the creator — usually the director — have? How can we grasp the meaning of what are called "works of theatrical art"? I think these work-oriented approaches are dated and far too limited for a serious discussion of theoretical issues as well as for the discourse of intercultural perspectives.

This need for theoretical reorientation became obvious to me while I was engaged in my own section of the theatrical field, the garden where I once planted my flowers and grew my own vegetables: reception research. This is not the time and place to expand on the wonderful questions of methodologies and practicalities of audience and reception research, but I think that some of the results could be illuminating for the discussion here.[11]

I was curious to find out why spectators like theatrical performances. The central point, the focus of attention, and the clearly decisive element for the spectator's overall evaluation of a theatrical performance is the acting. A spectator's value judgment of the entire performance is most directly influenced by what the spectator attributes to the performers. This is true regardless of the theatrical genre or the sociocultural background of the spectator (at least in Stockholm). I could only find two exceptions: classical operas — Mozart is always considered to be superb — and very young spectators, who for the most part will not express any judgments about the performers at all. Otherwise, a play, a musical, a modern opera, and a classical ballet are never considered to be better than the standards with which they are performed. This goes even for Shakespeare and Calderón! *How* something is performed is obviously more important than *what* is performed. There are a number of reasons which can explain the spectator's tendency to privilege the performer over the play. The only encounter which the spectator experiences directly is the acting. A spectator does not meet the director; nor does the script become visible as such — it exists only through the interpretation of the performer. Therefore, the fiction can hardly be judged higher than the formation it derives from. (It needs a very well trained spectator — like a scholar — to distinguish the play from the playing.) It is the live performer who is the main interest of the audience, as well as the gauge of judgment. Furthermore, I have noted that a spectator only shows interest in the content of a performance when s/he finds the quality of the acting sufficiently high. If the spectator is not pleased by the "how" of the performance, the "what" becomes secondary and at times even irrelevant. In other words, plot and characters, drama, and text are of little interest unless the overall presentation is satisfying.

Following these observations, I would like to suggest a theoretical reconsideration of the conceptualization of theatre, rather than discarding theatre altogether in favor of a new and not always so clear paradigm of performance. It would be pretentious to offer a solution to these complex and much debated problems. What I would like to point out in conclusion are some distinctions which I have found useful while dealing with theoretical problems of theatre scholarship.

First of all it is necessary to develop systematic theories of the theatre. By systematic theories I mean exactly what Dietrich Steinbeck suggested thirty years ago: the study of the concepts and the terminologies we use when we speak and write about theatre.[12] The risk is that we work with a number of conventional assumptions about theatre which are rarely reflected upon, although they are constantly in use. One could possibly talk about paradigms which are not made manifest as paradigms. Our forebears in theatre studies, for example, frequently spoke about theatre as a "compound" work of art (meaning that theatre comprises literature, music, design, acting, technology, etc., which, considered together, establish the art of theatre). The spectator was found necessary, but had no real place in that concept. The spectator is still not accounted for, only "assumed" or "implied." All the emphasis is placed on the production and the meaning of text and performance. This might seem odd as a theory of theatre, but it has been practiced for almost a century.

If, for a moment, we neglect the existence of a text and the intentions of a director, we still have some kind of performer and some kind of a spectator. How can we describe such an encounter — not beyond specific genres, but within them! Are there really differences between experiencing an opera singer, a performance artist, a shaman, a goalkeeper, and an actor? And if there are differences, in what categories and in which terminology are we dealing with them? Maybe the meaning of "performance" as an accomplishment, like that of the aforementioned athlete, could be considered. I think the personal encounter between a performer (a specific person) and a spectator (also a specific person) has to be studied much more closely in terms of psychology, gender relations, class formations, genre expectations, and other contextual conditions.

We have to reconsider the entire theatrical event as the intersection of production and reception, or, when contemporary events are in question, of presentation and perception. This also brings up the question of fictionalization. The character is one of the paradigms of traditional theatre studies, but there is no character on stage — just a performer in costume; neither is the character only a product of the spectator's fantasy. The character is not explained by the "agreement" between performer and spectator or by the so-called framing that leads us to consider something "theatre." It is a much more complex interaction between those elements mentioned, but further systematic theoretical research is needed to develop a terminology which allows us to discuss these issues in terms like performativity, referentiality, theatricality, or liminality. There have been a number of interesting articles on these issues, from Josette Féral's ideas on theatricality in 1988 to Ian Watson's most recent contribution in *New Theatre Quarterly* entitled "Naming the Frame: The Role of the Pre-interpretative in Theatrical Reception."[13] I have tried to work on this issue myself for a while, and some of my considerations are collected in this book. I am not advocating some new form of essentialism (knowing full well that essentialism is out in this period of poststructural thinking). Instead of counting genres, which may be included or excluded from some type of studies, I suggest systematic inquiries into the concepts we apply. It is part of the epistemological foundations of our discipline as well as the basis of the empirical work we accomplish. If something is essential to me, it is to give up the narrow production- and work-oriented perspectives and to bring into focus the contextual events as objects of our studies, the live interaction between stage and auditorium, or, more generally speaking, the specific doings of all participants in a performative or theatrical event, the effects of these doings, and their contexts. I agree with Schechner's view that as we should leave out the "Eurocentric string quartet" of playmaking and that our discipline first and foremost should be an integral part of the humanities. To abandon theatre as a concept altogether and to turn all our attention toward performance seems an unnecessary split to me. I think what is needed is a broader concept of theatre and a more thorough systematic investigation into the wide field of theatrical events.

I have been asking myself whether I have been trying to cover up a political position in the field of theatre and performance studies by introducing another scholarly argument. I am probably no different from anybody else who has been engaged in this controversy. I would, however, like to suggest another metaphor: I just wanted to open another gate in the fence, to let theatre studies out, to let performance studies in, to let ideas and theories flow in a more fruitful circuit. I don't believe in the closing of concepts: I believe in fruitful encounters.

# 3

# Reacting
# to Actions
## Concepts of
## Theatricality

The term "theatrical" is widely used, appearing in casual language to describe a variety of situations and behaviors, which often have nothing to do with theatre. Graduation ceremonies can have a theatrical touch; a scoring team excels in theatrical hugging and dancing; a politician might deliver excuses in theatrical poses; mourners can cry out their sorrow in theatrical gestures during a funeral; and even an actor can be accused of being theatrical on stage. In all of these cases the adjective "theatrical" has negative implications, marking something exaggerated or formalized, something which is not serious, not expressing real feelings. "Theatrical" carries the stigma of pretense, which is contrary to deeply felt emotions and honest concerns.

Transformed into a noun, the term "theatricality" assumes a different significance: it is no longer a negative description of a nonreality-based behavior, but an artistic or scholarly concept. As a concept, theatricality is meant to represent the essential or possible characteristics of theatre as an art form and as a cultural phenomenon.

While "theatrical" denominates a more or less generally agreed upon notion of shallowness and exaggeration, there is no agreement about "theatricality" as a possible theoretical paradigm within the field of theatre studies. On the contrary, concepts of theatricality have been presented and debated throughout the twentieth century.

## Categories of Theatricality

In *Theatre Research International*, Erika Fischer-Lichte presented a collection of articles on this elusive topic.[1] In her introduction she referred to some classical and some more recent discussions on various concepts of theatricality. These articles and books, augmented with a few others, could be summarized under a few headings to bring some order to the diversity of opinions.

One way of using the term "theatricality" is to give it a *metaphoric* meaning. One of the first to apply theatre as a metaphor of social behavior was Erving Goffman; he found many followers who told us how people enter the stage of life, how they approach the footlights to be exposed to the public, what they do behind the wings, and so forth. The anthropologist Victor Turner and the philosopher Bruce Wilshire — discussed by Marvin Carlson in the above mentioned issue of *TRI* — can also be included within this category. The problem with metaphorical applications is that most of these scholars from various disciplines have a very limited view of theatre. What they refer to is the most traditional domestic drama, enacted in a realistic style on an American mainstream stage or maybe in a BBC family series. The actor is thought of as a person who pretends to be someone else — in other words, the theatre remains unproblematized, and theatricality is reduced to mean something which is pretended.

Another group of applications could be labeled *descriptive*. We find this attitude most clearly expressed in Roland Barthes' writing, stating that theatricality is just "le théâtre, moins le texte."[2] Such a view was already held by Georg Fuchs at the beginning of this century; it was repeated in Patrice Pavis" *Dictionaire du théâtre* and also in a recent German *Theaterlexikon*. In this latter article, Hans-Thies Lehmann defines theatricality as everything on stage which is not the drama text and draws the conclusion that in modern theatre theatricality is mainly the business of directors. Within this definition, theatricality is more or less equivalent to what other scholars call *mise-en-scène*.

A third category of definitions of theatricality could be called *binary*, because they are directed against something which is considered nontheatrical. Theatricality in this sense was mainly thought of as an antithesis to naturalism, and the term was frequently used by the Russian avant-garde at the beginning of the last century. Theatre should not reproduce reality on stage but become a reality of its own, become theatrical or, in Nikolai Evreinov's term, retheatricalized. Gordon Craig and Antonine Artaud could also be mentioned as sharing such a view on theatricality. The Canadian dance scholar Michèle Febvre has reversed this idea, encircling theatricality in dance by emphasizing the narrative aspect of theatre as opposed to the abstract forms of contemporary dance.

Another important group of writing I summarize as *epochal*, because most of these discussions of theatricality are characterized by the attitude that there is no general definition of this term, only temporary concepts. Each epoch develops certain indications of what theatre is and understands theatricality accordingly. Helmar Schramm has studied the use of the term theatre since the Renaissance, when *theatrum* was still a showcase, where anything worth watching was shown. In her 1972 book on this topic Elizabeth Burns defined theatricality as a "mode of perception," which Joachim Fiebach extended to also include a "mode of behavior and expression." These modes will change continually; therefore theatricality can only be defined within a certain time and a certain culture.

Some scholars think that a general concept of theatricality could be described — for instance Josette Féral, who underlines the bodily presence of performer and spectator and their specific relationship to each other.[3] Erika Fischer-Lichte looks at theatricality from a semiotic point of view, stating that it is a "particular mode of using signs," namely, that theatrical signs are always signs of signs. It is not my idea to establish a bibliography on theatricality; nor can these writings be presented adequately in this context. I am interested in categorizing the different approaches in order to find my own position (i.e., looking for a terminology which is conceptual on a general level). If the concepts of theatricality change from epoch to epoch or from culture to culture, there might nevertheless be a common axis along which the definitions and concepts travel.

Trying to establish a concept of theatricality — in dialogue with those who have already worked in the field — I find it worthwhile to observe that theatricality is described as part of the performance on stage, including a specific style of theatrical representation, or as a mode of perception. In other words, theatricality has been related either to the stage or to the auditorium. Only Josette Féral underlines the necessity of the physical presence of both performer and spectator as a prerequisite of theatricality. In my own attempt to contribute to this discussion earlier, I have tried to construct a bridge between style and perception, but this construction seems too weak for the heavy traffic of theorizing.[4] In this essay I follow two different pathways (i.e., the performer's and the spectator's activities), placed in what I hope are recognizable contexts.

## Theatricality as Actions and Reactions

Employing a phenomenological approach, I have attempted to describe theatre as the communicative intersection between the performer's actions and the spectator's reactions. I think it would be useful for the discussion of theatricality to investigate the possibilities such an approach offers for constructing a reasonable model of theatrical processes, which may illuminate some aspects of theatricality itself.

### ACTIONS

What does a performer do when he or she appears on stage? For conventional reasons I assume at this point that the performer is a traditional actor (later I consider how the model can be applied to the speech of a politician, the acts of a circus artist or a magician, performers in non-Western theatre, and the entertainment of a stand-up comedian). I am also aware of the fact than any space might become a stage, according to Peter Brook's famous statement, although the transition from space to stage is more problematic than it looks at first sight.

The very appearance of the performer on what we assume is a stage already has a number of implications. Just to be there on a spot where hundreds of eyes can watch means that the performer has to show him/herself, with the emphasis on *him/herself*. The performer exposes both physical appearance and mental condition. Despite the possibilities of makeup and costume, the actor's bodily appearance is exhibited with all its beauty and faults. Sarah Bernhardt has pointed out this fact: Had Beethoven or Berlioz, Michelangelo or Raphael, been clubfooted, it would not have made any difference in respect to their art, but an actor cannot afford such a "handicap."[5] Even in more liberal times, the physical self of the actor has a major impact on the impression the performer is able to create. Women's and men's bodies are perceived through culturally conditioned norms, and every performer's body is exposed to the view of an audience according to these norms. I call this basic part of the performer's appearance on stage *exhibitory actions*. The term "action" should not confuse the reader: to appear on stage is here considered an action, even when the performer does not do anything particular. Although the performer does not act, there is an act of showing which I include in the term "exhibitory actions."

These kinds of actions are not limited to the performer's physical qualities, but also include the performer's mental status at first appearance and throughout the performance. An actor may feel very self-assured and confident when appearing on stage, but can also suffer from nervousness or from a more destructive stage fright. Even when actors try to conceal such emotions before the eyes of the audience, it certainly will affect their exhibitory actions. What will be visible is the degree of their concentration and attention, which is directed toward their own self, toward other actors, and toward the audience. Actors are usually employing different techniques to reach full concentration, an aspect which is well known, but important to note in this connection.

The actor's basic appearance is also affected by such personal things as voice and bodily movements. On this level, however, we can already speak of the actor's expressive means, under the heading of *encoded actions*. Looking, for example, at gestures, it is most likely that hand movements are partly conditioned by the actor's "natural" behavior, partly by cultural patterns. This is not always obvious, since it is hard to distinguish involuntary movements from consciously expressive gestures. What seem to be individual or sometimes even personal movements can very well be prepatterned though the cultural environment. A look at the hand movements of newscasters on television — probably involuntary movements and definitely not meant to be artistic expressions — reveals such cultural patterns, when comparing programs on Swedish Television, the Italian RAI, or CNN. Learned behavior, stereotypes, and international influences can easily be seen when traveling from country to country.

The encoded actions of a performer are to a high degree determined not only by individual and cultural conditions, but also by the aesthetic norms of the particular performance. Here I think primarily of the requirements of certain genres, styles, and periods. There are numerous conventions about how to perform in comedy, drama, farce, or tragedy — which, of course, change from period to period and from region to region — there are major styles (realism, minimalism, expressionism, etc.), and there are, last but not least, different types of theatrical expressions (such as opera and music theatre, spoken drama, ballet and dance, mime, and puppetry). Every one of these categories presupposes a set of aesthetic rules and norms, which the performer has to follow or, in exceptional cases, can consciously moderate.

All these ingredients are present at the very moment when a performer performs. Assuming the performer is an opera singer, the singing contains the individual voice of this particular performer, a personal timbre, recognizable in whatever he or she sings and changing only slightly over the years. There is a definite difference between Maria Callas and Birgit Nilsson. But their voices do not sound "natural," since they were trained according to the norms of opera singing, which follow certain aesthetic ideals as well as differences in taste and preferences of the singers themselves, their impresarios, the repertoire they perform in, the managers of opera institutions who hire them, and the audiences in various countries which applaud them. The example of the opera singer is meant to point out the complexity which is immanent in every encoded action on a stage.

An important aspect of encoded actions is the skill with which they are performed. Whereas certain genres require special techniques and long training — such as opera singing or ballet dancing — others can be executed by amateurs and even children. Ian Watson has given a wonderful example of how his four-year-old son behaved as a puppeteer and how the older sister corrected him, because he was not strictly keeping to the rules of puppet theatre:[6] there are certain conventions of the genre which the performer has to follow, even when lacking artistic skills. The question of the skillfulness of encoded actions is important for the performer and maybe even more so for the spectator, but whether it is of any concern for the problems of theatricality remains unresolved at this point.

The exhibitory actions and the encoded actions are normally not performed without purpose. They are at least intended to signify something which is beyond the directly perceivable appearance of those actions.

But exhibitory and encoded actions do not automatically convey such a symbolic level. It therefore seems useful to me to introduce at least one more type of actions, which I have called *embodied actions*.

In the narrow sense of the word, embodied actions are actions in which the performer chooses consciously to signify "something." There are certain intentions on the part of the performer to produce some kind of symbolic or fictional meaning. Some embodied actions can be described as real actions (i.e., the performer carries out something on stage which is meant to show exactly what it is): when the actor sits down on a chair, it does not mean that the actor is tired, but that the performer is presenting the act of sitting down. Other embodied actions are not real actions, but pretended ones. The performer acts as if doing something, but does not do it in reality. Both pretended and real actions can be used as embodied actions.

At this point it might be important to make a distinction between embodied actions, which I sometimes have called "performative" actions, and performativity as such. Embodied actions are presented by the performer in order to show something. The act of showing is always directed toward someone who can see it. Thus, embodied actions are intended to be perceived by another person, called the spectator when speaking about theatre. Despite the performer's intentions, there is no guarantee that the spectator is able to decode and understand the intended meaning of a certain embodied action. This does not alter the status of the actions as being performative.

Performativity, in contrast, in my view is a much larger concept which belongs to the communicative process in theatrical situations. Performativity relates to performative, embodied actions as intentionality relates to intentions. Intention belongs to a psychological category, expressing an act of will, whereas intentionality is a philosophical term, describing the basic hermeneutic experience of understanding — knowing that an expression is an expression for something. The spectators in the theatre know that the expressions on stage presented to them are meant to signify something. This means that everything on stage, produced consciously or just there, is open for interpretation. In that sense, performativity describes the interaction between stage and auditorium, saying that practically everything can contribute to the production of meaning. From the perspective of theatrical communication, exhibitory and encoded actions can also assume symbolic meanings and thus be integrated into the performativity of the theatrical event. So far, I am still dealing with the performer's actions, and I think it is useful for the discussion of theatricality to distinguish the three major modes of actions which I have presented here — exhibitory actions, encoded actions, and embodied actions.

I am consciously avoiding two terms which most scholars might find adequate in this discussion: "playing" and "character." The notion of playing is far too wide to describe in detail what the actor is doing on stage. Of course, there is a play element involved in theatrical activities, as Aristotle pointed out, and this has fascinated many anthropologists. Hans-Georg Gadamer, however, has made it clear that playing is the basis of all art forms and as such is always directed toward another individual, the other; so far I have hardly mentioned the spectator.[7] The concept of character is a paradigm of Western theatre and theatre scholarship, which is not very accurate and which I would like to question as an ingredient of theatricality.

When an actor speaks a line such as Shakespeare's famous "A horse, a horse, a kingdom for a horse," he is simultaneously carrying out the three actions described above. He uses his voice as part of the exhibitory actions, delivers the line according to codes determined through individual, cultural, and aesthetic choices, and gives them a embodied quality partly though the use of real actions (for example, shouting the line) and pretended actions such as indicating despair. All the three types of actions described here are involved in this act. I think it is only possible to distinguish them clearly in analytical terms, while a real experience in the theatre easily might blur the distinction.

If I accidentally witnessed an actor speaking this line for practice in a dressing room or in a remote corner of a park, I might find the situation "theatrical," but I would not necessarily perceive it in terms of theatricality. In my view, theatricality is not something which is produced by the performer alone, but is established through the interplay between performer and spectator. Looking into the performer's dressing room leaves it open to the onlooker to determine whether the event carries an element of theatricality. This means that it is not sufficient just to observe a theatrical process: one has to participate in it to be defined as a spectator. As Josette Féral has suggested, only the presence of both performer and spectator seems to be a reasonable ground for speaking about theatricality. An onlooker is not yet and not necessarily to be defined as a spectator.

## REACTIONS

How does a spectator participate in the theatrical event? In a number of reception studies there are frequent references to four characteristic responses from the audience: reflections of prior experiences, emotional reactions, cognitive reactions, and value judgments.[8] Since prior experiences, producing expectations, preferences, and prejudices, have a strong impact on both emotional and cognitive reactions during and after the performance, they become part of the actual theatrical experience and can be dealt with as direct responses to the performer. Value judgments, in turn, influence as well as result from the emotional and intellectual effects of the encounter with the performer and can therefore be seen as part of these reactions. It seems relevant for this discussion to concentrate on those central involvements, which deal with emotion and cognition.

Emotions are a complicated matter, because they range from intuition and vague feelings to strong responses and psychic crises. As a scholarly field of investigation the study of emotions and feelings has mainly occupied disciplines like psychology and psychoanalysis, but even in the field of philosophy and aesthetics there are numerous examples of studies such as Jean-Paul Sartre's attempt in 1948 to launch a phenomenological theory of emotions. As far as theatre is concerned, there have been many discussions about how to present emotions on stage and how this affects the spectator, but more empirical studies about what kind of emotions a spectator actually does experience are — with the exception of an attempt by Meyerhold to measure audience reactions in the 1920s — of a very late date. Most theories of emotions agree upon a kind of chain of responses and reactions, which produce and resolve emotions. A typical emotional process starts with a stimulus, which is analyzed, compared to other experiences, evaluated, and finally transformed into an adequate feeling or a conscious/cognitive action.[9] In the process of a theatrical performance many such emotional chain reactions can be observed. The most frequent emotions in the theatre are pleasure, sympathy, empathy, and identification.[10]

Since the stimuli produced and presented during a theatrical performance are quite different, according to the distinctions used here between exhibitory, encoded, and embodied actions, it seems reasonable to assume equally differentiated emotional reactions from the audience. As cognitive processes occur and intermingle with emotions, information is accumulated and processed intellectually. These two parallel modes of reactions — the intuitive and the cognitive — can only be separated on a theoretical basis, whereas they continuously interact in the spectator's mind.

Exhibitory actions immediately trigger positive or negative feelings. Besides their physical necessity, exhibitory actions have the purpose of calling upon the spectator's attention. This attention is crucial for the entire theatrical communication. If the actor fails to affect the spectator, there will not be any communication at all. The importance of the stage personality and its capacity to get the audience's attention is a well-known fact for every casting director, film producer, or entertainment manager. This immediate feeling, which the spectator focuses on the actor, can cognitively be completed with notions like recognition, comparison, expectations, and also wishful identification with certain aspects of the body and personality that the actor exposes. To mark this level of communication I have used the term *sensory*, indicating that the perception of a stage personality in the exhibitory moments causes both automatic responses, which only gradually are processed into understandable cognitive knowledge, and persistent feelings that remain active during an entire performance.

Encoded actions produce different kinds of reactions. Here the emotions range from sheer enjoyment of what one hears and sees on stage to more sophisticated comparisons with earlier experiences. The presentation of encoded actions requires a certain competence on the part of the performer — even skills, as mentioned before — and a similar competence is also necessary on the spectator's part, if the emotional pleasure of the experience is to be transformed into an intellectual evaluation. The frequently reproduced caricature of the theatre critic who first obviously enjoys the show, only to criticize it later as not being in agreement with certain norms, comes very close to the actual interplay between emotional and intellectual responses to encoded actions which many experienced theatregoers may register. But aesthetic norms are flexible — the breaking of norms might be an expected feature of certain performances: the insufficient versatility of performers is fully acceptable when watching amateur and child actors, whereas technical perfection is absolutely necessary in classical ballet. Needless to say, the expectations as well as the actual pleasure vary according to the background of every spectator. I summarize this point of theatrical communication as *artistic* level.

The reactions to embodied actions are even more complicated, since they are in principle twofold. On the one hand, the spectator observes the embodied actions as such, realizing, for instance, when the actor really carries out certain actions but pretends to carry out others. On the other hand, the spectator is made aware that these actions symbolize actions of a different kind — that they are signs of signs — which are open to interpretation both emotionally and intellectually. This transformation of embodied actions into symbolic or fictive meaning can only take place when the spectator is given recognizable references. Such references can derive from various sources which — and this is important to emphasize — the actor and the spectator share to a large extent as long as they belong to the same cultural sphere. Although a complete similarity of references is hard to find, empirical reception studies indicate that the understanding of a performance in fictional terms is relatively uniform for all the spectators present. Still, the same fiction can be interpreted in various ways. I have called this type of communication the *symbolic* level, but it could be argued that a division of this level into two — an embodied and a referential level — could be useful from an analytical point of view. Personally I tend to see the referential processes as responses to the performative behavior of the actor, which the spectator is free to engage in or not. A discrepancy between intentions and responses, for instance, is obvious as soon as a spectator watches foreign theatre, when it is simply impossible to grasp the meaning of certain conventional expressions. But even a spectator who lacks the necessary competence can still enjoy other aspects of such a performance.

To speak about the performer and the spectator might seem appropriate in this theoretical context, but this singular constellation is rather exceptional in the life of theatre.[11] Therefore I would like to mention some features which concern the audience as collective. While an individual spectator very well can experience tension during a performance, the collective tension of many spectators grows into attention or attentiveness which directly affects the performers. The contrary reaction from the audience, inattentiveness, also affects the actors. To underline the actual mutuality of the theatrical communication, the interdependence between actors and spectators, I would like to mention Erland Josephson's experiences while performing in Peter Brook's production of *Cherry Orchard* in Japan. The Japanese spectators fell asleep, which was signaled to the actors when they heard the receivers of the simultaneous translation equipment dropping to the floor. Josephson describes how the actors became aware of the situation, how they communicated unnoticeably with each other on stage, and how they succeeded in re-engaging the spectators in the performance.[12] Many actors who have performed before young audiences have experienced the problems of inattentive spectators getting up from their seats rather than falling asleep. Meyerhold's study of audiences, mentioned earlier, used a scale from absolute silence to climbing onto the stage to register the behavior of his spectators at intervals of five minutes. In the end, there is nothing more rewarding than stormy applause, which confirms for the actors that they have done a good job and for the spectators that they have seen a wonderful performance.

## Theatricality and Style

A specific problem of theatre studies concerns the investigation of how daily life is reflected in theatrical expressions. I have developed a simple scale to indicate this relationship. I see this addition as a complement to the model of theatrical communication, and I consider it helpful in a study of theatrical style. It gives some explanation of how expressive means can be understood by the spectator.

First of all, playing is distinguished from everyday life, including the playing character of the theatrical event. The playing of games is a different activity compared to other social ways of behaving; as far as the performative arts are concerned, both the performer and the spectator are aware of this distinction. In other words the expressions on stage are artistic expressions and are understood as such by the spectator. At the same time, it is also clear that these artistic expressions are created by human bodies, which resemble other human bodies. It is difficult to imagine an abstract performer, in the sense in which a painting can be nonfigurative. Theatre, thus, always shows a certain resemblance to its nontheatrical environment (there are exceptions, which can be discussed as such).

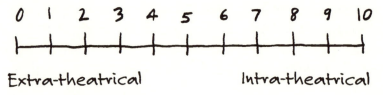

4. *A simple scale of theatricality.*

If I assume — although only for theoretical reasons — that performing could be equal to "life," I could use this "total similarity" as one possible fixed point in my understanding of style. If I also assume that performing could be "only" art without any resemblance to life, I could place this other fixed point opposite the first one as extremes on either end of a line. Since I know that all acting always contains both ingredients — life and art — to various degrees, I put a scale on this line not to measure but to distinguish different "mixtures" of life and style or, as it would have been termed in the nineteenth century, "nature and art." I have called the extreme points of this scale extra-theatrical and intra-theatrical, meaning that the understanding of expressive means either comes from outside the theatre, recognizable from some kind of "reality," or comes from within the theatre and its own conventions (see figure 4).

As I mentioned, this scale is not to be understood as an exact measurement of the artistic means of expression, but it could be used as an indication of different ways of perceiving styles of performing. Spectators and even scholars are never totally independent persons, but they watch a performance in a special theatrical and social context. The place which a particular style occupies on this scale depends on a number of contextual parameters, of which I would like to mention a few:

1. the theatrical conventions (for instance, the major Western conventions of theatrical genres);
2. the performative genres (such as music theatre, spoken drama, dance, mime and pantomime, puppet theatre, but also Happenings, performance art, ceremonies, and sports events);
3. the codes of everyday behavior in typical and significant national patterns (such as verbal and gestural expressions, movement patterns, proxemic relationships, dress codes, and color codes);
4. the social context, of which the performer and the spectator/the

audience are part (specified through gender, ethnicity, religion, class, etc.).

A few *ad hoc* examples may clarify how the scale could be used. I believe that opera, operetta, and revues occupy a more intra-theatrical range on the scale than many realistic drama performances, which at times try to get as close to zero as possible. Avant-garde performances tend to exceed the extremes on both ends: there are experiments which try to transform a performance into an entirely nonhuman expression — for example Wassily Kandinsky's *Der gelbe Klang* from the 1910s — and there are performance artists who neglect the performative aspect and become a reality beyond reality — for instance, Marina Abramovic's *The Lips of the Holy Thomas* from 1975 in Innsbruck, where the Yugoslavian artist actually cut a bleeding star into her stomach. The distance between two persons speaking to each other signifies different relationships in different countries. A loud voice and a face very close to the person one speaks to might just be an angry utterance in a southern European culture, whereas it would be considered an insult and a sign of disrespect in a Nordic country. Such behavior is of course interpreted differently according to the gender of the speakers, their age, their class, and the circumstances of the situation.

## Variations of Theatricality

A preliminary conclusion concerning the problems of theatricality would definitely support the idea that it is necessary to be able to speak about theatricality with the presence of both a performer and a spectator. It is a necessary condition, but not sufficient. The performer has to be defined as a performer, which I have tried to do by describing the various actions required in the process of performing. At the same time I have attempted to show in what ways the spectator becomes involved in these actions. The intersection between the performer's actions and the spectator's reactions — which I see as the core of theatricality — is characterized by three interactive levels, called the sensory, artistic, and symbolic levels of theatrical communication. These levels can only be activated during the process of a theatrical event. It is the very "eventness" of all theatre, the interaction between performer and spectator, which facilitates theatricality.

In the following I would like to present different situations to which it seems reasonable to apply a concept of theatricality, although certain elements of the above-described model might not be obvious at first sight in these experiences.

Some years ago I saw my first live Nō performance in Japan. My Japanese friends were worried that I might find it very boring, since I would not understand either the language or the theatrical codes of Nō. To their relief, I was very enthusiastic the next morning — I had a marvelous experience and was very pleased. They were wondering how I experienced such a performance, which even some of them find rather exotic. Trying to explain my experience, I compared it to hearing a symphony by Gustav Mahler: I responded to the sounds and the sights, tried to relax and not to exaggerate my attempts to understand, but just to see and hear. Some pictures created free associations in my mind; the voices gave me other impressions; I could feel the rhythm of the performance between tension and relaxation; and so forth. What I lacked were clear references, my only reference being a leaflet with a short note on the plot — which, I understood soon enough, was the least interesting aspect of the performance. It is, in other words, fully possible to have a rich experience of a theatrical performance without engaging in the referential system the performance is employing. I do not deny that a profound knowledge of the art of Nō gives a very different and probably much richer experience, but for my personal pleasure at that time the lack of references was no obstacle to gaining access to the performance. I could see the performative character of the actions; I could understand their performativity, but not their references. This is at least an indication that the fictional level can be suspended to a certain degree, assuming a much more general symbolic quality.

As long as we experience theatre in conventional theatrical environments, we do not have difficulties in applying models of theatricality. But how do we recognize a theatrical situation in the street — or, on the contrary, how do we know that something which happens on a conventional stage is not theatre but just stagehands working on some equipment? This question has made me wonder if the encoded actions and their recognition as encoded actions occupy a central position in the establishment of theatricality. Street performers usually give me a cue in the form of spectacular costumes or by shouting in a "theatrical" way or by other encoded actions which signal "street theatre." In Agusto Boal's

Invisible Theatre, which he uses as a pedagogical and political means to provoke discussions in public places, no such cues are given, although the performers use pretended actions. As performative actions, they might not be different from embodied actions in a recognizable theatrical situation, but since they are not encoded they remain "invisible" as theatre. Although there are exhibitory, encoded, and embodied actions, in this case these actions do not activate the different levels of communication. Provided that there are people who engage in this situation, only the sensory level comes into play, but not as theatrical communication. While the players use theatrical means of expression, the other participants treat them as ordinary people. The onlookers' referential system remains the same as in a real situation. They might react emotionally and intellectually; but, unlike a theatrical situation, they interfere with the actions of the performers. It certainly would be worth a closer examination, but my point in question here is the position of encoded actions. By making actions encoded (i.e., recognizable as encoded actions), theatre becomes theatre, political speeches appear as political speeches, circus acts remain circus acts. The type of encoding indicates genres, styles, professionality, and the type of performativity, which directs the spectator's expectations and ability to decode whatever happens from there.

Another complicated case is the performance of a stand-up comedian, although here the situation as such is very clear. Unlike Boal's invisible performers, here the comedian is obviously performing. The exhibitory aspect of the actions is dominating — the ego of the comedian not only is the focus of attention, but very often is also the issue which is talked about: the comedian refers to himself or herself even when jokes are told which originate from other sources. The comedian on stage is himself, like Lenny Bruce, who was frequently fined for what he told his audiences, and Jesper Odelsberg, a young Swedish comedian with cerebral palsy and severe impairments of movement and speech. Odelsberg sits in a wheelchair and makes fun of the term "stand-up"; he even makes fun of disabled people. This is acceptable only because he is disabled himself: his own movements assume the quality of exhibitory actions, which certify the reality of his embodied actions. Instead of functioning only as exhibitory actions, they are transformed into performative, embodied actions which need to be interpreted by the spectator. When he tells us that women are erotically interested in him, not because he is a lovely fellow, but because they want to enjoy his spastic movements, this drastic joke is only acceptable because the exhibitory and embodied actions coincide.

The following examples involve events which we normally do not consider "theatre," although they obviously carry certain traits of "theatricality." My purpose here is not to transform them into theatre, but to investigate what a concept of theatricality might add to the understanding of these events. This an important point, which at the same time tries to set limits to this concept of theatricality: it is not an attempt to make theatre into an all-embracing concept, but should be understood as an extension of what theatre studies could achieve when looking into other public events.

Since the times of Olof Palme, Swedish party leaders have gathered in the Hanseatic city of Visby on the island of Gotland in the Baltic sea. During one week, every one of them gives a speech on consecutive afternoons in the lush park of Almedalen, where local people mix with numerous tourists and a massive invasion of journalists. The next morning, the speeches are analyzed and evaluated on the editorial pages of almost every Swedish newspaper. A few years ago, Kurt Johannesson, professor of rhetoric, published a comparative study of these political events.[13] Unlike the editorial comments of the political journalists, his analysis concerned less the political content than the rhetorical means which the politicians employed to convey their political messages. Did the politicians wear a casual summer shirt like their listeners or did they dress up for the television cameras? What kind of metaphors were they using? Were the speeches related to the situation of standing and sitting on the green lawn of a park or were they no different from what is usually said in parliament? Did they address the people or the media? Were their gestures more expressive, more "theatrical" than in a regular political surrounding? The answers to these questions not only were highly interesting for Swedish readers who know the politicians, but might also contribute to the present discussion about concepts of theatricality.

The problem here is not whether a political speech qualifies as a theatrical event according to the principles of theatricality given above. I would rather suggest a contrary approach: if one uses the description of theatricality as the intersection of presentation and perception, seen through various levels of communication, then what does such a point of view say about political speeches? When Kurt Johannesson analyzes

*5. Olof Palme in the role of political orator. Photo by Bertil Wöllner.*

the "costumes" of the speakers, their way of addressing the people in the park, their use of their own summer and vacation experiences to illustrate their political points, their gestural language as designed for an open-air appearance, he depicts elements which clearly bear a resemblance to the sensory and artistic levels of communication described above. It is also clear that there is a great amount of interaction with the audience, at least in the case of certain politicians (not least in the case of Olof Palme, who was still alive at the time). But can we detect a symbolic level in these speeches — a level which transgresses the information which is given in them?

This question has at least two major aspects. First, I would have to find out if the rhetorical means of such speeches produce embodied actions, and, second, if such actions can be perceived in terms of symbolic or even fictional content. What can be described as embodied actions in the speech of a politician? If, for instance, the speaker uses a recent experience of a boat trip to illustrate how quickly a storm can threaten the idyllic pleasures of a summer vacation, he might demonstrate the storm with his voice, his gestures, by slowing down the delivery of his speech, by registering the horror of the situation in his own face, and so forth. These ways of illustrating a story to a listener can very well be accepted as embodied actions, and they will certainly be perceived as such, even if one listener believes the story while another takes it as a simple rhetorical trick.

There are also impersonating actions that will not be as obvious as the story of the stormy sea. The conclusion of this same story might eventually be used to give the audience the feeling that the speaker is a competent captain who knows how to handle a critical situation — the listeners therefore need not worry about future political crises as long as the speaker is in charge of the national boat. This symbolic message is in its way also a kind of fiction: its purpose is to keep the audience confident and calm. The spectator can take this message at face value (i.e., feel confident and calm) or can realize the theatricality of the speech and relate to it in terms of symbolic communication.

Analyzing the act of a circus artist through the glasses of theatricality reveals similar problems — namely, the question of whether a level of symbolic communication exists. There is no doubt that circus performers first and foremost display their skills, be it horseback riding, rope dancing, trapeze flying, or lion taming. The tension which these acts produce in the spectators derives to a large extent from the fact that the audience knows that these actions are not pretended actions, but actually require a high professional competence. Watching an artist swinging high in the cupola of the circus tent provokes both admiration and anxiety, pleasure and wishful identification. Does such an act also result in any kind of interpretative response from the spectator? Can the visitor to the circus perceive embodied actions, or are these restricted to the clowns only? I think the circus is a good example of a situation in which theatricality is largely determined by the attitude of the spectator. Many acts in the circus can be interpreted in terms of symbolic actions, showing the human capacity to overcome the laws of gravity, to — almost — fly like a bird, or to control tricky objects. In relation to such symbolic notions, the skills of the circus artist assume performative qualities, which are often supported by the artists' way of exposing their bodies by their costumes, by gestures of welcoming the audience and concluding the actions, by the dramaturgy of building up more and more daring exercises, and so forth. In other words, elements of theatrical display are easily found when looking at each act from the perspective of theatricality.

While circus artists make great efforts to show us their special skills, a magician invests great efforts in hiding skills from the spectators.[14] The acts of a magician are supposed to look "natural," but the spectator is expected to know that they are not. The magician's skill is not to let the spectator detect his or her "magic" doings. Here it is no longer a question of pretended or real actions — the embodied actions are meant to create an illusion of magic.

The experience of films reminds me of the same "magic illusion" that the magician creates. Film artists also do their best to hide the "tricks" through which they create illusion, whether this illusion is related to the "real" world or to the imaginary realm of virtual realities. Of course, the artists are not standing in front of us like the magician, but they seem to us to be present via the screen. On television they might even be present "in time." I consider these implications of presence — between the creation and the experience of an artifact — in chapter 5, which deals with human encounters and cultural events.

What do politicians, magicians, circus artists, and other performers have in common with a stand-up comedian or with my experience of a Japanese Nō performance? They are all in a sense performers who present actions to spectators who interact with these actions on various levels of communication. Is it meaningful to speak about these interactions in terms of theatricality?

Questioning theatricality as the communicative process between the performer's exhibitory, encoded, and embodied actions and the emotional and intellectual reactions of the spectator is an effective tool to analyze and understand events of a performative nature. Such events include both performances of a more conventional type, which we find in theatre buildings, and encounters between less traditional performers and their audiences in streets and other loci, on podia or in stadia.

As I have pointed out earlier, it is important not to confuse this concept of theatricality with possible definitions of theatre. Although this model has been constructed out of my scholarly experiences of performance analysis and reception studies, it is not confined to conventional forms of theatre productions. Sometimes I have found it applicable in connection with performances that were far from regular theatre experiences, and sometimes it has demonstrated to me aspects of theatricality in situations that are not normally associated with theatrical events at all.

In other words, theatricality can easily be detected outside the theatre, and as a concept it is applicable to many kinds of events. Theatricality is, however, something that takes place *between* actions and reactions. Unlike Erika Fischer-Lichte, who distinguishes between performative and referential signs, I do not think that the use of signs designates theatricality. Nor do I think that theatricality is a specific "mode of perception," as Elizabeth Burns uses the term. Theatricality, in my view, includes both perspectives, both actions which become signs and reactions through which these signs are perceived in a special way. But theatricality is not restricted to the production and perception of signs; it also includes the performer as person and artist, and it includes the spectator, who enjoys and understands the presentation.

## *The Turkish Tailor*

Instead of a conclusion, in which the matter under debate is condensed, simplified, and organized for suitable quotations, I prefer to present a concluding example. It does not add any more theoretical points or give more sophisticated explanations, so the hurried reader might as well proceed to the next essay. For those who take the time to continue reading, I want to demonstrate the interdependence between performer and spectator through the levels of sensory, artistic, and symbolic communication by describing my personal experience of a "performance," which did not take place in a regular theatre, but in a seminar room. The following happened during a conference on reception research in Munich many years ago.

Peter Stapele from the University of Leiden in the Netherlands was known to me and at least to some of the other participants as a scholar of semiotics, often writing in a difficult academic idiom. When he was due to give his paper, approximately twenty-five participants were assembled in a seminar room. Dr. Stapele approached the front desk: a relatively short, relatively heavy man in his mid-forties, wearing gym shoes and a thick Norwegian sweater.

Peter Stapele started to tell us about the Turkish Tailor, a story he knew from his grandmother, although she never could explain why the tailor had to be Turkish. While he was talking, he removed his shoes and took off his sweater. So far I only thought that he would feel more comfortable this way, but I also remember that I was surprised by his fairly muscular body, which became more visible when he wore only a T-shirt. He also took off his socks, a move which went beyond my assumption that he wanted to be comfortable. He quickly jumped onto the table — again I was surprised at how easily he moved his body — and sat down cross-legged.

So far Peter Stapele had been able to create an interest in his doings, indicating that we were to expect a theatrical event, but restricting himself to exhibitory actions: exposing his body and showing how easily he could control it. The spectators were responding with curiosity, registering details (which I still remember). The only unclear move to this point was his removal of his socks, an action I stored for later "use."

Sitting cross-legged on the table was for me an obvious reference to the title he had mentioned, since tailors — at least in our fairy-tale fantasies — used to sit cross-legged on their tables. Now he pulled out an invisible thread with one hand and cut it off with a two-finger pair of scissors and took a likewise invisible needle from the sleeve of the jacket which he was not wearing.

Two observations are in place here: at this point the spectators had a clear view of the encoded actions he was using — pantomime — and he also demonstrated his skills in doing so. These are two separate responses. One has to do with the choice of a specific mode of theatrical expression; the other concerns the mastering of this expression. The first is a cognitive process of recognition, which, furthermore, also holds a key to understanding an earlier moment, depending on the references of the spectator. For me, pantomime is originally a Roman genre; the actors of the Roman mime were called "planipes" — people in bare feet. Other spectators might have thought along other lines — for instance, that many actors practice in bare feet to avoid slipping on the floor. The second reaction mentioned above refers to his mastering of pantomimic movements. In that case both pleasure and value judgments are involved. How much we appreciated his performance depended to a high degree on the skillfulness of his presentation.

The performance went on. He took the imaginary needle and pierced it through his little finger, pulled the thread straight, and continued with the ring finger, repeating this maneuver through all his fingers including the thumb, which seemed especially painful because it is thicker than the fingers. There was much laughter in the auditorium at his comical enactment of this absurd sewing process.

So far we had experienced a fascinating set of actions: the exhibitory actions were still present (and for us in the seminar room he remained Peter Stapele, entertaining us) and the encoded actions were well executed and appreciated, but at the same time indicated embodied actions of a special kind. His imitation of sewing was clearly a pretended action, and this was important for the spectators: we would not have liked him to pierce his fingers with a real needle in front of us! The references he evoked were nevertheless "real-life" actions, imitating the way we might imagine a tailor sewing (albeit few of us had ever seen a tailor working, let alone a Turkish tailor). Pretended embodied actions were perceived as references to something we could only refer to in our fantasy, but the symbolic level of communication certainly worked perfectly. The theatrical conventions of pantomime mingled freely with the spectators' stereotyped images, creating fiction as well as entertainment.

To me this is an excellent example of the spectators' capacity to make distinctions. We had no problems in observing the different kinds of actions and their effects on the sensory, artistic, and symbolic levels. Theatricality was created by the vivid interaction between performer and spectators, and neither could have done without the other.

Peter Stapele brought his show to an end. He finally pierced his elbow with the needle — which was extremely difficult "to do" — stuck the needle back into his imaginary jacket, took the loose end of the thread with his hand, pulled, and thereby flipped open the fingers connected with the pretended thread. After a few flippings he hastily jumped down from the table. We laughed and applauded, but Dr. Stapele blushed and put on his socks. The theatrical event was over.

# 4 | *Theatrical Events Revisited*
Playing Culture and the
Historiography of Early
Nordic Theatre

In February 1908, the National Theatre of Sweden moved to a new, Art Deco–inspired building in Stockholm. The first play to be presented there was August Strindberg's *Master Olof,* his famous vision of the Reformation in Sweden. The first scene of the prose version of the play starts with a quotation: two schoolboys are reading the doggerel verses of the earliest printed drama in Swedish, *Tobiae Comedia* from 1550, written by the title hero of Strindberg's play, Master Olof or Olaus Petri as he was called in Latin.

Master Olof's practicing with schoolboys had been a well-established didactic method of education since the Middle Ages. Although *Tobiae Comedia* represents the oldest printed Swedish drama text, it certainly does not imply that Swedish theatre actually started then. A number of documents point to the existence of liturgical drama, profane entertainment, pagan rites, and heathen celebrations from earlier times. But the picture of the theatrical activities predating *Tobiae Comedia* is blurred by the attitude of researchers who have spent energy establishing a chronology, although the material is not very clear in this respect. What kind of questions can reasonably be asked? It is my conviction that the conceptualization of the object of studies — the theatrical event — directs research and leads to completely different results. Although I refer to early theatrical practices in the Nordic region, I hope that my argument will also apply to other periods and countries.

## Some Sources

Let me give a few examples which might illustrate the material from the period, which is still called the Dark Age despite its many splendid innovations (also in the field of theatre), even on the margin of Europe, represented by the Nordic countries. There were of course religious plays, including those early liturgical dramas called *Visitatio sepulchris*, the three Marys visiting the tomb of the Lord. There is a palimpsest with agricultural records from 1574, covering fragments of an Easter Play from about 1250 with dialogues written in black ink and stage directions in red ink. This parchment comes from a bishop's town, Linköping, which in those days had both a monastery and a school. Different material documenting a similar theatrical event is found in a chalk painting from the twelfth century in the small, rural church of Fornåsa, not far away from Linköping in southeastern Sweden.

On the western side of Sweden, facing Denmark and the North Sea, the local law was written down at about the same time as the *Visitatio* play was put on parchment a few hundred miles away. In the so-called Law of Western Gotaland from about 1280, the following statement records how to treat "players" in court. The Swedish word for "player" is *lekare*, which also means player of instruments, acrobat, juggler, jester, storyteller, and so forth. In other words, it suggests what the Latin word *joculatores* would cover.

The paragraph concerning players reads as follows:

> If a player is hit, all claims shall be revoked. If a player is hurt, one who travels with violin or drum, then a non-domesticated heifer cow should be brought to the court. Then her tail shall be shaved clean of all hair and it shall be smeared with grease. Then he may get newly greased shoes. Then the player shall hold the tail of the heifer, while another man hits the heifer with a whip. If he can hold her, he may keep the good animal and enjoy her as a dog enjoys the grass. If he cannot hold her, he will have to endure what he got and the shame and the damage. He may never ask for more justice than a beaten wife of a serf.[1]

Another document from the same time is the *Codex Regius*, containing the poetic *Edda* with numerous poems and tales from ancient Norse and

Icelandic times. For one and a half centuries scholars have debated whether these texts, which might, in part, originate from the eighth century and even earlier, could be considered dramas. In *Nordic Theatre Studies*, two eminent scholars have resumed this discussion: were *Edda* songs performed; were they the beginning of theatre in Scandinavia; was there anything prior to these possible performances?[2] Do the figures on the stone coffin from Kivik in southern Sweden represent dancing maidens? Do the figures of the rock carvings from western Sweden show dancers wearing birds' masks? It might be difficult to give a definitive answer, but it is clear that these petrographs (discussed below) are from the Bronze Age, approximately 1300 B.C.E.

What can we know about these early traces of theatre in Sweden and Scandinavia? What do we want or need to know — what kind of answers are we looking for? These questions raise some general problems in theatre historiography and in theatre studies at large. The issues I want to discuss here can be summarized as follows:

1. Narrow definitions of theatre emanating from the pattern of the written culture limit the historical perspectives to questions of chronology and developments which cannot be answered adequately due to the lack of material, especially concerning the oldest periods.

2. By positioning theatre within the traditions of playing culture, it seems possible to open up broader perspectives.

3. The theatrical event as a theoretical concept concretizes the frame of playing culture and permits new interpretations of some of the oldest Scandinavian material concerning the performing arts, the rock carvings of the Bronze Age.

4. The concept of historical horizons helps to bridge the gap between past events and the present scholar.

5. Theatre history will most probably change its narrative when looked upon as a series of theatrical events and as manifestations of a playing culture.

The following section examines the two articles mentioned above in order to discuss the significance of the conceptualization of theatre that every scholar implicitly expresses in his or her writing. Therefore, rather than considering the specifics of evidence and documentation, I focus primarily upon the historical models and assumptions of these scholars. In the last section I try to reevaluate possible approaches to theatre historiography.

## Two Approaches

The two researchers who examine this medieval material represent two historical approaches, which can be identified as a normative, formal-aesthetic view (Terry Gunnell) and a genealogical view, coupled with certain anthropological attitudes (Sveinn Einarsson). Let me immediately point out that I deeply respect these two scholars and their wide knowledge in this field. The primary issue here is not a matter of who is right or wrong; what concerns me is the way that certain historical arguments and assumptions guide these two research projects.

Let me very briefly characterize Terry Gunnell's attitude. In his article he is investigating "The Play of Skírnir," one of the texts in the poetic *Edda*. Gunnell seeks to determine whether these songs were performed in a theatrical performance — whether they can be considered dramas. To be able to solve this problem, Gunnell has established rules or norms for what a drama is, just as Aristotle did 2,330 years ago. Gunnell lists the elements which according to him define a text as drama (i.e., make it "performable"). These elements are the dialogic character of the text, its present tense, and its representational function (i.e., no narrator is necessary). Last but not least, Gunnell asks himself if a text actually would allow for or even require two or more actors in a performance.

The author has a clear idea of what makes a text into a theatrical text, what makes it performable and therefore likely to have been performed. Although such a view seems logical, it clearly puts the emphasis on the performing of written texts. Gunnell intends to prove that for these lines "some form of dramatic presentation must have been essential" (p. 22); accordingly he finds it necessary to examine them "from the viewpoint of the *demands* of performance" (p. 21; my emphasis). For Gunnell, there are clearly defined formal elements which give normative answers to what can be accepted as theatre. Gunnell is very well aware of the connection between the Eddic texts and folk drama and also finds possible roots in the sacred marriages as well as the mock-weddings in many Scandinavian games. But eventually he relies on the text: "The strongest evidence for such performances, however, is in the poems themselves.

Whatever their origin, and whatever their context, there seems to be little doubt that they were not only regarded by the thirteenth century scribes as being dramas of some kind, but that they were also presented as such" (p. 32).

Sveinn Einarsson represents another attitude, both modern and traditional, which is expressed in the title of his essay: "How Old Is the Theatre in the Nordic Region?" In consequence, theatrical expressions are considered something deeply human, something which Aristotle had described in terms of the idea of *mimesis* and which Gustaf Ljunggren described in the following way more than a hundred years ago: "The mimetic urge to imitate, the desire to disguise and to represent another person is common to all people on any level of education. A human being is born with such desires. Somewhat more developed, it is to be found in the custom of reproducing religious myths and real life events through songs, dance, mime, and gestures. Such embryonic theatrical performances can be found everywhere, among the savages of America, the original inhabitants of Java. . . ."[3]

If all human beings and even the "savages" have this mimetic capacity and desire, then it would be strange if the Scandinavians were the only people who were left out. Sveinn Einarsson argues along the same line when he comments on the traditional view that Scandinavians learned court dances like the *carole* from the French, but that this influence could not reasonably be the origin of dance in Nordic culture. "If the Nordic tribes did not get to know how to dance until they came under the influence of the French court, then they must have been almost the only people who did not express themselves through dancing or used dance-like movements in their cult customs."[4]

The key question for Einarsson is not *if* the Nordic people had theatrical activities, but *when* these activities started. In turn, he wants to know what kinds of theatrical events occurred, when the first drama emerged, and if dance developed earlier than ritualistic drama. Einarsson illuminates his investigation with many learned references and introduces an interesting distinction, although he does so implicitly rather than explicitly. This distinction concerns the functions of performances.

Einarsson notes the various accounts of the Blót celebration in Uppsala, which occurred during the time of the Vikings. He suggests that dancing and costuming were part of these ceremonies; but because of the lack of evidence, he cannot determine what kind of performances took place. At best, only conjectures can be made. He is also quite sure that traveling jesters were in Scandinavia, but they belonged to entertainment rather than to theatre. He includes Sami shamanism as a possible source for the Scandinavian theatre, but just like the witchcraft of the Norse *sejd*, these activities functioned within the framework of religion and, for Einarsson, had no aesthetic pretensions.

On the one hand, Einarsson is prepared to accept a definition of theatre similar to the one Gunnell put forward, but he is prepared to extend his concept of performance history: "In using this term [theatre] I apply the classical criteria, namely the presence of dialogue and impersonation. I am, however, fully aware that these criteria will not apply in all of the borderline areas with which I shall mostly be dealing" (p. 7).

On the other hand, he continues to raise a series of concerns and questions about cultural activities that bear many similarities to theatre:

Let us now deal with the question of whether the *joculator*, or — more natural for us — a scop, a bard, a scald, is really to be regarded as a player or actor. In our days the monologue has enjoyed a renaissance and nobody doubts its place in the theatre, but can we use the tastes of our own time as a touchstone when judging phenomena from the past? Can we draw the line (between the dramatic monologue and poetic recitation) at the point where the performer goes to the trouble of "staging" his material, dresses in a special costume or in some way indicates the appearance and characteristics of the characters who may appear in the monologue? (p. 12)

Together, Gunnell and Einarsson represent a common attitude among theatre scholars, who firmly believe that all human beings from prehistoric times to the present have a mimetic ability. Nevertheless, they both argue that certain criteria must be applicable to transform an activity into theatre; these normally deal with questions of representation and the dialogic nature of dramatic texts. Only when such criteria are met does a national or regional theatre come into being. Accordingly, the historian seeks to determine when these kinds of elaborated dramatic traits first occurred. An origin is needed. A specific condition is realized for the birth of theatre. The research thus attempts to point out the exact time and place of this moment of transition. In turn, the research also tries to identify foreign influences that contributed to this decisive advancement. By showing how and when this process of theatre developed, the historian indicates that theatre liberated itself from cultural activities and functions of rituals, ceremonies, competitions, and so forth. Theatre attains a higher or different function as an aesthetic activity, and drama becomes an autonomous work of art.

## A Playing Culture

Is such a conception of theatre an adequate way of looking at theatre history, especially early theatre history? From my perspective, this emphasis upon the distinct aesthetic qualities fails to do justice to all aspects of the historical evidence. Also, this aesthetic approach reflects some attitudes and assumptions of our own modern perspective. If we are not careful, we may lose sight of the fact that "the past is a foreign country," to quote David Lowenthal.[5] We need to recognize that cultural activities that are distant — in time and space — may have functions and meanings that do not fit our aesthetic categories and working assumptions about the evolutionary development of theatre.

I suggest that theatre in general and remote theatrical events in particular should be liberated from the historical model of written culture, in which they have mostly been placed, and should be reattributed to the playing culture to which they belonged from the very beginning and belong even today. What does it mean to look at theatre as part of the playing culture rather than as part of the written culture? There are historical, general, and theoretical reasons to argue for such a point of view.[6]

To illuminate the *historical* role of games and playing, I would like to quote once more from Gustaf Ljunggren, who in 1864 discussed the dramatic disposition of the Scandinavian people as they were expressed in the songs of the *Edda*. He came to the following conclusion: "Although some of these oldest literary monuments show early manifestations of a dramatic seed, we will get to know such dispositions much better when we look at the pastimes and games which the Nordic people have been playing and loving from the oldest times up to our own days."[7] Ljunggren reports on hundreds of different games that were played during various seasons in celebrations, but also as competitions or simply for the sake of entertainment. While his presentation of the Eddic songs takes nine pages (and he is skeptical about our ability to know anything substantial about their performances), he devotes forty pages to the description of playing games, all originating before or during the early Middle Ages. It seems fully reasonable to have this kind of entertainment in mind whenever we discuss the theatrical activities during this period.

What are the *general* implications of a playing culture from a theatrical point of view? I would like to underline a few features, although I do not intend to provide a historical survey of the many aspects of playing in early cultures. First, it seems obvious to me that the playing culture is something very *physical*. The body becomes a centerpiece of playing, which includes physical closeness, touching one another, and the development of activities done in unison. Not only are movements acted out according to certain rules, but the lyrics which are sung and recited take on a verbal, rhythmicizing function and the verses are subordinated to the physical procedures of the game to be played. The bodily experience of playing is not confined to those who "perform," but also involves the spectators in both emotional and physical ways. The experience of others, present in time and space, becomes a strong sensory encounter.

The playing culture is mainly preserved through *tacit* knowledge. While rhetoric is documented in books since the days of Aristotle and while Quintilian in particular used the actor as a model for the speaker, there is very little written about the skills which are the basis for performers. They were rarely discussed in public, because they were handed down from generation to generation. This seems true for all kinds of players, whether it concerned the learning of musical instruments, dancing, competing in various sports, acting, or singing. It is equally true that the art of acting was rarely written about until the times of Antonio Francesco Riccoboni, Denis Diderot, Eduard Devrient, and finally Konstantin Stanislavsky. This explains the lack of documents, but does not permit us to think that there was a lack of skills.

It is also obvious — and Mikhail Bakhtin has given many examples of this — that the playing culture often contains *subversive* elements. Theatre history and genres within popular culture are full of instances in which the world is shown upside-down, power is criticized, and the last will become the first. The carnivals, the *festa stultorum*, the donkey feasts in the abbeys with the garbled holy masses, the mock sermons, the improvised dialogues of the French *sotties*, ancient Nordic dance games, and the fights between Winter and Spring accompanied by satiric verses are some well-known examples from the Middle Ages. Written culture is openly exposed to censuring authorities, but playing culture can never be fully controlled.

The culture of physicality, tacitly transferred from generation to generation and often used for subversive purposes, constitutes only some aspects of the general culture of play that permeates so many activities in a society. Perhaps it would be appropriate, therefore, to try to understand the ways in which theatre was integrated in this complex culture of play.

According to Gadamer, playing is a purpose in itself, without any superior aim, and also something that takes place independently of the consciousness of the player. The game plays the player, who accepts and adopts the playing. Gadamer continues: "From this we can note a general characteristic of how the essence of playing is reflected in the playing attitude: *All playing is a being played.* The impulse toward playing, the fascination which it exerts, comes exactly from the fact that playing masters the player."[8]

In consequence, Gadamer argues, it is typical for the human playing that *something* is being played. This means that there is a certain order of movements or other rules to which the playing is subordinated and from which the player has the possibility to choose. From this choosing, Gadamer concludes that playing is or at least can be a "presentation of self."[9] Because of this, playing can become a purpose in itself. From here Gadamer makes an interesting conclusion concerning the arts: "All presentation carries the potential of a presentation for someone. That this potential as such is envisaged constitutes the specificity of the playing character of the arts. The closed room drops, so to speak, one of its walls."[10]

The presentations of cults and dramatic acting obviously do not have the same meaning as the playing of children. Acting is not simply an activity, as when children are playing for themselves. Acting exposes itself to those who participate as spectators. "[Acting] is not confined to presentation, but points beyond itself to those who participate as observers. Playing is no longer the mere presentation of regulated movements, nor the mere presentation which absorbs the playing child, but it is a 'presenting for. . . .' This aspect of all presentation is hereby realized and becomes constitutive for the Being of Art."[11]

The actors play their roles, but the playing is a totality of performer and spectator. And it is the act of playing, rather than the specific interpretation of its meaning, that most interests Gadamer:

> Also dramatic acting remains playing, i.e., it has the structure of playing as a closed world. But cultic or profane playing, although representing a closed world, is open toward the spectator. Through him it achieves its whole significance and meaning. The players play their roles as in every playing, and so the playing is presented, but the playing itself includes the wholeness [*Ganze*] of player and spectator. Yes, playing is experienced and its "meaning" presented for the one who does not play, but watches. For him playing is, so to speak, lifted to its ideal state.[12]

I do not go as far as Gadamer does in his famous book, from which I have been quoting, where he argues that the experience of art is the only truth which humans can encounter. For my discussion here it is important to insist that theatre, like any other art, is constituted by the encounter between performer and spectator. The major difference between Gadamer's view and traditional communication theory is that in this model of communication there is not first a sender and than a receiver; it is the simultaneous encounter between performer and spectator in the situation of playing which constitutes theatre as art. I call this encounter a theatrical event.

## Theatrical Events

The concept of the theatrical event is here presented as an alternative to normative theories of theatre, which aim at defining what is to be counted as theatre (and what not!) on formal aesthetic grounds; these formal aspects normally only concern the performer's expressions — the theatrical "work of art" — not the spectator's experience of these expressions to make it a whole theatrical event. The concept of the theatrical event is also meant as an alternative to the anthropologically oriented attempts to establish a genealogy of theatrical genres and to construct chronologies based on developmental perspectives. I think it is essential to conceive of theatre as communicative theatrical events within the framework of playing culture and with multiple functions at work simultaneously.

I have argued for a description of theatrical communication on three levels, which together can be understood as the theatricality of the event.[13] I think that this description can be expanded and completed, but I also believe that the three levels of communication emphasize some very crucial points of contact between the performer and the spectator. Even in the current discussion I think that the levels of sensory, artistic, and symbolic communication can be used to distinguish different functions which a theatrical event of any kind can have.

These functions, which I assume to have been present in all kinds of playing activities and thus — from my point of view — even in rituals and ceremonies, games, dancing, singing, and acting, can be studied in what are probably the earliest documents of such activities in the Nordic countries: the rock carvings of western Sweden (Bohuslän). These petrographs were cut into the coastal cliffs between Gothenburg and Oslo during the Bronze Age (1800–500 B.C.E.). Although some of them are older (7000–8000 B.C.E.), most of the carvings were created successively from the thirteenth to eighth centuries, among them the 22-meter-wide carvings of Vitlycke with more than 300 figures. There is a younger one — probably created by only one artist — from about 600 B.C.E. in Fossum. This period coincides approximately with the building of Stonehenge, the war of the Greeks against Troy, the foundation of Jerusalem, and the first Olympic Games.

A male figure from Backa (see fig. 6), typical in its gesture of raised arms, is wearing an axe, a big helmet on his head, and a sword at his side and has an obvious symbol of fertility extending in front of his body. All these details are easily described as symbolic attributes. No such symbolic value has been attributed to the very marked and swelling calves. It could be the clumsiness of the stone cutter, were it not that these types of calves appear on most petrographs of the time. They were not just a male attribute, but appear even in the few pictures of women which can be found — for example, the famous woman from Fossum, greeting with a raised arm (see fig. 7). There has of course been some guessing as to what this dominant form of calves might signify; the most convincing suggestion so far is that this particular shape of the legs simply equals the ideal beauty of the time. They have what I call a *sensory function*: they depict something which was considered beautiful and which calls for the attention of the observer. This is why people of all times seem to put some effort into the shaping and reshaping of their appearance, both in

6. *A male figure from the Backa rock carvings.*
*Courtesy of Bohusläns Museum.*

7. *Female figure from the Fossum rock carvings.*
*Courtesy of Bohusläns Museum.*

everyday life and not least in extraordinary circumstances, such as the occasions to which these rock carvings refer.

The sensory level of communication is extremely important in all kinds of human encounters. It describes what we find interesting in a person, why we attend to a communicative situation, and what keeps us in it. The sensory aspects include both physical features (appearance, movements, voice, facial expressions, etc.) and psychological characteristics (mood, temperament, intensity, energy, etc.). These traits, which

8. *Dancing figures.*
*Courtesy of Bohusläns Museum.*

9. *A voltifactor doing somersaults.*
*Courtesy of Bohusläns Museum.*

could be summarized as personality, are the clue to any relationship, be it an occasional meeting, a long-lasting friendship, or an encounter during a playing activity, which defines one of the participants as performer and the other as spectator (i.e., a theatrical event). In such an encounter it is, for instance, important if the performer and the spectator know each other beforehand (as in amateur performances, school performances, shamanistic rituals, etc.), or if the spectator looks at a stranger such as a medieval jester or a newly arrived priest. Recognition, attention, attraction, joy, fear, curiosity, and repulsion are some of the functions which can be described on the sensory level.

Two groups of figures might illustrate my point as far as the *artistic level* of communication of the theatrical event and its artistic functions are concerned. The first one shows two men, holding a stick in their hands and bent into a "sit-up" position (see fig. 8). There is hardly any doubt that these figures are involved in some kind of dance (i.e., using a prepared pattern of movements which they execute with some degree of skills). The same can be said of another figure, a so-called *voltifactor* (a person doing somersaults; see fig. 9). These acrobats appear quite frequently in the rock carvings — sometimes even doing their jumps in

*10. Footprints: imprints of the gods. Courtesy of Bohusläns Museum.*

boats, which symbolized the voyage to the realms of death — but there are few interpretations which would exceed the entertainment aspect of such activities.

While the long "faces" of the dancers can be interpreted as masks — probably depicting some holy birds — and thereby point to a ritual purpose of the dance, the dancing itself is made up of movements coordinated between the participating dancers and thus a premeditated artistic expression. Such a choreography might have pleased the gods, but it certainly also pleased the spectators, just as the acrobats did with their control of their bodies. Through the use of artistic means of expression, these performers clearly distinguished their presentation from the doings of everyday life, calling upon the special attention given to a theatrical event. The functions of the artistic level include entertainment, skills and appreciation, pleasure and judgment, as well as the distinction between theatricality and everyday life.

As mentioned before, many or perhaps most of the rock carvings also have a *symbolic meaning*. Even when we are not sure of the interpretation, it is easy to see that there are symbolic values attached so many icons. That the footprints of figure 10 indicate the presence of gods is known not only from the Nordic countries, but also from other religious iconography (for example, from India). The figure with a large hand (see fig. 11) is not playing: the twenty-nine balls in four rows of seven shallow holes probably represent an early example of a moon calendar. The two standing figures, kissing, embracing, and making love (see fig. 12), are not merely engaged in the pleasures of everyday life, but represent a holy wedding, bringing fertility and prosperity to the country. The aspect of symbolic intercourse is emphasized by a figure standing next to the couple with a raised axe, who possibly consecrates the act.

*11. A moon calendar.*
*Courtesy of Bohusläns Museum.*

*12. The holy wedding. Courtesy of*
*Bohusläns Museum.*

When interpreting these petrographs, I am not claiming that these pictures refer directly to activities outside of this pictorial world. But it would be a very narrow perspective to think that the figures of the rock carvings have nothing to do with any reality which the people of those days experienced. Most of the figures seem to have a relationship to cults and ceremonies, but there are some which clearly refer to everyday life, such as a deer caught in a net or a ploughman with two oxen. I think it is safe to assume that the pictorial world of the rock carvings is expressing spiritual as well as everyday life experiences of the people, sometimes perhaps both, and it is up to the observer to interpret the situation. Recalling Gadamer's statement that art always carries the potential of presenting something for someone, the symbolic level marks an important series of functions (accumulative information processing, identification and empathy with fictional phenomena, interpretation and understanding, the affinity with or distance from representations of the spiritual world, etc.).

## Historical Horizons

As I have attempted to indicate, the rock carvings of western Sweden have sensory, artistic, and symbolic functions for those who created them and for those who subsequently experience them. It should also be clear that the activities of playing within a society can be shown to have relevance to our historical attempts to understand the development of theatre. For the participants, the act of playing may occur just for pleasure and entertainment or as a part of ceremonies, didactic practices, or shamanistic experiences. Still, we can begin to see how the act of playing, involving both players and spectators, provides a model of theatricality and thus a way for us to expand our study beyond models of aesthetic form based on such criteria as Aristotle's definition of drama.

When events have taken place a long time ago, leaving only accidental traces, the question arises how a scholar can (re-)construct and interpret such events. Here, too, I have found it useful to consult Hans-Georg Gadamer, especially his idea of the fusion of horizons, which provides at least a plausible attitude, if not a practical methodology, for historical studies. Gadamer departs from the reception history (*Wirkungsgeschichte* or history of effects) of a historical phenomenon. Although reception history describes the various effects a historical event or artifact has had during certain periods, Gadamer does not think of reception history as a complement of historical research, but as a central problem of all inquiries into the past. For him reception research is not a special branch of history, but a methodological consciousness which informs the scholar.

Why is such a consciousness necessary? Because even the researcher belongs to this reception history, representing the last link of a historical chain, so to speak. As I understand it, Gadamer's point of view comes very close to Michel Foucault's concept of discourse, inscribing all understanding into one's own historical position.

Every historian is writing within a certain situation, whereas the historical event he or she is writing about took place in a different situation. How do these two situations relate to each other? Traditional historicism claims that scholars leave their own position and (try to) assume a new position, which is thought of as being contemporary with the historical event. Through empathy and imagination the researcher in a sense relives the historical moment. Gadamer denies such a possibility: there is no way to step outside of our own situation — the encounter with history follows another path.

Gadamer uses the term "horizon" to describe a more adequate approach to historical events. Just as a hiker sees the horizon of a landscape, so the scholar's perspective is confined by a virtual horizon. Two characteristics of a horizon are noteworthy: the horizon moves as long as the hiker/scholar moves, and it is also possible to enlarge the horizon by positioning oneself at a point that allows an overview.

Instead of re-creating the horizon of a historical event, as the historicists suggested, Gadamer has a vision of the "two" horizons melting together in the process of understanding. "The horizon of the present cannot take shape without the past. There is neither a horizon of the present as such, nor a historical horizon, which should be gained. *In fact, understanding is always the process of fusion of those horizons, which are assumed to be separate.*" [14]

The two horizons of the present and the past exist only in theory, because in practice our view of a historical horizon is already a transformation of our own horizon. That is why Gadamer emphasizes the importance of reception history: the historian's consciousness grows out of the historical discourse, which, in turn, affects the perspective on history. This attitude is less controversial today than it was when Gadamer wrote his book, but certain aspects of the historical event — be it theatrical or something else — are still worthy of reflection. This concerns especially the question of when a historical event starts and when it ends, or, as Gianni Vattimo has phrased it, the "actuality of the historical event." In Vattimo's view, every interpretation of a historical event is in itself an event, which maintains and underlines our links with history. At the same time, all interpretations express an attempt to formulate a different and new aspect of the historical event, in relation both to the event itself and to all earlier interpretations of it. "The interpretation of history is rather a dialogue in which the real *Sache,* the real question at issue, is that 'fusion of horizons' discussed by Gadamer."[15] Through a series of interpretations, the historical event is kept "alive" — there is a continuous "actuality" of history, as long as we renew our understanding of it.

We can see such a permeating continuity of history in the Royal Dramatic Theatre's performance of Strindberg's *Master Olof* in 1908. Through Strindberg's use of Olaus Petri's play *Tobiae Comedia* from 1550, itself the result of medieval practices, the actors and audiences at the beginning of the century represent a link between the early period of Swedish theatre and today's researchers and readers.

If a historical event has made a lasting imprint on the scholarly discourse or at least returns to the historical consciousness of a certain scholar, it might be necessary to enlarge our perspectives, to widen our horizon to reach out to the historical event, to enhance the fusion of the horizons. The development of new theoretical approaches is one way to extend the understanding of theatrical events.

## New Perspectives?

The problem I have addressed in this essay is "what we *can* know" about past theatrical events, especially when the information is so scarce as in the case of the very early theatre in Scandinavia. I have pointed out that it depends on what kind of questions one wants to ask, which in turn depends on how one conceptualizes the object of study. I have tried to place the theatrical event within the framework of playing culture and have described various functions which simultaneously are fulfilled in such situations. I also have discussed the historiographical problems caused by the extreme time span between the creation of the events and the traces they have left and the experience and interpretation of the source material by the scholar. Gadamer's fusion of horizons and Vattimo's prolonged actuality of the event point to possible conceptions of history that must be explored further.

Provided that these theoretical and methodological considerations constitute an acceptable framework for historical research in theatre studies, what consequences would this new model produce for the theatre historian? So far I can only describe the advances of such an approach in general, while the discussion about the source material of the Bronze Age, the Vikings, and the early Middle Ages must be reexamined by those who are specialists in the field. To me, such a reexamination looks very promising, because some of the dearest hobbyhorses of traditional humanist research could eventually be abandoned.

First, the hegemony of chronological thinking could be broken. Not that I think chronology should be abolished altogether, but the primacy of chronological order — what comes first and what comes next — has dominated traditional research to such a degree that it has inhibited more inventive and productive ways of thinking. I would favor a historical perspective in which all genres exist parallel with each other, where dance, song, spoken lines, ritual movements, and ceremonial orders, are all very close to each other, underlining different functions without excluding others. Within such a view, we should also reevaluate our familiar categories of periodization. For instance, we would examine whether the distinction between pagan and Christian eras really is useful in relation to theatre history. Another reevaluation concerns the sources, especially iconographic ones. The dependence upon written documents should be supplemented by a wider use of pictorial materials, including those from later periods: How have visual artists from various epochs interpreted past theatrical events? What do such pictures tell us about the reception history of those events?

The concept of the theatrical event would make the question of "what is the oldest" irrelevant and outdated. It was my ambition to show that an opposition between theatre in the traditional sense and other forms of performances can be dissolved by looking at the multiple functions every performance has for both the creators and the spectators.

We also have to accept that the documents we have from theatre history need not coincide with the time of the theatrical event itself; on the contrary, it is likely that many sources were created later than the events. It is obvious that the thirteenth century has left traces which are extremely valuable for Scandinavian theatre historians: the palimpsest from Linköping and the chalk paintings from Fornåsa documenting liturgical Easter plays; the law text concerning the juridical treatment of players; the texts of the poetic *Edda*, including parts of what can be looked upon as dramatized stories. At the beginning of the same century, Saxo Grammaticus wrote his account of the Blót celebrations in Uppsala; at about the same time Iceland's great chronicler Snorre Sturlasson wrote his sagas and accounts of life and history in Norway and Sweden.

From the perspective of a theatre historian, this outpouring of written texts in the thirteenth century raises two major problems for us. In the first place, although these documents appeared in the thirteenth century, many of them actually refer to and are derived from earlier historical epochs. It is commonly assumed that the songs of the *Edda* probably existed half a millennium prior to their notation. The celebrations in Uppsala were typical of the pre-Christian era. The Christian *Visitatio Sepulchris* plays were popular divertissements with the monks in numerous European monasteries at least three hundred years before the Linköping parchments were produced. So it is most difficult to determine which moment in history these artifacts refer to. They demonstrate the process of fused horizons of consciousness and history, as they embody the thirteenth and earlier centuries simultaneously. In addition, most of them are not artifacts of theatrical activities; nor do they inform us about practices of their times. But if we bring to them our expanded ideas of a playing culture and of the theatre event, they do begin to indicate aspects of performance in these earlier societies. And so, 800 years later in our own time — yet another fusion of horizons — they provide traces of a history that we are just beginning to see in the documents. The past remains unseen until one shifts perspective to include a "continuous actuality of history."

From the perspective of playing culture, the concept of the theatrical event opens up a broader view of these activities, which does not require a differentiation of all the genres in question, their origins, and their mutual influences. The concept is broader than the traditional concept of theatre as an extension of written culture. For too long we have been looking for the autonomous "works of art" and the intentions which their creators might have had. Why should we not count dance games or public recitals of poetry as forms of theatre, seen as diverse forms of the playing culture?

Let me give two unorthodox views of this problem. In many handbooks of theatre history, the early liturgical dramas are presented as a form of *Biblia Pauperum*, a visual explanation of the incomprehensible language of the Gospel, Latin, for the illiterate populace. How unreasonable such an argument proves to be is demonstrated by the simple fact that these plays were performed in exactly that language, Latin. And furthermore, where was the population to which the Gospel should be explained at four o'clock in the morning, when these Martines were celebrated in the churches of the monasteries? If there were some peasants standing in the back of the church, they were not the audience for whom these quite elaborate dramas were performed. There were many funny scenes included, such as the Three Marys bargaining with the Mercator, the lame Petrus rushing to the Sepulcher, the scarred soldiers asking for mercy, or the shepherds of the Christmas plays quarreling over a ram before the angel Gabriel announced to them, "Gloria in excelsis deo" — the Lord has been born! These plays were performed for the monks of the cloisters by the youngest novices in a combination of piety and pleasure. The second example concerns our own time. In 1997 Dario Fo was awarded the Nobel Price in literature for his work in the theatre. This work consists of a considerable number of monologues, which Fo has been performing himself. In these monologues, he appears as the narrator, who consecutively impersonates, one after the other, the characters of the story. Anyone who has seen Fo himself perform such stories (or some other gifted actor like Björn Granath in Sweden) has no doubt that we are participating in a theatrical event — so why should the bards and scops of the *Edda* have been doing anything less than Dario Fo? Who needs a costume, a dialogue, and several impersonators in order to recognize a theatrical activity — the audiences of the *Edda* songs or today's scholars?

I would like to summarize my outlook on theatre history in the following way. We accept the variety of theatrical forms and functions at any given time, looking for material which can indicate the existence of these performances. The simultaneous existence of a broad repertory of events seems to me a fruitful point of departure for both early and later periods of theatre histories. The periodization, in its reevaluated form, will account for discontinuities and sudden changes, either stimulated through foreign influences or impaired by domestic censorship. These changes — especially those which were brought about through the import of artists, plays, and technologies from abroad — could create short-lived fashions or long-lived conventions. More often than not, these influences created discontinuities, which seem more interesting to me than the continuities we so often have seen constructed between unrelated activities, just to create some kind of development in chronological order.

In addition to the variety of performative events and the discontinuity caused by the continuous transgression of borders and limits, I think it is also valuable to think of discontinuous patterns in theatre history in a number of opposing areas. If theatre is primarily an urban phenomenon, then how does theatre work in rural areas? Is the theatre of small towns in the countryside essentially different from the mainstream theatre offered in the cities? Is it useful to speak about a center and its periphery? If so, there is at least a series of centers, which have created differences not only between the city and the country side. Stockholm has not always been the center; but, as the capital of Sweden since early modern times, it has certainly become the theatre center of the country, with royal play and opera houses as the focus of attention. Stockholm, however, can be seen as marginal when compared to other European capital cities like London, Paris, or Vienna. But not all new creativity comes from the center, at least not all the time. Which ideas have been absorbed, which repelled? What, from time to time, is flowing from the periphery to the center? As far as prehistoric periods are concerned, archaeological research has made it obvious that Scandinavia was far from being an isolated, cold place in the North. On the contrary, 3,000 years ago the climate was similar to that of southern France, the vegetation was lush, and the gods were many: there was also a regular exchange with foreign people, contacts with foreign cultures, and hence cults and pastime activities which could absorb the novelties of the time.

I think it is possible to imagine a rich cultural life at any point of history. Culture is not an organic phenomenon, which develops from a primitive embryo to a mature period to finally being taken over by a stronger and better culture. In my opinion, it is more reasonable to assume that all people everywhere in the world produced exactly the culture which fulfilled their needs for rituals and ceremonies, artistry, and entertainment — all that was necessary for a good life.

# 5 | *Culture as Human Encounter*
### Theatrical Communication as Model of Cultural Events

When Signorina Gherardini left Naples to marry a merchant in Florence, she did not know that one day she would become world-famous. Probably she never had a notion of this future fame, and her husband even less so. The fame is not so much related to her person as to her name — her Christian name, to be more precise. And even that Christian name, simple as it is, would mean nothing to the world were it not connected with her face — not her real face, but the portrait of her face. I am, of course, speaking of Mona Lisa.

*Mona Lisa* is an oil painting on canvas by Leonardo da Vinci, approximately 50 by 35 cm in size, hanging in the Louvre Museum in Paris. It is an object of art history, endlessly reproduced, described, analyzed, repainted, travestied, even attacked, mentally as well as physically.

This painting belongs to the masterpieces of European art, according to the canon of art history, but its fame exceeds by far the usual fame of such a masterpiece. It has become an icon of everyday life. Many people want to see the original painting. Standing in the Louvre, watching the line of visitors slowly approaching the heavily guarded canvas, can be an exciting experience in itself. Almost everybody responds visibly or audibly in front of the famous Mona Lisa. Everybody seems to have expectations, which are or are not met by the real painting. The surprise or the confirmation of one's expectations concerning the small size, the darkness of the colors, the enigmatic smile, and the distant gaze of the lady is often shared with others standing in line, even strangers.

The object on the wall is not just hanging there — it obviously does something to the beholder.

We do not know exactly the nature of the relationship between the artist Leonardo and the wife of the merchant Giocondo. Leonardo was a mature man in his fifties, Mona Lisa still a young woman. The only thing we know is that Leonardo's encounter with Mona Lisa made him paint her portrait, a portrait which thousands of people are patiently waiting in line to see, despite the fact that they know it from books, journals, and advertisements. These visitors are looking for an encounter with Mona Lisa, although different from Leonardo's. Possible reasons for this fascination with this particular painting are not discussed here, but what I find striking is the nature of our encounters with art, which I think is of profound significance for our view of cultural behavior.

## Creation and Experience

Art cannot be properly understood as a collection of dead objects on the walls of exhibition halls or museums, but should be seen as a series of activities, which, in my view, also always include the beholder. This is a classical problem in aesthetics: Is the painting in the attic which nobody sees or the poem in the drawer which nobody reads to be considered a piece of art? I would answer that these works are simply not interesting, unless they are brought to the fore. The argument can be enlarged to include all kinds of cultural objects: the ruins which have not been excavated are not very exciting (except to the few specialists who know about their existence); a church service without a congregation is meaningless; stained glass windows without light, folk dancing without music, and storytelling without listeners are dull exercises, because they are deprived of their communicative potential. Furthermore, the communicative aspect of culture is to be considered not only a potential, but the *raison d'être* of culture. In this sense, culture in general and the arts in particular are a mode of communication. When I speak of culture in general terms, I am not aiming at the anthropological notion of culture, which would include all human behavior in the framework of a civilization. My perspective is limited to the arts and to activities which bear some kind of similarity to the arts: organized places allowing for activities with a beginning and an end. This is not meant to represent a definition of culture. I just want to describe what I have in mind when I leave Leonardo's *Mona Lisa* and bring up other examples of cultural encounters.

Culture understood as communication has been described in terms of the traditional scheme of the communication triad of sender-message-receiver. The portrait of Mona Lisa could easily be interpreted in those terms. Leonardo is the sender, who transformed his feelings for Mona Lisa into a painting, the message which we, the receivers, look at and decode almost half a millennium later. This scheme conceals, like all simplifications, a few problems. First of all, the process might very well be reversed: the starting point can be the visitor in the Louvre who is looking at the Mona Lisa, which happened to be painted by Leonardo, albeit not to show it in a museum (the history of this canvas is quite another story). Cultural messages are not always "produced" for the purpose they might be used for; nor are we, as members of a culturally defined community of another epoch, always interested in the original messages.

Instead of a message, carefully wrapped by the sender to be unwrapped by the receiver, I suggest the human encounter as the center of the communication process. At one end of this process, something is *created*, either by a single artist, as in Leonardo's case, or by a collective of artists and artisans, who together created Gothic cathedrals or who present performances in a theatre, evening after evening. While the cathedral can be described as an artifact, the theatre performance is rather to be seen as an event — and every evening there will be another event. Creation in the field of culture thus refers to both artifacts and events, historical ones as well as contemporary ones.

What is created will, at some point, be *experienced* by readers, listeners, and spectators. These observers experience cultural creations at a certain point in time and in space, but the temporal and spatial encounter with artifacts and events does not necessarily coincide with their creation. Since I consider these differences in time and space between the creative act and the public experience to be a major feature allowing for the distinction between different art forms in terms of their communicative functions, I would like to exemplify and systematize these differences.

This differentiation poses two specific scholarly problems. First, the actual encounter with a cultural artifact becomes a cultural event and thus the focus of cultural communication. In that sense, cultural encounters function like theatrical events, but this does not mean that they are the same. What interests me is the possibility of applying my model of theatrical communication to other cultural events. I am not subsuming all these other cultural events into some limitless definition of theatre; on the contrary, my concept of the theatrical event remains the same. My curiosity is aimed at the effects of such methodological transfers: to see what I can learn about the functions of cultural encounters. Second, it is obvious to me that the conditions of such cultural encounters are different for different cultural expressions. The distinction between the time and place of the creation of a cultural artifact or event and the time and space of their experience can be described in four categories: creation and experience coincide in time and place, occur at the same time but in different places, happen at different times but in the same place, or, finally, are separated in time and place. The following discussion includes some examples of each category, including both traditional art forms and other cultural expressions.

Certain art forms as well as other types of events have been called "cultural performance," a phrase that Milton Singer introduced in the 1950s.[1] These are presentational in the sense that they are created in front of their audiences. Such art forms include all kinds of theatre (music theatre, dance, puppets, mime, etc.) as well as all live musical performances. Theatrical performances or musical concerts do not exist physically except in the moment when they are presented publicly. They do not have any concrete duration after the fall of the curtain and the concluding applause. Of course, they might have been prepared for a long time, but as cultural events they only come into being during their presentation. This is also true of ceremonies and rituals, parades, circus acts, shows, and magicians, as well as weddings and funerals. A wedding, for instance, demonstrates very clearly when the act is carried out: a wedding is usually prepared for a long time (including the creation of specific dresses, flower arrangements, music, etc.) and might even be rehearsed by the participants; but both from a legal point of view and in the mind of agents and bystanders, the actual wedding only takes place once. As cultural event it is created and experienced at the same time and the same place. In this particular sense — but only in this sense — a wedding is similar to theatre without being theatre. The question is what we could learn from the similarities and differences between these two types of cultural events.

Through various media developed during the twentieth century it has become possible not only to experience events, but also to observe artifacts and documents as they are created, although they are created in a different place. Through radio and television we have become used to watching royal weddings, sports events, political speeches, and even wars at the very moment when these events actually occur, although they may happen on a different continent. The fact that Europeans had to watch the Olympic Games in the middle of the night to receive them live from Atlanta or Sydney is a clear reminder of the simultaneous creation and experience of such events over a distance of thousands of miles. New electronic media increase the number of objects we are able to observe without a time lapse between distant places.

There are, however, many cultural objects which no longer can be experienced simultaneously with their creation. Some of them even have to be seen at the very place where they have been created. This is normally the case with architecture. To see a Gothic cathedral, we have to visit the city where it was built; the pyramids of Egypt and Mexico have to be experienced in those countries; to study the original Baroque stage machinery, one has to come to the Drottningholm Court Theatre. The same can be said about archaeological sites: even when the pottery, coins, and statues have been exhibited in museums, the place of the excavations can only be viewed at the original location. This is also true of all places where historical events happened, be it the battlefields of Waterloo, the birthplace of Shakespeare, or the house in Mexico City in which Leon Trotsky was assassinated. Whatever impressions a visitor to those places receives, and whatever relation one has to the events which occurred there, such experiences cannot happen somewhere else.

Many artifacts and documents — probably the majority of all cultural goods — are experienced through encounters which coincide neither in time nor in place with the acts of their creation. Such major art forms as painting and sculpture, all literary genres and other books, journals and leaflets, film, television programs, and videos are hardly ever experienced at the time and place where they are produced. Who will read Strindberg's chamber plays sitting at the desk where they were written, even a hundred years later? Who will watch Alfred Hitchcock's *Psycho* in front of the original bathroom at Universal Studios in Hollywood? The spatial and temporal distance between creation and experience is not only a significant trait for many art forms, but also the basic form of communication in practically all museums, with the exception of those mentioned as the site of specific events. In a museum the visitors are invited to bridge the gap in time and space, to take part in the exhibition of things which otherwise would be concealed by temporal and spatial distances. The endeavor to bring remote objects close to the visitor is what characterizes museums, art galleries, reconstructed buildings, and public archives.

Schematically the temporal and spatial differences between creation and experience could be depicted in the pattern shown in figure 13.

As soon as such a pattern is established, I can easily detect a number of exceptions and irregularities which make this scheme even more interesting. Observing a certain mobility between those neatly designed categories points in the direction of dynamic shifts within the traditional patterns of cultural communication. A few examples indicate such possibilities.

A historical event can be transformed into a contemporary experience by someone who re-creates it through a narrative document such as a participant's memoirs or through a scholarly study. In this way the event enters today's discourse about this event.

A live transmission of an event is reprogrammed by a television channel. What was formerly a simultaneous experience of a distant event now becomes also temporally distanced. The time span between the event and the repeated showing of it can range from the replay of a football goal scored just a few seconds earlier to the use of television archives showing interviews which have been conducted several decades earlier. The advanced use of television cameras during sports events and even rock concerts has changed our perception of these events in many ways. The exciting moments on the sports field or on the concert stage can simultaneously be watched on large television screens, many times more detailed than what can be seen from one's own seat in the arena. But the screens only expose the choices of a TV producer, reducing the spectator's own views to a secondary experience.

Buildings are not always what they seem to be. Large sections of the "historical" inner city of Warsaw have been reconstructed after the Second World War; the ancient temples of Aswan have been moved from their original site to give way to the exploitation of the waters of the Nile; Swedish cottages, stables, and manor houses have been reassembled in the open air museum of Skansen; Antonio Gaudi's cathedral La Sagreda Familia in Barcelona has been under construction for de-

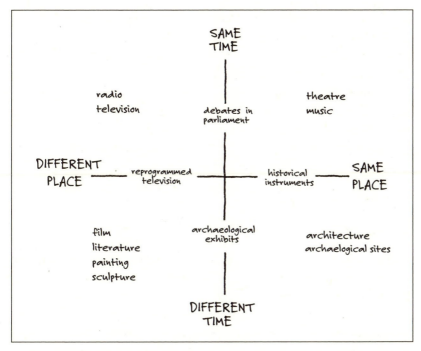

*13. The spatial and temporal relationship between the creation of and the experience of cultural artifacts and events.*

cades, and if it is ever finished, its character as "living," growing architecture will be transformed into something else.

Old celluloid filmstrips of silent movies are restored and recolored and shown to new audiences; music is performed on historical instruments; medieval frescos are freed from centuries of iconophobia and layers of old paint; baptizing rituals are re-created according to the first Swedish Protestant prayer books of the sixteenth century. But our eyes are no longer used to the eighteen frames-per-second movements; our hearing is distorted by loudspeakers; neither the child nor the congregation is patient enough for a baptizing ceremony of more than one hour — in other words, the preservation of artifacts and the repetition of ancient rituals speak to us in a very different manner than they did to their contemporaries. Being aware of the continuous changes in the beholder's context, we nevertheless can appreciate and enjoy the encounter with many cultural expressions, created in remote times and places. The basic condition for such cultural encounters is that the observer is actually confronted with these objects — wherever and whenever they have been created. But we must wonder how the temporal and spatial distances affect and change the encounter: in every case we have to assume an activity on the observer's part. The communication process can be started only when attention is given to a cultural object. This is also true of instances when we discover such objects by accident — a television program we happen to switch on, a wedding we happen to pass, a theatre performance we happen to encounter in a park — we still need to give some attention to the artifact or event we happen to observe. An old church we hardly notice while passing is comparable to the poem in the drawer: no communication takes place; no cultural encounter occurs.

## Models of Encounters

Historical cultural objects, artifacts, or events do not provide any explanations or interpretations — history does not understand itself. Through the encounter with these objects, it is up to the observer to search for these explanations and interpretations. Only through repeated encounters with historical documents can a continuous discourse with cultural history be established. This discourse builds upon our own as well as past generations' confrontation with artifacts and events, both historical and contemporary. The time and space relationship to cultural objects has been emphasized above, because it is of major significance for our ability to communicate within our cultural framework. At the same time, it is also obvious that the cultural encounter always takes place *hic et nunc*, seen from the observer's point of view. The here and now of cultural experiences, in turn, is the basis on which we can enter the cultural discourse. It is, therefore, essential to any study of culture to understand the nature of the cultural encounter itself.

Theatre is one of the cultural manifestations which always take place here and now, an art form in which creation and experience occur simultaneously. Therefore, I would like to suggest the use of the model of theatrical communication as a model for other cultural communications. Once more I want to point out that this step does not imply an extension of the term "theatre," but only a methodological application to the larger field of cultural encounters. The following is an attempt to transcribe my model of theatrical communication into a general model of cultural communication.

The basic assumption in this model is that in the theatre the performer on the stage and the spectator in the auditorium are related to each other through a number of communicative levels, which vary in emphasis over time, but which are activated synchronously through the theatrical event. The communicative levels are, in turn, also influenced by an expression of the conventional, structural, and conceptual contexts of which the creators and the perceivers of the theatrical event are part. These contexts determine in which way the communicative levels are activated — how a theatrical performance is presented and how it is perceived by various members of the audience. At this point I want to underline that even cultural objects other than theatre have a presentational side — nothing appears *per se* — and always are part of their specific contexts.

The sensory level of communication describes the immediate impression an observer gets from an object. This level is very often also the first level to be activated in a communicative process. When we encounter an artifact or an event, we intuitively grasp some of the sensory qualities which the object displays or exhibits (its shape and size, colors, rhythm, material, location, sounds, etc.) — in other words, what the observer experiences primarily with his or her senses. These impressions provoke our attention and make us interested in an object or an event. From these direct and mainly intuitive impressions, the sensory perception is extended to emotional and intellectual responses. The color can be perceived as warm, the material as smooth, the rhythm as contagious, the location as exceptional. While these notions affect us emotionally — resulting in feelings like curiosity, affection, enchantment, but also repulsion or disgust — even cognitive processes are triggered. Intellectually we might react with recognition, surprise, interest, or disinterest. The intellectual responses necessarily include the activation of our prior knowledge, our preferences and prejudices, our taste and our earlier experiences. A comparative element enters into a preliminary judgment, which is not yet an aesthetic or ethic judgment, but rather a question of liking or disliking what we see or hear or touch or smell. By comparing it to similar objects or experiences, we place this new experience in a certain frame. Experiments have shown that these preliminary judgments are vital for the further development of our relation to an object.[2] We will not readily change our mind again — unless overwhelming new information is added — but will keep this first impressions on the sensory level alive during the entire process of communication.

*14. A baptismal font in Bogsta church, from the twelfth century. Courtesy of Sörmlands Museum.*

Visiting a number of country churches in the rural districts south of Stockholm — most of them built during the early medieval period and remodeled and enlarged in the consecutive centuries — I always kept looking for the baptism fonts, which were placed either at the left side of the apse or at the rear end of the churches. My immediate impression of these fonts was a sense of great weight, a heavy piece of gray sandstone in the shape of a drinking cup on a high foot. Despite its weight, the material is smooth, almost soft. Also striking are the harmonious proportions of the pieces, making them steady and at the same time erect and uplifting, rather than bound to the ground. Having seen one, I could easily recognize the others, but I soon realized the subtle variations each one of them displays.

The next aspect of the communication process is the artistic level. It recognizes the fact that the artifact or event of our encounter is a cultural object, something which is human-made. My analysis here does not engage in the Kantian discussion about whether we can experience nature in an aesthetic manner or the debate about whether *objets trouvés* are to be considered art. The artistic level deals with the observer's notion that the object at hand is created by someone according to some rules or norms which exceed the mere functionality of the object. The very appearance of the object is shaped by its creator(s) to fulfill the artistic and aesthetic requirements of a certain period or style, usually completed with the personal taste and skills of those who have created an art work or who are executing a ceremony. While different modes of aesthetic expression require specific kinds of competence from the creator(s), a similar competence is required from the observer to be able to appreciate the object fully. Even on the artistic level, emotional and intellectual processes go hand in hand. While a cultural encounter produces pleasure in the mind of the beholder as an intuitive response to the artistry of the object, a comparative process relates the present experience to past experiences, which eventually leads to evaluations in terms of both aesthetic positionings and value judgments.

Looking more closely at one of the baptismal fonts, I realized that their well-proportioned shape follows the conventions of medieval sculpture, including certain patterns of decorative elements. Even the simplest pieces normally are beautified with an engraved decoration, combining, for instance, a chain of rings with stylized crosses. To look at these simple but nevertheless delicate ornaments is a pleasure, but I must admit that the more sophisticated these patterns were, the more I enjoyed the font. The skills of the artisans certainly have an impact on my appreciation of their work — even 800 years later. From an interpretative point of view, it does not require a lot of education in art history to realize that the artists combined pagan elements, which can be found on other artifacts of the Viking times, with the still relatively new symbol of the cross. I observe and admire the specific location where the ornamentation has been placed on the font, the size of the figures that the artist has chosen, and the skill with which the engravings harmonize with the overall impression of the stone piece. The anonymous artist has thus articulated individual aesthetic taste and qualities within the culturally conditioned conventions and codes of twelfth-century religious society.

The third level of cultural encounters concerns symbolic communication. While the sensory and artistic experiences of cultural objects are essential for the observer's attention and appreciation, the communicative process normally does not stop at this point. One also asks if there is a meaning to the object which cannot be perceived immediately. Meaning in this context does not necessarily imply a specific content or function, but must be seen in a wider sense as a symbolic meaning, which can be imaginary, spiritual, or even fictional. Many times such a symbolic meaning coincides or is combined with very concrete functions which the object has been created to serve. Even on the symbolic level, the observer is engaged both emotionally and intellectually. Through free associations as well as through well-argued interpretations, the symbols of an artifact or an event can be illuminated, explained, and debated. Interpretative activities are highly related to the referential system — the knowledge and judgment — of the beholder. But interpretation is not merely an intellectual process; instead intuition, the desire to understand, the ambition to know, and the identification with the object as well as fantasy and imagination are all part of interpretative processes. It is also important to remember that there are no true or false interpretations, only more or less convincing ones. A specific symbolic meaning will be reasonable for one observer, but not for another, depending on the references and inclinations of the interpreting beholder. From my point of view, interpretations have very little to do with the intentions of the creative artists — here the time/space relationship between creation and reception, the varying cultural contexts, and the sometimes limited views of the artists themselves are to be accounted for.

Standing in the cool apse of a small country church as an interested tourist looking at the baptismal font might make me meditate about the struggle of the early church to incorporate paganism into the art of the time. I can imagine how the artist worked on the block of stone, how pleased the parish priest was when the font came into place, the pride of the congregation, and I also wonder who paid for the finished piece. These historical considerations were swiftly blown away when I was invited to an actual baptism, when proud parents brought along an infant and even prouder grandparents attended the act, which symbolized the acceptance of a little child into the Christian community. The font was no longer only an art object, but assumed a central function in an event which signified Christian faith, ancient rituals, and cultural performance.

Both as a cultural tourist and as a participant in a traditional ceremony I experienced an artifact as well as an event on the levels of sensory, artistic, and symbolic communication. In both cases my experience was conditioned partly by the immediate circumstances of the situation and partly by the cultural contexts of which I am a product socially, aesthetically, educationally, economically. I do not think of myself as an exception, and my experiences are rather to be seen as typical in the sense that they followed general patterns and conditions. The temporal and spatial relationships between the creation of cultural objects and the actual reception of them in the here-and-now situation of the observer cause a fascinating dynamic exchange, which connects the past with the present, regions with continents, individuals with collectives, and artifacts with events.

## Studies in Cultural Politics

I have tried to situate cultural encounters as the focus of studies of culture. In my view, the direction of such studies will have implications for the analysis and understanding of cultural politics. It would be ambitious but not fully realistic to hope that this kind of study also will have an impact on a country's cultural politics.

The focus of studies in the arts and in other disciplines of the humanities has traditionally been the creation of arts and artifacts, their preservation, and their meaning in the past. According to the agenda that I have sketched here the main issues would be to include the reception of arts and artifacts, their presentation, and their meaning for today's encounter with them. Keywords for such research endeavors would be the availability and accessibility of cultural encounters, the concrete reception during cultural experiences, and the contextual conditions under which such experiences are made, which exercise a strong influence on why and how such experiences take place.

The ancient theatre of Epidauros is one of the most well preserved examples of Hellenistic theatre buildings. As a theatre historian, I thought I knew something about this historical monument, but approaching it by car on a tour over the Peloponnesos radically changed my understanding of this theatre. There are no major settlements in the area, so I started to wonder why such a theatre had been erected at this place. Two circumstances — which had not been mentioned in any of the books I had read — explained the special position of this theatre. One of the first things I realized was that it belonged to the precinct of Asklepios, the god of health and recreation, to which tired and stressed Athenians retreated as a kind of *Kurort*, a spa of the late Greek civilization. The remote location of the place saved the theatre from destruction — its building materials were not used for fortifications or churches, but were only slightly damaged by weather and wind. My encounter with the site of Epidauros did not change the theatre as artifact, but it considerably changed my understanding of it. This dynamic interplay of knowledge, references, and experiences shapes our cultural encounters, although the monuments remain exactly the same. But I had to go to Greece to find out, to the place which archaeologists had prepared long before I arrived.

Göran Nylöf of the Swedish Cultural Council has developed a very simple model for the study of the relationship between the availability of cultural products — in his case mainly art, literature, theatre, and film — and the interest which people have in these products. By distinguishing between high and low interest, on the one hand, and between a high or low availability of cultural objects, on the other, he could easily point out when a cultural situation is satisfactory or frustrating, when people think there is an abundance of cultural objects or when their own disinterest makes the availability of artistic experiences altogether negligible. Nylöf has suggested an easily accessible tool for the study of how attitudes toward cultural encounters are developed in various situations (see figure 15). The expressed feelings resulting from these combinations of conditions are of course only approximate examples.

Nylöf does not take into account the different natures of various cultural events. A cultural event is also characterized by the "input": what

| | Availability | |
|---|---|---|
| | rich | poor |
| **Interest** high | SATISFACTION | FRUSTRATION |
| low | ABUNDANCE | INDIFFERENCE |

*15. The relationship between interest in and availability of cultural products.*

is to be seen, heard, read. Most people have very clear preferences as to what they want to experience, what genres, styles, and type of contents they expect from a cultural encounter. These preferences are not as personal as we might think. Pierre Bourdieu has shown that what he called the "economic" and "cultural" capital of a person has a crucial influence on the developments of taste.[3] It implies a different social status to go to the opera, to see action movies, to attend a soccer game, to visit a church service, to play in a bingo hall — and it is fairly predictable which activities will be most popular in certain social strata.

When I speak about cultural politics, it is obvious that I have a European perspective in mind. I am well aware that the political and economic conditions of culture are very different in other parts of the world. In a country like Sweden, cultural politics include the arts, historical and other museums, public television, subsidies for the press, international exchange, and many other items, which are handled by a special public authority. The Swedish state provides money for all these activities, but the counties and the municipalities also contribute a considerable amount of money. While public money is invested in public culture, it is at the same time very important to guarantee political and ideological freedom to these institutions. But it has not always been this way. Although royal theatres were established more than 200 years ago, the financial support from king and parliament was minimal and often debated during the ninteenth century. Around 1900 both theatres were leased as private enterprises before the state took back its responsibility and extended the subsidies to cover more than 80–90 percent of the budget. This was in the economically expansive 1970s, while today's politicians urge the theatres to raise their box office revenues.

There are, of course, already considerable differences between Western European countries, Germany and Great Britain representing two extremes.[4] In Germany there are almost 100 city theatres with the potential to present operas, musicals, and spoken drama, and in addition every state of the federal republic has its state opera and state theatre. By contrast, the long-lasting problems in establishing an English National Theatre are well known, and the rebuilding of the Globe through a private foundation is also an indication of how difficult it is to gain support from the "public hand" in that country. In Eastern Europe all theatre was state-run before 1989 — in both economic and ideological terms — whereas it now has become an area of free enterprise, causing enormous difficulties for many formerly famous companies. In most African countries cultural politics ends with signing far-reaching documents, since there is no public money to support such plans. I do not need to give more examples to stress my point. I am not in a position to present an overview of cultural politics from a global perspective, but there are some problems which might concern many parts of the world.

Cultural arbitrators face a number of dilemmas. On the one hand, for instance, it is not sufficient to restrict cultural politics to the problems of distribution. It is certainly not enough to provide money for the dissemination of cultural "products," because they will most likely resemble the established canon of hegemonic culture (i.e., already acclaimed and approved artists, museums, prints, etc.). The allegedly high quality marks the selection, which — at least in Europe — is handled by professional cultural managers. Even the selection of avant-garde art follows this pattern. As a result, there is a risk that cultural politics may follow the old ambition of giving "good art to the people," which in reality means to a few people, while the majority simply is not interested in this kind of culture.

On the other hand, it would not be acceptable in a democratic society for cultural politics in any tangible way to determine the content of cultural production. The freedom of expression is one of the major guarantees of democratic constitutions, which cannot be undermined by political decisions. On a less dramatic note, one can remark that there is considerable awareness of the limits of political interference with culture. As soon as any politically chosen board member of a public cultural institution tries to impose a political view on the artistic or cultural management of that organization, there is manifest opposition to all such manipulations. But this attitude does not always operate in all democracies.

How can cultural politics combine a wider responsibility with less interference? I would deserve an immediate engagement at the Ministry of Culture if I could offer a solution for these problems. Of course, there is no simple way of dealing with these questions. I would like to point out a few topics for further investigation.

There is also a scholarly problem to be added: if people in general are prejudiced about their interest in various cultural activities, so are the researchers dealing with cultural issues. I would like to share two observations from my own research. An extensive analysis of the social spectrum of visitors to the Royal Opera in Stockholm showed an educationally, economically, and socially much broader audience than anybody, including the opera management, would have expected. A comparison between the preferences of theatrical genres and the actual evaluation of performances which the same spectators had seen showed a significant difference. Someone might have strong opinions about what kind of theatre he or she likes, but once in the auditorium might very well appreciate a performance that the person would never have visited it otherwise.[5] I am mentioning these two cases just as a reminder that it is useless to speculate about people's cultural behavior — extensive research is necessary to gain insights into public tastes and habits. This is, of course, not only true of Sweden.

I think that culture has to be defined over and over again. There is no constant which we call culture, but a continuous discussion about how we — society, politicians, scholars — look upon culture, what we see as necessary inclusions as well as exclusions. The Swedish debates during the last three decades have produced all kinds of attitudes, from a concentration on the high arts to the extension of *cultura* to all human activities. Neither extreme can be applicable as a basis for either cultural studies or cultural politics. While it is relatively self-evident that the arts — high as well as low, if such a distinction is at all appropriate — are part of culture, it not so clear what else should be included. I cannot provide an answer, but I would like to note that the cultural performances mentioned above — ceremonies, rituals, celebrations of the life cycle, holidays, anniversaries, inaugurations, championships, and many other occasions of regional, national, or international interest — should be considered culture. But even if we define these events as cultural encounters, to what extent are they the objects of cultural politics?

No answers can be given without thorough investigations into the nature and specifities of cultural encounters. How can we improve our understanding of cultural behavior? How do the temporal and spatial distances affect the experience of cultural artifacts and events, past and present? Such studies could provide a basis for the redefinition of cultural values, which I find absolutely necessary to break down the hegemonic dominance of established cultural forms, which are privileged by cultural politics. We must be more observant concerning the contextual conditions for cultural creation and cultural experiences.

Context is not just a trendy academic term which can be translated into something fashionable. Regarding cultural politics it would mean — in addition to the before-mentioned investigations — that special care has to be invested in the presentation of cultural objects, both material and spiritual. The events through which the observers (i.e., citizens, who have paid taxes for cultural politics) find access to cultural artifacts, documents, stories, and performances have to find their audiences. Marketing is not only a commercial enterprise, but can also be used to serve public interests. Even here research is required — culture can learn from the market, but has to transform its mechanisms into public service.

Last but not least, we must ask what roles the academic scholar could or should play in the cultural politics of our era. Besides playing the important pedagogical role of educating students, what are the possible functions and duties of the scholar in the political arena? Scholars already provide commentary — program notes for the performing arts, catalogues for art museums, guidebooks for architectural monuments. And they provide critical evaluation and analysis of cultural events and artifacts, from theatre productions and movies to gallery shows and jazz concerts. But beyond these roles, they could also provide a more direct political involvement in the city, province, and state institutions (including political legislatures, assemblies, and parliaments) that make the decisions about the place of culture in society. Do we need to become active politicians, writing and acting like the established political decision-makers? Maybe that would be a good idea, but it would not automatically guarantee any immediate success or even a deeper understanding of the problems. Nevertheless, research into public affairs like cultural politics is bound to become part of the political debate. We are responsible for the results of our research, even when they become part of politics. This is the path I see ahead of us: to contribute to decisions in cultural politics which are based on knowledge and on the debates about knowledge rather than on popular opinions and fashionable trends.

# Part II

## Theatrical Events
### *Applications*

# 6

## *Sarah Bernhardt in Phenomenological Perspective*
### To Study a Living Legend

> Oh! Sarah! Sarah! Sarah is grace! Sarah is youth! Sarah is beauty! Sarah is divinity!
>
> I am mad, I am beside myself! I no longer know what I am doing, I no longer think of anything. I saw Sarah Bernhardt last night.
>
> My God! What a woman! Sarah . . . Sarah . . . when shall I see you again. I weep, I tremble, I grow mad, Sarah, I love you! (Otis Skinner, p. 241) [1]

This entry from the diary of the then eighteen-year-old writer Pierre Loüys is one of the most frank and enthusiastic responses to the actress Sarah Bernhardt. But more mature men such as Mark Twain also greatly admired her:

> There are five kinds of actresses: bad actresses, fair actresses, good actresses, great actresses — and then there is Sarah Bernhardt. (Gold, p. 3)

When Victor Hugo's famous and scandalous play *Hernani* was revived in 1877 with Bernhardt in the role of Dona del Sol, the aging writer sent the young actress the following note:

> Madame, you were great and charming; you moved me, me the old warrior, and, at a certain moment when the public, touched and enchanted by you, applauded, I wept. This tear which you caused

me to shed is yours. I place it at your feet. Victor Hugo. (Otis Skinner, p. 110)

Even earnest Sigmund Freud obviously surrendered to captivating and powerful stage art:

> I can't say anything good about the piece itself . . . But how that Sarah plays! After the first words of her lovely, vibrant voice I felt I had known her for years. Nothing she could have said would have surprised me; I believed at once everything she said. (Gold, p. 4)

Alexandre Dumas *père* called Sarah Bernhardt his *petite étoile*, his little star, and a star she became. For today's historian she clearly overshadows her predecessors and successors such as Rachel and Adelaide Ristori and even the celebrated Eleonora Duse, if not as an artist then at least as a phenomenon. In Swedish pastry shops one can find small chocolate biscuits with a paper strip attached to them reading "Sarah Bernhardt" — not as a proof of her superior skills, but as proof of a prevailing myth, seventy-five years after her death. I don't think there is any other actor or actress, dead or alive, who can challenge her fame during her own lifetime and after.

Sarah Bernhardt's career is indeed an unprecedented success story. From the day she conquered the West Bank audience of the Odéon Theatre in Paris in 1868, her theatrical achievements were the talk of the town. Her life in the theatre included setbacks, at times even on a disastrous scale, but these meant nothing compared to the recognition and admiration she received from all the world.

During her stage career, which lasted more than sixty years, Sarah Bernhardt (1844–1923) created more than 130 characters. About half of them were original parts, often written especially for the star. No less than 25 creations were so-called cross-gender roles, in which she portrayed men — from the young Florentine poet in *Le passant*, her first great success in Paris, to Goethe's *Werther* and Shakespeare's *Hamlet*. Even after she had one leg amputated in 1916, she premiered more than a dozen roles in her Parisian theatre as well as in the field theatre of the First World War. During all her life she was surrounded by eminent partners, both on stage and in private, including Jean Mounet-Sully, Edouard de Max, Lucien Guitry, Jean Richepin, the painters Gustave Doré and George Clairin, writers such as Dumas *père* and *fils*, Hugo, George Sand,

Victorien Sardou, Edmond Rostand, and many other celebrities of the time.

Sarah Bernhardt's fame was, in the true sense of the word, worldwide, due to her extensive traveling. The London audiences were even more enthusiastic than those in Paris; her tours took her everywhere in Europe, from St. Petersburg and Stockholm to Rome and Athens. Between 1880 and 1918 she toured North America six times; on a two-year tour, which brought her even to South America and Australia, she was to earn 3.5 million francs. She spent money as easily as she made it.

Without doubt, Madame Bernhardt was an extraordinary artist with great acting technique, an actress who provoked strong response from her audiences, but she was elevated above cult status. Can one explain this entire phenomenon of the actress, woman, and star? Not if by explaining we mean finding a neat formula, giving the key to her success by pointing out a single cause. But if we look at her career as a historical phenomenon, we might be able to understand some of the factors which made this success story possible: the personality, the theatrical structures and the conditions of life just before, during, and after the *fin de siècle*.

It is undisputed that, besides the clever management and the extensive marketing, Sarah Bernhardt had something to offer her audience which went far beyond the surface of her legend. She was actually able to communicate with her public in a very particular way. How can this amazing ability to exert an irresistible grip on the spectator's attention be described and understood? Although we might never be able to analyze all aspects of the phenomenon, we must move beyond the biographical narratives and follow a more theoretical path.

To begin with, we should focus on the theatrical event, which always includes both the actor and the spectator — the actions and the reactions. Since semiotics has taught us that the actor is to be understood as a fictional sign, which signifies something else, it seems easy to agree that theatrical communication includes a fictional or symbolic level. But not everything in a theatrical performance is fiction. It also includes artistry, skills, and beauty. These aspects are less frequently incorporated in the discussion of the communication between actor and spectator, although the artistic and sensory aspects of a performance can hardly be excluded from the theatrical event.

In order to understand the phenomenon of Sarah Bernhardt, we need to consider not only the sensory, artistic, and symbolic aspects of her acting techniques, as she presented herself in performances and as spectators reacted to her, but also the conventional, structural, and conceptual contexts that encircle the individual performances like layers or spheres, each communicating its own set of significant codes and meanings to the theatre event. A theory of theatrical communication would remain incomplete if only the theatrical event itself received our attention.

The theatre is not simply a piece of art or an art work, but an event in time. Thus, Sarah Bernhardt, like any other actor, should not be reduced to an art work, a show piece, or a static image. Instead, the actor is one part of a theatrical communication which, as intended by the actor and as perceived by the spectator, has a clear time dimension; therefore, it is necessary to acknowledge that the spectator also communicates with the actor — stage artists are not only aware of the audience's reactions but also incorporate these reactions into their own behavior on stage. It goes without saying that both actions and reactions are patterned by the contexts in which they occur — historical time and place is always a prime condition in the analysis of a performance.

There are recordings of Sarah Bernhardt, both tapes and silent movie scenes. Listening to her or seeing her today conveys nothing of her grandeur. These recordings are inadequate historical documents, in part because of their poor technical qualities. But they also hinder our historical understanding because they now exist as self-contained artifacts, detached from their historical moment. They are no longer dynamic events. We cannot adequately understand theatrical presentations of the past unless we attend to both the action and the reaction. Therefore, a statement by a historical spectator often tells us more than the finest recording: again, theatre has to be understood as an event, not as a piece of art.

Last but not the least, it is essential to take into account the circumstances and conditions which surround theatrical life. Edmund Husserl uses the German term *Lebenswelt*, meaning simply the world in which we live, or, to use the English translation, the life-world. Sarah Bernhardt's life-world benefited greatly from several conditions that proved to be prerequisites to her worldwide career and fame. And part of her talent was her savvy ability to use, adapt, and translate these conditions for her expansive presentation of self.

The first and foremost condition for the appearance of the star in every major city of Europe and North America was the access to railway lines and ocean steamers. These facilities were not only conveniences in regard to her excessive traveling; those journeys would simply have been impossible during a period in which horse carriages and sailing boats provided the only means of transportation. The railway networks were part of the recent industrial and technological revolution, which were primarily developed to serve capitalism.

Two other factors which greatly contributed to the worldwide fame of the actress were also technical inventions: the press and photography. The rapid growth of the newspaper business during the second half of the nineteenth century guaranteed continuous publicity, another condition of the star system. The easily accessible reproductions of photographs of the star in her various roles sold by the thousands. Renowned photographers such as Félix Nadar in Paris regularly produced artistic reproductions of stage artists, thus providing wealth and status both to his still new trade and to the subjects before his camera. And Sarah Bernhardt used this new medium of representation as well as anyone, even exploiting it in a scandalous manner with her famous shot of herself posing dead in her coffin.

Another factor that contributed to her career, directly and indirectly, was the rapid emancipation of women toward the end of the century. Not only were the suffragists striving for equal political and legal rights for women, but women were also becoming more noticeable in the cultural field. Although few in number, female writers and dramatists were beginning to make a place for themselves. In the theatre, the actress had conquered the stage some hundred years earlier, but many young women were now exploited in the commercial theatres of the late nineteenth century. Sarah Bernhardt, the successful and significant woman, was perceived as a necessary counterimage to these insignificant chorus girls. She was used as a symbol of independence by American women's liberation movements, an involvement to which the actress willingly contributed. As Elaine Aston has shown in her recent book, the spoiled celebrity was very well aware of her capacity as a model for self-conscious and expansive female enterprise.

## The Sensory Performer-Spectator Relationship

Starting from the sensory level of communication, we have to ask ourselves what it means to see the actress on stage. It is not the private person of the performer we observe upon her *entrée*, but the performer as actress. The performer exhibits her acting personality, her physical as well as mental qualities, displayed through what I call exhibitory actions. In other words, the actress is staging her own performer personality.

Sarah Bernhardt was very much aware of this fact. In her book for aspiring actors and actresses, *The Art of the Theatre*, written toward the end of her life, she outlined what she thought were the prime prerequisites for any stagecraft.[2] Her first chapter deals with "the physical qualities necessary to the actor": memory, physical proportions, voice, pronunciation, and gesture. These five basic factors determine the success of an actor. Without an excellent memory a young person should not even think of going into the theatre — she herself learned her parts by reading them, in a concentrated manner, four times!

An equally important factor for the stage artist is physical appearance, and Bernhardt had a clear and outspoken conception of how crucial the performer's looks are within this peculiar trade of the theatre. A physical handicap for other artists, she writes, it would not have made any difference in respect to their art. But the actor "must be tall, have good figure, an expressive and pleasing face and nothing that distracts from the general harmony of his body" (p. 42). The male performer is nevertheless privileged:

> From the actress the spectator demands even more. So far as she is concerned, the most perfect technique cannot compensate for the physical grace, the charm, and the fascination that emanates from woman. No doubt by will power she may prolong her youth, and even after middle age give the illusion of freshness and adolescence. But if she lacks the necessary figure, if she is without the minimum of gracefulness, or is defective in originality, if nature has endowed her so unkindly that she cannot appear on the stage without repelling the audience at first sight, she will do wise to abandon all her hopes of succeeding as an actress. (p. 43)

Bernhardt here stresses the general importance of a performer's physical appearance, necessary to succeed in exhibitory actions and to be able to launch a vivid impulse on the level of sensory contact with the spectator. Her description reflects the consensus of her own time and its conventions, but the following might apply even to other periods: "Perfect beauty is not essential to the theatre; an actress may have an ordinary face and yet be perfectly charming on the stage, provided she is well proportioned, that is to say, if she has a small face, a long neck, a short figure, and long legs and arms. It is rare for a woman's face to be entirely ugly, especially if she is animated by the desire to please; and that should always be the aim of an actress, whatever her part, even if it be that of a mother-in-law" (pp. 45 f.). She clearly differentiates between the actress as a private person and the actress as a stage personality. Whereas physical proportions cannot be altered easily, the main point for the actress is the "desire to please," her willpower, her ability to use exhibitory actions. The body and the face are to be used to stage the performer's self as favorably as possible, to exhibit the entire stage personality to the audience.

It is remarkable to read how consciously Sarah Bernhardt relates the actor's sensory abilities to the communicative aspects between performer and audience. In regard to the actor's voice she states frankly: "The voice is the dramatic artist's most necessary instrument. It is the voice that fixes the attention of the public, and effects the contact between the artist and the audience" (p. 50).

After criticizing the voices and the various practices of several of her contemporary fellow actors at the Comédie Française — with an astounding sensitivity for all kinds of variations — she returns to basics: "To know how to use the voice, it is needful to have a musical ear (this is not an injunction to practise music!). This musical ear co-ordinates the natural sounds which the vocal chords emit; it guides them, subjects them to a rule, and preserves them pure and healthy. It enables the speaker immediately to adapt himself to altered acoustics consequent upon changing his theatre or upon variations in the size of the audience" (pp. 58 f.).

Summing up the experiences of an actress who has served the stage for six decades, Sarah Bernhardt describes the relation between what can be learned by the actor and what has to be there from the very beginning: "Gesture, like delivery, can be mastered by dint of study and becomes perfect in course of time. But in no case can study take the place of nature, the innate gifts which constitute the very essence of talent or of genius" (p. 80).

With an almost brutal openness Bernhardt points out the secrets of the performer's trade: talent or genius. It does not seem very encouraging for young artists — at the time of her own first triumph on the stage

*16. Sarah Bernhardt, 1902. Courtesy of Drottningholm Teatermuseum, Stockholm.*

she was already twenty-six years old and a more general recognition of her genius did not occur before she was thirty-three. Nevertheless, she touches a crucial problem in histrionic history: the natural disposition of the performer, the impact of natural gifts, the dependence upon such conditions as the form and size of one's body, the scope of one's voice, the relation between given conditions and acquired skills — all adding up to what we sometimes call the aura of an actor, the radiation emanating from the performer, the basic facilities which make the spectators listen to and observe the stage actions.

All this seems outside the reach of scholarly apprehension, although it is the very basis of theatrical communication. Researchers leave it to writers of biographies to cope with such "strange" qualities as the sensory presence of an actor on stage, relying on numerous anecdotes of success, instead of realizing one of the most basic conditions of the theatrical event. Spectators and researchers alike are exposed to the intentionality of the performer's physical and mental presence addressing us across the footlights.

It is not possible fully to reestablish this peculiar presence of Sarah Bernhardt so many years after her death, but we have to acknowledge its predominant significance for the theatrical events in which she featured. Some photographs of her, especially those taken by the Nadars, give a hint of that special stage personality to which her contemporaries surrendered. Some of the paintings also transmit an inkling of the intensity of Bernhardt's exhibitory actions, even when she posed for an artist.

Sarah Bernhardt's way of displaying her costumes — as a way of staging her personality and creating a fictional character — contributes to the sensory impression she achieved. Even in pictures and photographs showing her as a "private" person we realize a sense of public presentation. Her hair, a wild, dark reddish bush which she never succeeded in taming into a proper hairdo, constituted a special case. Even her mother had failed to suppress these agonizing curls into something suitable according to the taste of the time. Over the years this "natural" hair became something of a trademark for her temperament, intimately associated with her private and public personality.

All these features add up to the particular image of presentation of Sarah Bernhardt as a performer. Together they constituted the intentionality of her exhibitory actions. Having described at least some features of her stage personality, we may now proceed to look at the responses to that personality, to see how this actress was actually perceived by the spectators of her time.

The excerpts from the diaries of Pierre Loüys and Sigmund Freud as well as Mark Twain's classification of actresses quoted in the introductory paragraphs of this chapter clearly indicate that Sarah Bernhardt was able to exert a major influence on these men's perception of her exhibitory actions. There was obviously strong and effective sensory communication between the actress and these spectators. Another famous writer could be added to this collection: D. H. Lawrence, who, at twenty-three years old, saw her as *La Dame aux Camélias* in Nottingham: "She represents the primeval passion of woman, and she is fascinating to an extraordinary degree. I could love such a woman myself, love her to madness; for all the pure wild passion of it. Take care about going to see Bernhardt. Unless you are very sound, do not go. When I think of her now, I can still feel the weight hanging in my chest as it had there for days after I saw her" (Gold, pp. 3f.). This happened in 1908, when the actress was far into her sixties. Lawrence underlines the emotional impact she had on him. I suggest that we, at least theoretically, distinguish two major modes of perception: an emotional perception and a cognitive one. Whereas the emotional reactions account for the appreciation, attraction, and other feelings provoked by the sensory communication, the intellectual reactions include the spectator's prior knowledge, expectations, and prejudices and involve the ability to register cognitively what we see and hear. Our appreciation of the actress is also founded on the perception of the exhibitory actions experienced in the performance, even before we become aware of the artistic means used to create a fictional character. The very appearance of a Sarah Bernhardt on stage resulted in a number of emotional and cognitive reactions, not only from young enthusiasts like Loüys and Lawrence, but also from mature theatre critics like Jules Lemaître, who realized that she put into her role "not only her soul, her spirit and her physical charm, but her sex. Such bold acting would be shocking in anyone else; but nature has deprived her of so much flesh and having given her the looks of a chimeric princess, her light and spiritual grace changes her most audacious movements into exquisiteness" (Otis Skinner, p. 107).

Lemaître writes here about Bernhardt's "physical charm," but these charms do not fit with the contemporary standard vision of female beauty. She is thin, and the critic uses the word "chimeric" to find the link between the physical, sensory appeal and the intellectual, artistic grip which Lemaître experienced when seeing her Phèdre. Francisque Sarcey wrote about the same performance of *Phèdre*: "This is nature itself served by a marvelous intelligence, by a soul of fire, by the most melodious voice that ever enchanted human ears. This woman plays with her heart, with her entrails" (Otis Skinner, p. 107).

Although these critics were men, it is not certain that they surrendered primarily to the charms of this woman. Sarah Bernhardt was not a woman endowed with features that automatically aroused the erotic feelings of her contemporary male spectators. Being small in stature, she was also quite thin; as Lemaître phrased it, "nature had deprived her of so much flesh" that not even her continuous eating of chocolates helped to put on weight. For most spectators her appearance on stage was nevertheless a source of pleasure and appreciation. Maurice Baring's remarks on the occasion of the opening night of Sardou's *Fedora* in 1882 are typical: "A secret atmosphere emanated from her, an aroma, an attraction, which was at once exotic and cerebral . . . she literally hypnotized her audience" (Otis Skinner, pp. 217f.).

Typically, each of the three critics tries a combination of intellectual and physical features to describe the enormous impression this actress makes on them. They use words like "intelligence," "cerebral," "spirit," and "grace" to characterize the basis of Sarah Bernhardt's mind. Her body contributes physical charm, the most melodious voice, an aroma, attraction, even sex. Somewhere in between intellect and the body are the heart and the soul. It is obvious to me that the three critics are seeking an ideal combination of mental and physical qualities to catch something of the power in her public appeal. As theatre historians more than 100 years later, we should try to listen to their endeavor.

Sarah Bernhardt's ability to make contact with her audience was the basic prerequisite for her success — through the sensory communication between the actress and her audience the whole process of the theatrical performance was built up and maintained. As all actors know, this contact is not something that automatically prevails during an entire performance; it can be lost or destroyed and then has to be laboriously regained. Otherwise the whole effort of performing will be wasted. The spectator's attention to the actor's activities, including the exhibitory actions, is the very foundation of the theatrical enterprise.

The sensory contact between performer and spectator is enlarged and emphasized by the theatrical situation. Sensory communication does, of course, even occur in everyday life, but the theatricality of the performance in a theatre legitimizes what in private would be classified as voyeurism. In the theatre we are supposed to watch the performer: the spectator's gaze is the *raison d'être* for the performer's exhibitory actions. But it is not the sole reason: we also want to experience the performers as artists and we want them to create their roles.

## Artistic Expression and Its Evaluation

What means of artistic expressions does a performer have at her disposal when she exhibits herself on stage? Sarah Bernhardt has already listed the "natural" conditions crucial to the actor's trade. Not even in her case was it enough to have a golden voice, to quote Victor Hugo's expression *voix d'or*; this voice had to be used in an appropriate way. What, then, is an appropriate way? In her case, it was the combination of what she had learned during her years at the Conservatoire of the Comédie Française and what she was able to add from other sources, including her own imagination. All in all, it resulted in a certain set of rules and norms, accepted or at least acceptable to her audiences. We sum up these expressions as encoded actions.

These encoded actions are most easily understood in the field of opera and dance. An opera singer not only has to display his own voice, but must learn how to use it to achieve certain artistic effects. Song and voice teachers train the young singer, adapt his vocal abilities to the codes of opera singing, and the more the young singer is able to learn the codes and to conform to the conventions of operatic expressions, the more the audience will appreciate his vocal skills. The singer will be judged by the standards of his fulfillment of the norms. On top of that, a personal transgression of these codes might be appreciated, as long as it does not depart from the acceptable conventions set up by contemporary spectators and critics. In the case of the classical dancer, the perfect mastery of the basic steps and figures of romantic ballet is indispensable; without these skills no advancement to solo parts is possible.

But not everyone who dances perfectly will become a star dancer. Here the interplay between exhibitory and encoded actions is decisive.

What kind of training did Sarah Bernhardt have? At the age of seventeen she entered the famous acting school of the Comédie Française. She enjoyed — and endured — the finest teachers, such as Joseph Samson, François Regnier, and Jean Provost, just like all the other beginners. During her career she worked together with many colleagues who had the same background and, thus, conformed to the same standards: Gabrielle Réjanne, Constant Coquelin, Jean Mounet-Sully, Lucien Guitry. Basically, she had received the same instructions as the great Rachel — still, Sarah Bernhardt was a very different actress.

In the classical training of French nineteenth-century actors, one tradition was always the *ne plus ultra* of stage actions: the gesture had to precede the word. Before an actor opened her mouth, her arms and hands were to indicate the mood and the significance of the words to be spoken. Sarah Bernhardt is said to have added something very essential to this code: facial expression. The white makeup of the classical French actor's face was not supposed to interfere with the gestural expressions, but lent her appearance a serenity and artificiality which was to distinguish stage actions from everyday behavior. When she added the mimic expression of her face to anticipate the gestures, which, in turn, were to precede vocal delivery, this certainly constituted a break with accepted codes. But her way of using her face also opened up new modes of expression: the face did not necessarily have to express the same mood as the gestures, which allowed for contradictory comments to the spoken lines. Obviously, this offense against conventions was acceptable: it was interesting and at the same time skillfully displayed.

The great Rachel, who died when Sarah Bernhardt was seven years old, was primarily a *tragédienne*, an actress who shone in the genre of tragedy, in which the spoken word was dominant. Her declamation was the prime source of artistic expression, but her full and deep voice was not fitted for comedy, according to the taste of her contemporaries. This was also what Bernhardt had learned about her predecessor as a leading lady of the Comédie Française, but she assumed that Rachel could have developed her voice to suit a lighter genre had she not died so young (p. 51). Obviously there were strict codes which the vocal expressions as well as the general mode of delivery had to follow.

The great Eleonora Duse, at times certainly Bernhardt's rival, although the two publicly appeared to be good colleagues and friends, was influenced by a later development in theatre history, commonly known as verism and especially fostered by Italian actors. For her the psychological dimensions of a role were the main impulse for the theatrical style. She played many of Ibsen's women, who suited her introverted and emotional acting manners. It would hardly have occurred to Bernhardt that a play by Ibsen could be a challenge to her artistic temperament. She was what in French is called an *artiste dramatique*, a dramatic actor. The meaning of this term becomes clear from the repertoire in which she achieved her greatest triumphs.

During the 1880s, Sarah Bernhardt premiered in plays by Emile Augier, Eugène Scribe, Alexandre Dumas *fils*, Henri Meilhac and Ludovic Halévy, Jean Richepin, Victorien Sardou, and Victor Hugo. All these dramatists are well known in theatre history as exponents of the French *drame*, the well-made play, which carried on the traditions from melodrama as well as the classical French tradition. Bernhardt's roles, including the Lady of the Camelias, Froufrou, Fedora, Theodora, Tosca, and Adrienne Lecouvreur, could be characterized by their combination of stunning *entrées*, tender encounters with lovers, profound conflicts with temperamental word battles, and magnificent death scenes. This variety of sentiments, arranged in a well-designed rhythm, gave her the opportunity to display her mastery of emotional expressions. Her talent for great death scenes led writers to include a tragic death scene in practically all these plays, which were written especially for her.

Sarah Bernhardt's use of impressive stage effects is described in a scene which can still be seen in many opera houses: Tosca murdering the police commissioner Scarpia. Cornelia Otis Skinner, herself an actress, describes the scene in the following way:

> With *Tosca*, Sardou had again created one of those tight-fitting garments for his star. And in one act her actual costume was dramatically tight-fitting. This was the dress for the supper scene. An Empire gown of sinuous lines, it had a long narrow train which she utilized to make an exit that no one could forget. After murdering the villain Scarpia (and her discovery of the knife on the table was said to have been a chilling moment) and placing the candles about his supine body and the crucifix on his chest, she slowly backed off stage, staring

in horror, her hand to her cheeks. The train which had swirled about
her feet trailed along like an undulating snake and even after she had
backed out through the door, the train continued to follow until the
curtain fell. (Otis Skinner, pp. 240f.)

This statement also points to some other artistic means which Sarah
Bernhardt was to use frequently: lavish costuming and excessive stage
design. The times and places of these dramas gave ample opportunities
for the most expensive and abundant stagings seen in Paris at the time.
She spent a fortune on these productions — which she controlled herself, when she had left the Comédie Française — and it obviously paid
off most of the time.

Of course, Bernhardt also distinguished herself in classical tragic roles
during her career. Among these, Jean Racine's *Phèdre* is best known, but
she appeared successfully in all of his tragedies, whereas she never appeared in a play by Pierre Corneille. She has a very clear explanation for
this fact: "I have often been asked why I have such a predilection for
Racine, and such a horror of Corneille. The explanation is simple: in my
opinion Corneille, the sublime Corneille, does not know how to make a
woman talk. None of his heroines (Psyche must be excepted) is really a
woman. They declaim, but their heart is not in their breast, it beats in
their head" (p. 125f.). After analyzing some texts of these dramatists, she
concludes that it was probably only Rachel who ever succeeded in performing both Racine and Corneille well. Bernhardt herself concentrated
on Racine's art, "to render it more obvious to the public that is too apt
to find in these tragedies nothing but school remembrances."

How did Sarah Bernhardt succeed in conveying her artistic talent to the
audiences? The fact is that the professional critics rarely describe her use
of encoded actions. There are several reasons for that, but basically the
lack of descriptions has to do with the specific mode of perception. The
spectator's response to encoded actions on the level of artistic communication can, again, be divided into emotional and cognitive reactions.
As far as emotional reactions are concerned, skill in the use of artistic
means gives the spectator the pleasure of recognizing artistry as such:
the harmony and rhythm of delivery, gesture, movement, the beauty
of the composition, the interplay of the details. Even the critic appreci-

ates the artistic perfection on an emotional level and expresses just an emotional response — unless this analysis is on a cognitive level, resulting in evaluations rather than descriptions. The critic is able to compare a performance to other performances and thus builds a judgment on comparative observations rather than on the deep structure of a single presentation. It needed a talented writer such as Anatole France at least to hint at the combination of exhibitory and encoded actions. In the *Revue de Paris* he described Sarah Bernhardt's *Lorenzaccio*, the Florentine youth in Alfred de Musset's play: "We know what a work of art this great actress can make of herself. All the same, in her latest transformation, she is astonishing. She has formed her very substance into a melancholy youth, truthful and poetic. She has created a living masterpiece by her sureness of gesture, the tragic beauty of her pose and glance, the increased power in the timbre of her voice, and the suppleness and breadth of her diction — through her gifts, in the end, for mystery and horror" (Gold, p. 261).

The English actress Ellen Terry was obviously able to penetrate even further into Bernhardt's transformative techniques. After having seen Madame Sarah as Marguerite Gauthier, Ellen Terry made the following remark: "On the stage she has always seemed to me a symbol, an ideal, an epitome rather than a *woman* . . . It is this extraordinary decorative and symbolic quality of Sarah's which makes her transcend all personal and individual feeling on the stage. No one plays a love scene better, but it is a picture of love . . . rather than a suggestion of the ordinary human passion as felt by ordinary people" (Otis Skinner, p. 205).

Ellen Terry clearly sees the connection between the sensory and the artistic aspects of acting. More than twenty years later, the German critic Julius Bab, not known to be one of the submissive members of his trade, points to a similar link in Sarah Bernhardt's acting in the same role. "And now this woman appeared, almost seventy years of age, in a youthful make-up . . . One sensed the whole repelling artificiality of a violent pretension. But then Sarah Bernhardt opened her mouth and began to move, and right there pretension ended and the art of acting began. And this was probably the greatest miracle of the art of acting which I had ever experienced. The old woman was gone, and in front of us stood the young Marguerite Gauthier who loved and suffered and forced us to suffer with her."[3] This short account moves our reflections onward to

the symbolic level of communication, in which the exhibitory and encoded actions are connected with the fictional character to be perceived
by the spectator.

## Where Is the Fictional Character?

There are many reports of Sarah Bernhardt's ability to transgress the
limitations of age and physical type. But while the 70-year-old actress
performed the 30-year-old Marguerite Gauthier, we also know that the
32-year-old actress had great success in playing a 70-year-old blind
grandmother. This happened in 1876 in Dominique-Alexandre Parodi's
play *Rome Vaincue* about a Vestal Virgin, whom the grandmother kills
rather than allowing others the chance to assault her. "The audience,"
wrote Sir George Arthur, "was electrified: Sarah's whispers, Sarah's gestures and Sarah's hoarse cry in this grim episode must be burnt into
memory" (Otis Skinner, p. 109). Bernhardt obviously had the rare gift
of bridging the gaps of age, but it is not simply a talent. I would rather
describe it as her capability to create a seamless flow between exhibitory
actions, encoded actions, and embodied actions.

Naturally, many of the actions an actor displays on stage are directly
expressive of the traits and actions of the fictional character. These "embodied" actions are mainly of two types: actions which are pretended by
the actor to indicate a character's movements or behavior and actions
which are in a sense real actions, but which signify something fictional
to the spectator. This means that embodied actions are either independent actions of the stage figure, which the spectator imagines seeing, or
exhibitory and encoded actions, which carry a embodied meaning. To
the former type belong all the activities which an actor pretends, such as
dying on stage or hurting another character or being drunk or smashing
a fist on a table. The spectator usually knows that these actions are not
real, but accepts them as outlets of the fictional character. These actions
can be carried out more or less skillfully, which is a matter dealt with on
the artistic level, but the logic of the fictional world on stage ties them
to the character. As mentioned, Sarah Bernhardt was a specialist in death
scenes. No matter how artistically convincing such scenes were, it was
the character who was to die. Marguerite Gauthier's beautiful deaths
were the tragic end of the heroine, not of the actress. Rather it could be

said that Sarah Bernhardt's embodied actions were a matter of well-enacted pretense, capable of provoking immediate response from the spectator.

The connections between embodied actions and the sensory and artistic levels of communication are very well illustrated by a scene which has already been mentioned: Tosca leaving the room after having killed the villain Scarpia. Bernhardt took this opportunity to reveal herself to the audience — almost in the fashion of a *tableau vivant* — including her splendid gown with the long trail. She exposed a fascinating series of slow movements, to make a lasting impression. Last, but not least, the embodied quality of the same action seemed to have been quite convincing, as was the case when she discovered the knife on the table. How closely these actions related to each other is not only manifest in the enthusiastic applause which used to follow this scene, but also in an illuminating anecdote told by Graham Robertson. He happened to be present during a photographic session, when this very scene of Tosca was to be shot and reported:

> Several times she fell into the pose of horror and triumph after the murder of Scarpia, but always seemed dissatisfied. "Come here, Graham," she cried. "Come here and let me kill you." Now, I had, on more than one occasion, figured as a corpse in Fedora and found the sensation of being wailed over by the distraught heroine thrilling, so I advanced cheerfully and with confidence. But when those awful eyes of Floria Tosca — full of terror and deadly purpose — blazed into mine at such close quarters, I became uneasy, and finally, as she seized me with her left hand and caught up the knife with her right, I disgraced myself. "Madame Sarah," I yelped, "do remember that you've got a real knife and not one that shuts up into the handle!" (Gold, p. 238)

This trivial incident illustrates the difficulties the spectator — or even a fellow "actor" — confronts when trying to recognize and separate the different communicative aspects. This does not mean that the actress herself had any problems in distinguishing the various layers of actions, but the acting should appear seamless: "In order to convince others, the actor must be convinced himself; but it is not sufficient that he himself feels the violent crisis of passion; he must give outward expression to them" (p. 79f.).

Here Sarah Bernhardt formulated one of the basic problems of acting, to which Stanislavsky was to dedicate his entire life: not the acting
methods or the relationship between the actor's own feelings, the sentiments of the role, and the "outward expression of them," but the communicative impulse an actor creates through embodied actions. How,
then, can the spectator's response be described? Again, it seems useful
to distinguish between emotional and cognitive reactions.

Emotionally the spectator relates to fictional characters as people in
general do — one likes them more or less. All kinds of feelings for the
imagined person are possible, from indifference to sympathy, empathy,
identification, or antipathy, disgust, and hate. From the intellectual side
the reactions may be described as understanding of the role, which
means to interpret and analyze the behavior and the circumstances. The
question here is if there is such a thing as a "role," and, if so, where it is
located.

Sarah Bernhardt is a good test case for illuminating the difficult question of the role. When people crowded to the theatre, they came to see
the real Sarah Bernhardt, but they also wanted to enjoy her skills and her
typical way of acting. Last, but not least, they wanted to see, for instance,
Phèdre — not just any Phèdre, but this particular one, which only Sarah
Bernhardt could create. Strictly speaking, not even she could create a
Phèdre on stage; she could only create an image which the audience
perceived as Phèdre, which means that in the end the spectator had to
create the fictional role. This role, of course, was based on the image
which the exhibitory, encoded, and embodied actions of the actress presented and which made it unique. Nevertheless, the fulfillment of the
fictional role does not take place on stage, but in the mind of the beholder. The fictional role would therefore be located in the relation
between performer and spectator, in the intersection between the presentation of the stage image and the reception through the audience's
emotional and cognitive responses.[4]

This point of intersection was reconstructed by Cornelia Otis Skinner, who saw Bernhardt's interpretation of *Phèdre* as a turning point in
theatre history: "Racine's women had hitherto been deprived of their
sex by two centuries of falsely noble interpretation, but Bernhardt's
Phèdre was all sex, a female devoured by insatiable lust and abject guilt"
(Otis Skinner, p. 106).

Lytton Strachey, the Bloomsbury essayist, sums up his impressions:

*17. Sarah Bernhardt as Phèdre. Courtesy of Drottningholms Teatermuseum, Stockholm.*

"To hear the words of Phèdre spoken from the mouth of Bernhardt, to watch, in the culminating horror of crime and of remorse, of jealousy, of rage, of desire, and of despair, all the dark forces of destiny crowd down upon that great spirit, when the heavens and the earth reject her, and Hell opens, and the terrific urn of Minos thunders and crashes to the ground — that indeed is to come close to immortality, to plunge shuddering through infinite abysses, and to look, if only for a moment, upon eternal light" (Gold, p. 126).

In this compassionate comment, Strachey obviously moves through all communicative levels presented here and also mixes his emotions with intellectual reflections. Such reactions to Sarah Bernhardt are typical, indicating her capacity to intertwine all types of actions into one strong flow of images. From an analytical point of view, these complex patterns can be separated by the model presented in the introduction to this book. In addition to the use of the sensory, artistic, and symbolic levels of communication, I would like to comment on two things.

First, we have to add the time aspect. Communication does not only take place on the three levels between performer and spectator; it also develops along the time axis. In the model time runs vertically in relation to the communicative levels, from the top down. This corresponds with our everyday experience in the theatre: first we see the actor appear on stage, then we register artistic expressions, and by accumulating all this information and transposing it to the symbolic level, we start to understand the image of the role.

Second, this process cannot be pictured as a constant course or a steady stream of actions and reactions. The different aspects of communication alternate and intermingle during a performance. Sometimes a specific aspect may disconnect, almost disappear, then turn up again later. As spectators we sometimes "forget" the artistry of a performer as we are drawn into the fictional world; at other times we feel only the uncomfortable seats of the auditorium and are unwilling or unable to follow the fictional significance of poor acting.

Sarah Bernhardt obviously succeeded in uniting the three communicative levels into one. At times, then, the spectator no longer was capable of — or interested in — distinguishing the artist from her role. Yet, paradoxically, spectators also remained entranced by her stage personality and always enjoyed watching her perform. This fusion of all expressive means into one great thrust appealed first and foremost to the emotional side of perception, which the numerous accounts give evidence of. Could this capacity be assumed to be the secret of Sarah Bernhardt as a stage artist? It would describe the magnetism she exerted on her audiences, thus the very essence of her position in theatre history, but not the phenomenon as such. To gain a wider understanding of her exceptional fame, we have to broaden our perspective to include the theatrical and extra-theatrical contexts which permitted such a phenomenon to flourish.

### Contexts of Presentation and Perception

In basic terms, I have identified three contexts beyond the immediate theatrical event: the conventional, the structural, and the conceptual. The conventional context refers to theatrical genres, periods, and styles and also to the skills acquired and displayed by individuals and ensembles. The structural contexts describe the organization of theatrical life at a given moment, including financial support and governmental policies, trade unions and education of actors, the position of directors and managing directors, and other structural features of theatre in a certain area. The conceptual context aims at showing the attitudes and appreciation which theatre receives in a certain society — the position theatre enjoys within the value hierarchy of other art forms and cultural events, but also in relation to other obligations for which a society is supposed to take responsibility. The private and public sphere interact, for instance, when Bernhardt's amorous adventures are discussed in the newspapers and thus stimulate public interest in her performances.

It is important to notice that each context extends to both the presentation and the reception side of the communicative axis, thus circumscribing each theatrical event. In other words, the contexts describe the immediate as well as the remote circumstances under which a theatrical event is taking place. Naturally, the conventions change more quickly than the structure, while the concept of theatre in a society most probably remains relatively stable during a longer span of time. The general cultural context, which connects theatre with other nontheatrical activities, is a more general layer to be considered (see figure 3).

Although separated for analytical purposes, these contextual spheres do not identify isolated levels of experience — there is a constant flow through these layers. There are no distinct border lines between them. There is, however, a time dimension: while there is a correspondence between the conventional context on the side of presentation and the side of perception, both influence the individual theatrical event, as do the other contexts, though less directly.

Returning to our discourse about Sarah Bernhardt, we might ask ourselves in what conventional context her career took place. There is no doubt that the Comédie Française played a central role in the establishment of the "phenomenon." Not only did she learn her artistic vocabulary in that theatre's acting school, but her whole idea of theatre relates to the conventions of the French national stage: the performer as the very center of theatre. There were no directors to distract either the actors or the audience from the focus of theatrical attention. This is also obvious in the organization of that particular theatre, in which the *sociétaires* were both managers and proprietors of the theatre — and had been so since the times of Molière. Although Sarah Bernhardt had numerous conflicts with the management as well as with fellow actors and eventually left the theatre, she was nevertheless shaped by the idea that the performer *is* the theatre.

Sarah Bernhardt followed the convention of the French classical tradition that the dramatist rather than a director was responsible for the interpretation of a play. She collaborated closely with numerous writers, including those mentioned above. A considerable change took place in her relationship with dramatists during the course of her career. In the 1870s she still took instructions from Victor Hugo, George Sand, and Dumas *fils*, who had not written their plays for her. Dramatists who entered later in her career mostly wrote their plays directly for her. Instruction, then, seemed to be superfluous. At the same time, these conventions changed considerably during the sixty years of Sarah Bernhardt's stage appearances. When she started, directors who were artistically responsible creators of productions hardly existed; when she died, Max Reinhardt was already an internationally celebrated director.

These changes hardly affected Sarah Bernhardt, whereas her contemporaries' taste for international guest performances was the very basis for her world fame. She was, of course, not the only guest performer who traveled on the newly erected railway network across Europe and who crossed the ocean to tour America. Henry Irving and Ellen Terry toured there eight times. This was also the period during which the Meininger Ensemble visited almost every European city, with its neo-classical production style. I have already mentioned Adelaide Ristori, Eleonora Duse, and Tomaso Salvini, and there were other, less-known ensembles and performers.

This international circuit also presupposes an audience to which this type of performing guests from foreign countries appealed. And there certainly was an audience, particularly in Sarah Bernhardt's case. The audiences included everybody interested in the theatre, from aristocrats to maids, men as well as women, although the latter are less well documented. With the construction of the railway network, not only actors and other theatre people but also members of the public who could afford it traveled to the European theatre centers such as Paris, Vienna, and London to see the latest trends. In Paris one could buy booklets with the complete *mise-en-scène* of a recent production to take home, to reproduce at one's own theatre. When an entire production from Paris or from Meiningen arrived in Copenhagen, Madrid, or Istanbul, there was a veritable rush to these events.

How eager these audiences were to see the stars and how much they were prepared to tolerate is illustrated by Ernesto Rossi's visit to Stockholm in 1886. One of the famous roles he performed was Shylock in *The Merchant of Venice*. In contrast to Sarah Bernhardt, he had not brought his own troupe with him: he performed in the production of the Theatre Royal. The Swedish actors played in Swedish but had to learn the cues in Italian to be able to follow their guest star, who naturally performed in Italian. Furthermore, the fifth act was omitted in these performances, since Shylock no longer is in the play. People came to see Rossi and his Shylock, but not necessarily Shakespeare's drama.

Another aspect of the conventional context concerning the audiences (their taste and habits as well as what they expected from the theatre) has to do with the gradual emancipation of women. It is certainly not without reason that many of these international stars were women. They constituted a special fascination for the male-dominated audiences, of course, but they seem to have been equally appreciated by the female part of the auditorium. It was not only the erotic tensions between the sexes which influenced the rise of the female performers. They were part of a profound change in the attitude toward women and at the same time influenced these attitudes. It was almost unprecedented — at least in the theatre — that women could achieve such an elevated position as Rachel, Bernhardt, or Duse. This was a phenomenon *per se* and helped to raise expectations long before a star arrived in a specific city.

An additional factor contributed to preparing the encounter between the star and the audience. Especially in Sarah Bernhardt's case, her private life was always as exposed to the public as her artistic achievements. Her lovers were the talk of the town and often added to the excitement of her performances, since they more often than not also appeared on stage with her. Long before her international career began, Sarah Bernhardt and Jean Mounet-Sully were the loving couple of the Comédie Française, both on stage and in private, and all Paris seemed to know. On tour, later, she used to bring along her lovers in the leading roles of her repertoire. Since the press spread such news well in advance, the advent of the star was prepared for in more than one way. Life, fame, and artistic presentation all mingled in the framing of the public's mind.

Beyond these aesthetic and social factors operating within the conventional context, there were aspects of the structural context that helped to shape both stage and auditorium. Not only was Sarah Bernhardt a fascinating woman for the male spectators and an encouraging image of femininity for female members of the audience, but she was also in charge of her own business. From 1880, when she dramatically left the Comédie Française, she was her own employer, manager, and producer. She was not the first actress in theatre history who achieved such a position, but she was unusually successful in doing so. She hired supporting actors, the crew, a manager, and all that was necessary to produce theatre in Paris and abroad. For her tours she cooperated closely with her agent, Edward Jarrett, a stern businessman who knew how to make a profit. In Paris she operated the Théâtre de la Renaissance and later the Théâtre Sarah Bernhardt. A woman star and a successful acting manager was, in part, made possible by the liberalization of the arts business during the nineteenth century. Impressive as she was in her own right, she also represented the business mentality of her time.

The key word for the liberal attitude toward business life is competition. Sarah Bernhardt was all competition. She failed to win a prize at the Conservatoire and never forgot it for the rest of her life: she made sure always to be the winner. This also relates to her situation as a tenant or proprietor of the theatre she ran: her theatre was to compete with other theatres, including the Comédie Française. Her tours had to compete with other theatre tours, but her tours were to be the most attractive and profitable ones. Were there enough spectators for all this competition?

This was indeed a period in which mass audiences gathered in the cities. Not only were the cities growing rapidly due to the massive expansion of industrialism, but the urban population was mobile. Transportation was no longer a privilege of the noble and wealthy; trams brought everybody to any place in the city, even to the theatres. The local theatres, which served mainly the inhabitants of the surrounding quarters, had to compete with open market theatres, presenting attractive productions with famous actors. All theatres competed for all potential audiences.

An important instrument in this competition was marketing, through the vehicle of the well-developed press. Production information as well as rumors, gossip, and slander were quickly circulated in the newspapers. A more or less new profession evolved from the newspaper world: the theatre critic. The critical acclaim was a necessary component of competition. It provided the consumer with information concerning possible choices.

Seen in a conceptual context, these changes marked a period of important transition in the history of theatre: the "official" theatre had already been torn out of the hands of the aristocrats and was now controlled by the free manager. Only in twentieth-century Europe did state and city authorities feel obliged to care for theatres as cultural institutions. During the late nineteenth century legitimate theatre was very close to popular theatre, and their status in society was very similar at the time. Everything was a free enterprise.

There were, as always, certain limitations to these liberal attitudes — for example, the question of language. Sarah Bernhardt spoke French and was very proud of being French. Her Dutch-Jewish background had very little impact on these feelings, although she took a firm stand in supporting the unjustly condemned Jewish captain Alfred Dreyfus, even at the cost of a long-lasting split in her own family. She saw herself as the ambassador of French culture, which still had a dominating position in most European and American societies at the time. French as a stage language was acceptable in the entire western hemisphere, including Latin America and Australia. So was Italian, the language of opera. Even in France Eleonora Duse could perform in Italian. German was much less acceptable. The Meininger troupe succeeded in its international ambitions, but no German actor became a star outside language barriers. Even more illuminating is the case of Helena Modrzejewska, who was frequently compared to both Bernhardt and Duse by those who saw her. But her international career was limited to playing for Polish immigrants in America until she learned English and then had great success in the United States. One can only speculate about what would have become of Sarah Bernhardt had her mother decided to remain in Holland.

The production of stars was aimed at a market in which the customer buys what seems the most attractive product. The buyer's money is what the dealer is looking for and has to adjust to, but the buyer's taste is beyond the reach of even the cleverest manager. Taste and preferences are shaped and changed by much more complex mechanisms than the marketplace's simplistic formula of supply and demand. In the end, it is a question of social rather than individual dimensions. While it is difficult — and, perhaps, not always necessary — to distinguish between the public and the private, it is equally difficult to see a clear dividing line between the structural and conceptual context of theatre. The following example shows the gliding scales.

Sarah Bernhardt's private affairs during the first guest appearance of the Comédie Française in London in 1879 caused certain disturbances in London, and quite a few members of the British aristocracy were upset. Lady Frederick Cavendish informed a friend about the latest craze in town: "London has gone mad about the principal actress in the Comédie Française who are here; Sarah Bernhardt, a woman of notorious character. Not content with being run after on the stage, this woman is asked to respectable people's houses to act, and even to luncheon and dinner and all the world goes. It is an outrageous scandal!" (Otis Skinner, p. 132).

The letter of this conservative lady hints at an important break in society's attitude toward the profession of actors. Sarah Bernhardt was not only asked to act in respectable people's houses — which probably seemed more excusable — but she was asked to dine with the aristocracy. In reality she contributed immensely to the social advancement of the acting profession. Instead of being degraded to a mistress who privately entertained and pleased the rich and noble — as so many of her colleagues had to do — she met princes, heads of state, and business leaders as her peers. Many a crowned head bowed down to kiss her hand, and one is said to have bent his knees in front of her. These anecdotes from her biography should not be dismissed as mere excesses of a star cult; instead they convey an important step in the emancipation of the theatre performer.

From the perspective of the entire cultural context, it is clear that Sarah Bernhardt's theatre occupied a prominent place. It compares well with the Salon and other famous art exhibitions, the literary journals, and the musical stage. Her celebrated world tours were as much the focus of attention as the world fairs which came into fashion during the same time. The major part of her career belongs to the period before the birth of film. Although she participated in some films in the 1910s, she understood quite clearly that her proper medium was direct contact with her audience. The remaining film clips reveal nothing of her unique qualities. Sarah Bernhardt as a personality, not as a moving image, could reach out to the world.

## Acting as Event

Sarah Bernhardt's phenomenal acting career cannot be properly understood as a series of works of art offered to various audiences; every performance she gave constituted an event. It is through the notion of theatre as presentational event that we can grasp the historical significance of this actress. Speaking of the theatrical event does not necessarily mean limiting the discourse to a single event at a given time and place. It is the characterization of theatre as an event, the communicative encounter between performer and spectator, which determines our "object" and its specificities. In Sarah Bernhardt's case I have collected material from many such events to gain a better understanding of her as a theatrical phenomenon. In addition, I have placed this phenomenon in various contexts to hint at the circumstances under which it could develop.

During Sarah Bernhardt's long career, these contexts underwent several changes, partly in her favor, promoting her success, and partly contrary to her interests. In the long run, it seems as if her career followed a progression from the inner layers of contexts to the more durable and general contexts. While she willingly changed the artistic codes of the

1860s, her new acting style later became a norm. At that point Sarah Bernhardt had already affected the conventional and structural contexts of French theatre and was on her way to gaining influence on a world-wide scale. After the turn of the century she had definitely entered the conceptional level, and as a phenomenon she belongs to Western cultural history, far from being limited to the French theatre of the nineteenth century. She had become an image of the acting profession in more than one way.

For many years Sarah Bernhardt portrayed her colleague Adrienne Lecouvreur on stage, first in the play by Eugène Scribe and Gabriel Legouvé, later in a drama she had written herself. Adrienne Lecouvreur's life in the early eighteenth century shows many similarities with Sarah Bernhardt's own life, both on the stage of the Comédie Française and in private. One can understand the fascination that this Baroque actress exerted on Sarah Bernhardt, yet their fates were very different after all. When Adrienne Lecouvreur died as a celebrated young actress in 1730, she was buried at night, outside the graveyard in an unmarked hole. Such was the status of the acting profession in those days. When Sarah Bernhardt herself was brought to her last resting place in the cemetery of Père Lachaise in 1923, the funeral cortege passed tens of thousands of people lined along the streets to pay their tribute to the dead actress. In 200 years the world of acting had become very different, and Sarah Bernhardt's own talent played a prominent part in changing it.

# 7 | Mistero Buffo, *1999*
## Dario Fo's Intercultural
## Transfer to Sweden

When Dario Fo was awarded the Nobel Price in 1997, he was informed that he was supposed to give a lecture arranged by the Swedish Academy and that he should send his manuscript one month before this occasion. Three weeks before Fo was expected in Stockholm, he had sent one sheet of paper, containing a colorful hand drawing. The secretary of the academy was not sure if this was a joke or a misunderstanding, so he sent Fo another message. He received two more papers of the same kind. When Fo arrived at the airport and was greeted by the secretary, he handed over twenty-five pages of drawings and handwritten headlines. The audience that entered the lecture hall of the academy received a handout consisting of these twenty-five pages, neatly reproduced in color.

This was not a joke; it was Dario Fo's manuscript. During his "lecture" he went along from page to page, occasionally reminding the audience on which page he was at the moment; but since there was not one single sentence in the manuscript, this meant that he was speaking freely, improvising the "scenario." I had seen Fo before, so I was not really surprised, although I must admit that I found it very daring of him to demonstrate his fabulous capability to improvise at this occasion. He certainly convinced every person in the auditorium that the Nobel Prize in 1997 had been awarded to an "oral" poet, a storyteller, a performer. There were many critical voices against the decision of the Swedish Academy. Detractors claimed that Fo is not a writer, that he does not produce literature, and in Italy there were also political and religious protests against the choice of the Swedish Academy. Theatre people, however, congratulated the academy for its courageous interpretation of "literature."

The attention of the audience was at peak level during Fo's presentation, which is hardly surprising. But even the 1,200 students who listened to his lecture in the Aula Magna of Stockholm University were spellbound by this eminent performer, who was in high spirits, although he recently had undergone serious surgery. The fact that an interpreter stood next to Fo, translating his dwindling harangues into Swedish, did not impair the direct contact he established with his audience. Again Fo relied on improvisation. He told us that he did not want to give a formal lecture and felt too weak to present a performance. He preferred to answer questions. In reality, he needed only one question to keep the audience in his grip for an hour and a half. I think it is appropriate to call Dario Fo a phenomenon comparable to few in theatre history.

There has been a consistent interest in Fo in Sweden, long before he became Nobel laureate. His plays have been performed for more than thirty years, not only by free theatre groups, but also by municipal theatres in many Swedish cities. Considering the cultural differences between Sweden and Italy, this interest seems remarkable. How is it possible to transfer the Mediterranean temperament, the political turmoil, the rapid language, and the expressiveness of the body language to a country in the cold North, with stable political conditions and a minimum of physical expressions in everyday behavior? Are these differences only clichés which have nothing to do with reality? I do not think so, even though the differences between North and South are easily exaggerated. There are other factors of class, gender, and ethnicity which make these countries comparable. It is not my intention to engage in such a comparison, but I would like to give an example of how Dario Fo's work has been transferred to Sweden.

## Mistero Buffo *in the Park*

Stockholm is generous enough to offer its citizens free theatre performances in the numerous parks which are located in the center of the city as well as in the suburbs. In the summer of 1999 the repertoire consisted of the musical *Hair* and Dario Fo's *Mistero Buffo*, which I saw, and a few other productions which I did not see. I attended both performances in the same large park together with approximately one thousand spectators. Benches are only provided for some hundred people in front of the stage, with the rest of the audience spread out on the lawn. While *Hair* with an ensemble of fourteen young actors and actresses and a live orchestra had great difficulties reaching out to this vast field of spectators — I got quite disinterested pretty soon myself — Björn Granath with his one-man performance of *Mistero Buffo* managed to hold the audience in a firm grip for almost two hours. People did not even leave during the intermission which the actor needed after the first hour. How is this possible — how does such a performance work?

I think that the answer lies in the dramaturgy of the performance itself, provided that it is presented by a performer with certain requirements (discussed later). First, I want to describe how the performance is structured.

Björn Granath enters the stage as "himself": he greets the audience, comments on the beautiful warm evening, asks if everybody can hear him, and makes a few similar remarks. Although he appears as "himself," we do not experience him as a "private" person — and he would not say, "Hello, Willmar, nice to see you!" if he happened to see me. He is professional, but professional as a private person: a performer. This is underlined by his costume. He wears a black pullover with long sleeves, despite the warm weather, and dark gray pants and black leather shoes; apparently he is not using makeup. He could very well wear this outfit as a private person — there is no costume designer mentioned in the program — but at the same time this type of clothing looks professional for an actor of his age, just as bank clerks wear a tie to signal their profession.

During this introductory small-talk Björn Granath also tells the audience that he will present three pieces from Dario Fo's *Mistero Buffo*, that these are monologues which Fo and some scholars have found in medieval archives, and that *mistero* means a religious play, relating to stories from the New Testament.

The piece he is to show now, Granath continues, is called the *Wedding of Canaan*, and he reminds us that this was the occasion during which Jesus performed his first miracle. He starts to tell us this story from biblical Galilee about the unhappy father of a bride who had prepared several barrels of wine to entertain the wedding guests. When the time comes to serve the drinks, the guests notice that the wine has turned into sour vinegar. The father swears, the mother cries, the guests are upset. Among the guests are Jesus and his mother, Mary. She realizes that the situation is serious and urges her son to work a miracle. Jesus orders the servants to bring in twelve jugs of water.

In this manner Björn Granath continues to talk about the story as it is related in the Gospel. He reaches almost the end of the "plot," including the miracle itself, before he tells the audience that he is now going to present the story to us. Actually, the presentation will be handled by two characters: Archangel Gabriel and a peasant who was among the guests in Canaan and who had a little bit too much of Jesus' wine.

At this point Björn Granath breaks the flow of his speech, moves to the rear end of the stage, and "reappears" as Archangel Gabriel, placing himself in the middle of the stage. This change is fully visible to the audience and does not include any change of costume or props. The transition is carried out as a pantomime — the embodied actions are all movement. Positioning himself at center stage, Gabriel gives a solemn speech about this first miracle, which Jesus accomplished almost 2,000 years ago. But Gabriel is not to speak for very long, because Granath suddenly leaps to the left side of the stage to impersonate the drunken peasant, who interrupts the archangel. The peasant praises the quality of the wine, but Gabriel will not permit such blasphemous remarks. So the actor swiftly returns to center stage to urge the peasant to remain silent. The archangel wants to tell his story, but the peasant is not very obedient.

In this way Björn Granath repeatedly changes position to illustrate the two versions of the narrative. At some point the archangel finds the situation too humiliating and decides to leave the stage. The audience cheers in support of the peasant, who immediately approaches the footlights to continue his tale.

The two characters on stage are created in distinct styles. The archangel is an upright, straight figure, lifting his arms when he speaks, throwing his head backward, raising his eyebrows and showing a more and more "sour" mouth, just like a mask of tragedy in popular sculptures. The peasant, in contrast, walks on unsteady legs, with his back bent and looking up at the majestic figure of Gabriel. When the archangel has disappeared, he stretches out his body, relaxes, and talks in a less drunken manner.

I realize how easily I am entrapped into trying to re-create in written language what I have seen on stage. No doubt, it was an inspiring performance. My intention, however, is not to describe the entire performance, but to analyze its communicative and intercultural aspects.

## Dramaturgy of the Performance

At first sight it might appear awkward to watch a performance in which the same story is told twice. The same dramaturgical method was also applied to the other two pieces, so this doubling technique was not accidental. The effects of this strategy can be illuminated from at least two unusual perspectives.

First, by narrating the story before acting it out, Björn Granath created a democratic platform, giving the spectators a fair chance to understand the background and the references of the story. Sweden is a secularized Protestant country where only a few people would know these stories from having heard them in church or in school, let alone having read the Bible. In this way, they received Version A of the *Wedding in Canaan*. Dario Fo also uses this technique, though he of course adapts his narrative summary to the knowledge and background of his Catholic Italian audiences. To make sure that the points made in the second, embodied version are brought home, it is necessary to create equal conditions for all spectators. Other monologues by Dario Fo that draw upon material such as the tale of *Daidalos and Ikaros* and the flight to the sun or the fable of *The Tiger* require some previous knowledge which neither the Italian or the Swedish spectators bring to the auditorium. The democratic aspect seems important to him, but it is not the only reason for the repetitive staging technique.

The other aspect I want to bring into the discussion is the Brechtian *Verfremdungseffect*. By impersonating a story which has just been told as a narrative, a new Version B is created. Version B is obviously not identical to Version A. The main difference is that a person who was involved in the story now enacts it. One of the major effects of Brecht's idea of distancing is that while the audience has been informed about what will happen in the following scene, the spectators' focus is no longer on the course of the story itself, but on how the actions occur. Instead of using all their attention to understand the story line, Brecht's spectators were supposed to observe the turning points in the story in order to figure out how and why the events occur and the characters behave as they do.

*18. Björn Granath in Dario Fo's* Mistero Buffo. *Photo by Tomas Borg.*

When the peasant talks about the wedding in Canaan, we hear the voice of a person who has been there. This contrast is starkly emphasized by the introduction and disappearance of Archangel Gabriel, demonstrating that this particular story can be told in many different ways. It is through the peasant that we are aware of what a disaster the father of the bride is facing. The problem of the bad wine is not a mere inconvenience in the eyes of the peasant — and here he represents all the guests attending the wedding, not the perspective of the archangel or the Bible. What the Bible and Version A considered a nice opportunity for Jesus to do a miracle was in the view of a common man a fatal situation: how can a young couple get married without the party getting drunk? Is such a marriage valid at all?

On the one hand, this point of view elevates the story, making Jesus' miracle all the more important. On the other hand, it is Mary who pushes her son to help in this precarious moment. Jesus himself is reluctant to carry out the miracle; "his time has not come yet," as he remarks in the Gospel. The question the peasant raises is not what Jesus does in the end — we already know that he will — but why he is reluctant.

From my own perspective, as I watched the performance, the peasant's interpretation of Jesus' motives suggests that Jesus was reluctant because the occasion did not warrant a "heavenly" intervention. For Jesus, if not the peasant, the act of turning water into wine is too trivial for a miracle, and it even comes close to blasphemy when done for the occasion of a peasant wedding. And, of course, from the perspective of the Catholic Church the transubstantiation of water into wine is a holy thing, one of the important dogmas to be celebrated in every mass. But given Dario Fo's political ideas and sympathies, and given the charm of the peasant character and the pomposity of the Archangel Gabriel (who seems to be a figure of the established church), we come to see Jesus' decision as a choice for the peasants. The fact that he proceeds with the miracle despite his reservations shows that he belongs to the common people and not to the Church Fathers. The story, as enacted, thus criticizes the church for neglecting the needs and pleasures of the lower classes.

### Storyteller and Impersonator

The performer is required to appear both as a storyteller and as an impersonator. Making this shift from one form of narration into a form of playing also gives the performer the advantage of presenting "himself" and helps the audience to understand that the performer operates through different modes of communication. The appearance of the "private" performer is an invitation to the spectators to play a game together. There is no doubt about who is in charge of the game and who will draw up the rules. Of course, this invitation to play has to be convincing.

Therefore the first requirement of the performer is that he is actually appealing to the spectators.

Björn Granath is a man approaching sixty and looks like — excuse this vague expression — an ordinary man. What I mean is that there is nothing in his physical appearance which would make it easy to describe him. He is neither tall nor short, neither fat nor thin, neither bald nor long-haired. Even if he does not look like a picture-book Don Juan, I consider him an attractive man. His voice is a harmonious baritone, and his movements are well-controlled. He is not a person who makes everybody laugh at first sight; nor does he appear to be eccentric in any other way. I mention these rather trivial details because I think it is important to understand the "material" he uses when he becomes a storyteller and an impersonator.

Granath attracts attention from audiences through the contact he establishes with the spectators. This contact aims at the entire audience, not only the spectators in the first row. As occasion permits, he comments on things happening in the park or noises coming from the surrounding city to keep people aware of the "here and now." Furthermore, his eyes are constantly directed toward the spectators, making us feel that he speaks to us, that he is performing because we are watching him. He makes the spectators feel important.

The introductory small-talk establishes the frame of the performance, a solid sensory contact which is continuously reaffirmed throughout the performance. It is also the stable basis on which he builds the storyteller. The shift from the introduction to the storytelling is insignificant, hardly noticeable for us. There is not very much difference between his talking about Dario Fo's research among medieval parchments and his tale of the father of the bride in Canaan. When I try to remember what might have changed, the only thing which comes to my mind is that he occasionally gives a "preview" of movements and phrasings of a character in the story, which the spectators might recognize when he starts to impersonate them. In other words, Björn Granath uses a minimum of encoded actions to establish a firm symbolic platform of fiction.

In contrast to the storyteller, the impersonator uses an abundance of specific and observable encoded actions. Through his choice of encoded actions, Björn Granath distinguishes a number of characters and meta-characters. I have already tried to indicate some of the movement patterns he developed to present the peasant and the archangel. These movements derive from the pantomimic tradition and work with farcical exaggerations. Unlike mime, pantomime here also includes facial expressions and is completed by a corresponding use of the voice. When the archangel has disappeared, the presentation becomes more complex. Now the peasant is acting as the storyteller, which means that Björn Granath impersonates a new storyteller. The storyteller-peasant in turn impersonates characters like the father and mother of the bride, but he remains at the same time the drunken peasant. In these moments the spectator watches Björn Granath, embodying a drunken peasant who talks about other people, whom he imitates in his drunken manner. Granath manages to present both his main character and the meta-characters without leaving the slightest doubt about who is "present" at each moment.

The sources of Björn Granath's use of encoded actions, which seamlessly connect the various degrees of impersonations, are to be found in two traditions. First, his own acting career bears witness to a multifaceted talent, capable of adapting to contrasting acting styles. Second, Dario Fo's performances contributed both stylistic inspiration and interculturally transferable material.

Björn Granath received his basic training as an actor in the workshop of the free theatre group Narren (The Jesters) in the 1960s. Physical training, inspired by Jerzy Grotowski's exercises from the same time, constituted the basis of the daily work of the group. Growing out of the Fluxus- and Happening movement, the Narren group very soon turned toward political theatre. Plays were created through research on the "reality" outside the theatre and improvisations on the stage floor. Performances such as *The Girl from Havana* and *The Miners' Strike* indicate the leftist political agenda of the group. The material for the improvisations and the productions were gathered on location — for example, the group members participated in the miners' strike in the north Swedish town of Kiruna, living with families involved in political actions. The training program and the productions served for a long time as a school for alternative actors' theatrical education. For Björn Granath, the Narren group also provided ample experiences in constructing a play, performing in many roles in the same production, establishing close contact with an audience, and improvising both in rehearsal and on stage.

In the 1980s Björn Granath worked in various constellations within the free theatre movement, participating in successful shows, including

*Under Three Kings*, a satirical chronicle of the political changes during the reign of the Swedish kings in the twentieth century. He had his first encounter with *Mistero Buffo* in 1978, performing some of the pieces on various occasions. In 1983 the two monologues *The Tiger* and *Ikaros* were very successful, not least with the 180 participants of the extensive reception study which I carried out during these years (see chapter 10). Later in that decade the National Theatre of Sweden, Dramaten, engaged him.

The stage of Dramaten gave Björn Granath the opportunity to develop his talent in another direction. The dominating acting tradition at the National Theatre can most adequately be described as psychological realism. Many of Ingmar Bergman's film actors have their "home" at Dramaten. A lavish and exaggerated theatre style has hardly any place in this traditional theatre, but Björn Granath proved to be as useful at Dramaten as he had been in the Narren group. One of his achievements was in the role of the wicked Krogstad in Ibsen's *A Doll's House*, directed by Ingmar Bergman and shown at many international theatre festivals. During these years he also created a number of significant film characters, (e.g., the fathers in *Pelle the Conqueror* and *Jerusalem*, the latter being an adaptation of Selma Lagerlöf's novel).

Occasionally Björn Granath returned to *Mistero Buffo*, rehearsing new pieces of this series of monologues and presenting them in various contexts, such as the summer theatre in the parks of Stockholm. In all his productions of plays by Dario Fo, he collaborated with the director Carlo Barsotti, an Italian who had lived in Sweden for many years. Due to his close personal and professional relationship with Fo, Barsotti and his wife, Anna, have translated many of his plays into Swedish, and he also directed a great number of their productions. Carlo Barsotti represented the bridge between the Italian performer and the Swedish actor. What consequences did this easy access to Dario Fo have for Björn Granath's acting style?

To claim that Björn Granath imitates Dario Fo's style of presentation would be an inappropriate simplification. There are expressions, movements, and ways of speaking in Granath's presentations which certainly are recognizable from Fo's repertory of encoded actions. The blocking patterns — sideways to shift between characters, frontal approaches to reach out to the audience — also are often similar to Fo's own choreography. At the same time, there are considerable differences, foremost in terms of the playing tempo and rhythm of the performance. The Swedish language does not lend itself easily to a high-speed performance, not because it actually impairs the rapid pronunciation of words, but such a high tempo would sound terribly alien to a Swedish audience. A quick speaking of Swedish would create the impression of imitating something outlandish. Instead Björn Granath approaches the audience in their own idiom, making them feel comfortable and open to what he has to say. In this way, Björn Granath and Carlo Barsotti virtually transfer Dario Fo's Italian temperament into a Swedish product.

I think this intercultural move would not have been possible without the basic training of the Narren group and Björn Granath's subsequent experiences there. But I also think that the intercultural bridge provided by Carlo Barsotti was necessary to implement enough of Dario Fo's expressiveness to make the performances work. Neither the imitation of foreign patterns nor the complete remodeling of the original expressions contributed to the intercultural exchange.

This exchange can be described as a chain of hermeneutical processes. At every link we can observe a "fusion of horizons" in Gadamer's sense. Carlo Barsotti's understanding of Fo depends partly on the director's Italian origin and his familiarity with the context in which Fo works, but also on his involvement with the free theatre group movement, which dominated Swedish theatrical life in the 1960s and 1970s. Björn Granath, in turn, engages with these plays again and again because he has a theatrical training which allows him a maximum of expressiveness, but also because he has a partner in Carlo Barsotti, who ensures him of a reasonable closeness to the original.

The collaboration of Fo, the Barsottis, and Granath is an excellent example of how private, professional, and cultural relationships can add up to an intercultural theatre. It also shows how the levels of communication — especially the expressivity of actions and the appreciative reactions on the artistic level — depend on the contextual integration. Cultural patterns and references are reshaped in the context of a new culture, at the same time adding different aspects to it. Religion is not a high priority for most Swedes; so if the "mysteries" remained in the context of the biblical story, they would not become relevant to the majority of the audience. Focusing on the class implications of the religious topic certainly brings these monologues closer to a Swedish spectator. In Italy, I assume, there are ties between church and class which a Swedish audience hardly is aware of. The class perspective is for a broad Swedish audience related to politics, to social democracy and trade unions. Class relations can be changed, as Brecht has taught us. For the Swedish spectator Brecht is closer, artistically and ideologically, than the Italian jester with family ties to the *commedia dell'arte*. It is a long way from the South to the North of Europe, but it is fully possible to pass through the many borders.

## *The End of the Story*

It would not be fair to deny the reader the end of the wedding in Canaan, or rather what we know about it from our eyewitness, the drunken peasant. Like many people who drink too much, the peasant fell asleep and had a wicked dream. He dreamt that he was standing in a huge drinking glass, in which he could not move. He saw a lot of other people in similar positions and saw that their glasses slowly filled with a red liquid, which he understood was blood. He could not escape from his glass, so he was certain that he had ended up in Hell. He felt the liquid reach his knees; he screamed, but nobody woke him up. The liquid reached his chest, and he realized that he would drown in his glass. He considered it an appropriate punishment for his excessive drinking, while the liquid reached his throat. He wished this pain would go away just when the blood reached his mouth. Then he realized that the red liquid was wine and not blood, that he was not in Hell but in Paradise.

At this point Björn Granath asked the audience to excuse him for a short break, because he had himself become very, very thirsty.

# 8

## Reflections on Miss Julie, 1992
### Sensualism and Memory

A Danish theatre group with a Swedish director, calling itself the New Scandinavian Experimental Theatre, presented a provocative staging of Strindberg's *Miss Julie* in Copenhagen in April 1992. It was received with enthusiasm by the scholars at the International Strindberg Conference being held in Copenhagen at that time. What was it that made this production so appealing?

More than a hundred years ago Strindberg wrote a short play to prove his naturalistic ideas about theatre. Today naturalism is gone, at least in the theatre, but the play, *Miss Julie*, seems to inspire endless numbers of directors, actresses, and, not least, audiences. Julie is the focus of the script — even Strindberg himself sensed that when entitling the play, in spite of the fact that he himself favored the servant Jean. This fascination with the play derives, in part, from features which make it so suitable for all kinds of theatrical companies: a clear dramaturgical line, only three characters on stage, a strong conflict, a self-evident peripeteia, an exotic environment in the Nordic midsummer night, and a tragic end. All this is well known, but do these features really explain the worldwide, continuous success of *Miss Julie*?

The stage history of various plays has taught us that the success of a play depends more on the vagueness of the script than on its evident merits. It is not the obvious interpretations that make a play attractive to directors and audiences, but the endless possibilities of reinterpretations. Reinterpretations are primarily the concerns of those who produce stage versions of plays: they use the script to express their own and their own time's realization of plots, conflicts, and characters. It is obvious, then, that the scholar studies the intentions of the producers as well as the intentionality of the historical play script — a field of research commonly described as historical studies of productions. A serious production history, in which theatre is perceived as an event, would also include information on what the audience thought about a historical production. Historiographers could, however, conclude more about historical audiences from various sources than is usually done.

Performance analysis, in contrast to production history, presupposes that the researcher experiences the performance, normally as a spectator (in exceptional cases as a member of the production unit). As far as the general response to *Miss Julie* is concerned, we can only operate at the level of compilation. Reception researchers may be able to find out what the spectators on the seats next to ours think. Performance analysis, in turn, provide descriptions, evaluations, and argumentations which reflect the observers' own experience of the theatrical event. What was it we found interesting while seeing the performance; what were we thinking about it afterward; what remained in our memory? What, of all this, is of any interest to anyone else?

Because I think I have something interesting to tell — rather than to prove a point — I would like to report on a production of *Miss Julie* which exceeded the expectations of most spectators who saw it (thus, the following is not a strictly personal but at least representative account). But what can I write about? I saw only one performance of the production in Copenhagen. Rather than trying to remember all the details of the production, I am staring at the program and the photographs by Roberto Fortuna — another spectator who was able to document his experience of the production (although independently of me).

The front page of the program shows a cut-out window, which forms a frame for the first of the program's photographs. Through the window only one detail of the stage action is revealed: the face of Berit Kvorning, the actress who performed the role of Julie (see fig. 19). The photo immediately acts as a reminder of a series of cognitive and emotional reactions I probably experienced during the performance. In order to present those to the reader, I have decided to group them on three analytical levels: sensory, artistic, and symbolic.

To me the face of Berit Kvorning represents a strong sensualism. Her lips are promising; her half-closed eyes seem to express some enjoyable

*August Strindberg*

# FRØKEN JULIE

**Nyt Skandinavisk
Forsøgsteater**

*19. The cover of the program of* Miss Julie, *Copenhagen. Courtesy of Strindbergsmuseet,
Stockholm.*

moment. The seemingly wet curls of her hair indicate some steamy and exciting activities. Now, all this might be interpreted as part of the role, something that the actress pretends in order to impersonate the character. I do not have any objections to that, but I know that there is something more to it. The woman on the stage, just as the photograph depicts her, actually addressed herself to me (and all the others in the auditorium) to attract my attention. This struggle with the audience does not have very much to do with the character the actress is playing, but with her ability to create a stable and positive relationship with the spectators. Of course, as an actress she does not limit her appeal to the male part of the audience; but, being a male spectator, I can only refer to that experience.[1]

The cognitive aspects of my sensory experience of this actress — knowing that she is well known in theatre circles as well as to the Danish television public — also supported my emotional response to Kvorning. Even the photograph expresses something of the beauty and attraction of this actress, although I am not speaking about her as a private person but as a stage personality.

It is quite illuminating to compare my own response with the director's intentions, which Staffan Valdemar Holm expressed both in a discussion after the performance and in a program note (I quote from the latter):

> It is an old tradition that Julie is performed by an actress who — from a realistic point of view — is too old for her part. Simply because the part is so demanding. But Julie's age is only important as long as one creates a realistic psychological performance. This I didn't want to do, but I rather wanted to emphasize the ritual aspects: both the sexual ritual and the ritual of death. Therefore it was important to find an actress who is technically capable of moving between the two levels I am working with in the production. Clearly we are also using psychology, but only as a fetish, when the figures are alienated. This would be very difficult to achieve if a very young and virginal actress performed Julie.[2]

This paragraph indicates two aspects of Berit Kvorning as Julie: she is a mature woman, not an innocent young girl; this maturity is certainly transposed to the character of Julie, but it also affects the real spectator in the audience. Occasional sighs from a middle-aged male spectator are not enough to establish communication between stage and auditorium, however. On the contrary, the maintenance of the communicative link with the audience requires a continuous effort from the performers: in this effort the sensory connections are a basic requisite.

As the director noted, he needed a technically skilled actress; in Berit Kvorning he obviously found what he was looking for. When one opens the cover of the program a photograph is revealed (see fig. 20), depicting distinctly artistic expressions (for a moment neglecting its fictional relevance). The actress is bent forward at a 90-degree angle in a manner which only ballet dancers are capable of executing. What seems to be a random moment of the performance proved to be one of its characteristics: a strictly choreographic pattern of movements, which required advanced skills from the actors and a great deal of precision. The stage actions became symbolic expressions, whereas the skills for expressing psychological aspects of the characters were rare, scarcely needed or looked for.

The photograph also shows the differences in costume design used in this production as well as the rectangular coldness of the background — the tiles are reminiscent of a slaughterhouse more than of a kitchen. Here I am already starting to interpret what I see in fictional terms, the third level of my description. What do the actors and the performance as a whole transpose into a fictional world; what is intended to be perceived as fiction?

It is clear that the situation depicted in the photograph is the turning point of the story — or, to be more accurate, I interpret it as the moment just before the turning point: the actress shows a Julie who still expects enjoyment out of the situation. Julie has not yet realized that the humiliating consequences of this act will reverse her world. Optically she is already on her way down, but she is still the main character, with Jean only acting in the background, slightly out of focus.

Maybe I chose this photograph just because it depicts this moment in which there is still some hope, still something to expect. Julie has tried to compensate herself for the unacceptable fiancé — she protests by exceeding the limits of her class. She is still physically enjoying what she is doing, according to my interpretation. The attraction, responded to on the sensory level, merges with the artistic expression to create a symbolic level on which all these features are brought together for a moment. Soon Julie, Jean, and we as spectators will be disillusioned by the fictional

20. *The full picture under the cover of the program of* Miss Julie. *Photo by Roberto Fortuna. Courtesy of Strindbergmuseet, Stockholm.*

reality: the decline is unavoidable, the end only a question of time, at least within the moral which Strindberg established as fundamental for the play. We might wish that Julie — like a modern woman — could just walk away, find herself a job, live by herself, or find herself a stable relationship in a more complex urban world, but these are all daydreams, emotionally apart from the Jean-Julie conflict on stage. Running away from the plot, escaping the sensual grip of the actors, still admiring their skills: this is what remains toward the end of the performance.

Maybe those who created the program felt the same way when placing this photograph at the very beginning. For me it has provided a catalyst that revived my memories of this extraordinary production of *Miss Julie*. I have tried to show how the sensory, artistic, and fictional levels were so tightly interwoven that they produced compact impression on the spectator. Although I realize that similar reactions can be assumed on the part of the program makers, the photographer, some colleagues of mine whom I spoke to, as well as the thousands of spectators who bought all available tickets for months, I still can only make statements about my own reactions.

Does my analysis of one single moment in the performance, accidentally documented by a photographer, explain anything about the success of Strindberg's classical play?

The answer is yes, I think so. It underscores the power of theatre, for which the play-text is the incentive, but which needs the fueling of theatrical means to establish communication with the spectators. Despite the hundreds of productions, only a few will reach the high level of communication which I experienced in Copenhagen. The text is no guarantee of a successful performance. Today it requires a team of creative practitioners, including a director with challenging ideas and performers who are capable of understanding and carrying out these ideas. In the end, however, it is up to the actors, evening after evening, to establish a vivid relationship with the audience during all those theatrical events which make up theatre history.

# 9

## *Museum-Stage*
### The Frames Move into the Exhibition Hall

A student who was writing an essay on the 1960s made the following remark: "In 1965, I was seven years old and I saw my Dad climbing naked along the walls of the Modem Museum, which was kind of nice, but I could not understand why he kept doing this. I was told that it was a Happening."[1] This student's memory probably is off by a few years or remembers the wrong place, since there was no such Happening at the Modern Museum in Stockholm in 1965. But it likely occurred there, because this museum had developed into one of the most important avant-garde stages in the 1960s.

Yet the term "stage" is misleading, because the events at the Modern Museum were not conceived as traditional theatre or dance or art or poetry, but instead were attempts, in the words of the Swedish art journal *Konstrevyn*, to move "beyond the limitations of genre." The most generally used term concerning the activities I am talking about was Allan Kaprow's accidentally invented term "Happening" — at least during the 1960s — and today we could add "Live Art," "Installation," and "Performance Art."

What most interests me about these activities or arrangements of the 1960s is the arrival of the performer in the art world. Certainly this was not the first time an artist could be observed at work (e.g. Jackson Pollock's action paintings in the 1950s or Jasper Johns' random material paintings). In these cases the process of creating an art work was demonstrated in a public gathering, but the result was still a work of art, a solid object, which could be put on the wall and sold for money. What happened in the 1960s was probably something different. It is not immediately clear what the arrival of the artist on stage meant. Therefore, I would like to present a number of examples from the Modern Museum (MM) in Stockholm, more or less randomly chosen and quite different from one another.

Founded in 1958 in a former military gymnastics hall, the MM immediately worked on completing its collection of works from what could be called the First Avant-Garde: Pablo Picasso, Georges Braque, Francis Picabia, Fernand Léger, to name a few. But the MM was eager to get hold of the evolving art scene of the Second Avant-Garde, which had moved from Paris to New York.[2] Thanks to curators like Pontus Hulten, Ulf Linde, and Carlo Derkert it was possible for the MM to mount some very successful and internationally respected exhibitions in the early years.[3]

*Movement in Art* (16 May–10 September 1961) showed 233 works by 80 artists from 19 countries, which all demonstrated various kinetic aspects of art. There were mobiles and machines, engines and cars, and all kinds of mechanical devices by artists such as Marcel Duchamp, Man Ray, László Moholy-Nagy, Alexander Calder, Viktor Eggeling, Vladimir Tatlin, Alberto Giacometti, the new generation of Jasper Johns, Jean Tinguely, Robert Rauschenberg, and of course a number of Swedish artists. Abstract-Rhythm-Films were shown; electronic music was played; Javanese shadow theatre was performed. No less than 70,000 people visited the exhibition. The debate in the newspapers was never ending: which of these weird objects were to be considered art?

*Five New York Evenings* were arranged a few years later (8–14 September 1964). Among the artists were the painter Robert Rauschenberg, the choreographer Merce Cunningham, the composer John Cage, and a few others, who were all connected with Black Mountain College, where Arnold Schönberg was among their teachers.[4] There they had carried out experiments with music, movement, and space since the 1940s. Each of the five events was presented once during this week, and two of them are of special interest here.

Rauschenberg arranged what could be called a Happening. From the ceiling of the large exhibition hall a long rope hung down, decorated with various textiles. Underneath the rope stood a low-wheeled wagon with an oil barrel placed on it. Rauschenberg started by climbing down the rope very slowly, until he eventually descended into the barrel. When

*21. Rauschenberg's Happening at the Modern Museum, Stockholm, 1964. Photo by Stig T. Karlsson. Courtesy Moderna Museet, Stockholm.*

he finally reappeared from the barrel, a live cow was brought in, wearing socks (to avoid harming the floor). It pulled out the wagon. When the audience applauded, the cow responded by leaving a nasty-smelling heap on the floor.

On another evening Merce Cunningham presented a ballet with professional dancers, who wore green full-body tights with white dots. Robert Rauschenberg designed these costumes as well as an expansive painted backdrop, also in the same green with white dots. When the dancers were moving in front of the backdrop, they were optically reduced to heads, hands, and feet, whereas their bodies merged with a background of static and moving dots.

*She — A Cathedral* was the name of a sculpture erected two years later by Niki de Saint Phalle and Jean Tinguely (4 June–4 September 1966). These artists — later famous for their sculpture group *Paradise* in Stockholm and many others around the world — had created an enormous and colorful sculpture of a woman lying on her back: she was 23 meters long and 6 meters high. In the course of this exhibition, 80,000 visitors went into this woman's womb through the "gate of life" to experience Greta Garbo's first movie, a planetarium, an exhibit of classical paintings (which were all copied by Ulf Linde), a Coke machine, a look-out balcony on top of the stomach, and an aquarium where we inspected the body's bladder. The visitors had to find their way around without any guidance and could never be sure of having seen it all.

*Massage* by Claes Oldenburg, a Swedish-American painter, was produced later the same fall (3–7 October 1966). It was again a Happening, but, exceptionally, it was repeated five times in a minor hall of the MM. The number of spectators, or rather participants, was limited to eighty each evening, because no more people could be accommodated on the mattresses, which were an essential part of the arrangement. At one point all the participants, who had been watching various activities, were asked to lie down on the mattresses and were given blankets. The light was turned off, and it became pitch dark — and remained so for a long, long time. Nobody could see what the other participants were doing on their mattresses, unless the participants turned on their flashlights, which they could find on the mattresses. Eventually the main light was turned on again, loud rock music was played, and the Happening turned into a general dancing party.

Summarizing these five events with regard to the performers, we can easily detect different patterns:

| | | |
|---|---|---|
| 1. | *Movement in Art* | No real performers, only moving objects |
| 2. (a) | Rauschenberg | One performer and a cow |
| (b) | Cunningham | Professional dancers |
| 3. | *She — A Cathedral* | The visitors search for hidden objects in the object |
| 4. | *Massage* | Interaction among spectators |

What I find most interesting are the different ways in which the objects and the performers communicate with their beholders. Coming from the field of theatre studies, I immediately observed that such communication occurs on several levels at the same time and that this communication is mutual.

The *sensory* level describes the physical and psychological interaction between performer and spectator, comparable to everyday situations. This interaction is also equally important when a performer and a spectator meet, although the situation brings about a certain theatrical effect.

In my examples, Robert Rauschenberg and his cow seem to be the most prominent performers, exerting an uninhibited impression on the audience. What the spectator sees is the artist himself as the main attraction of the event. The artist makes himself visible in person, which is a sensation in itself, satisfying both trivial aspects like the curiosity of the spectator and deeper-felt sympathies (or antipathies) toward the personality of the artist. Rauschenberg was a well-known figure in the Stockholm art world of those days. Rauschenberg's personality was at the same time the very object of the show. The audience was not watching the process of creating another art work, such as Pollock's action paintings; the sensory experience of the artist was the "content" of the Happening. Being an amateur as a performer, although professional in another field of the arts, Rauschenberg at the same time demonstrated the then popular notion that "everybody can do it," even a cow!

Cunningham's dancers were professionals, but in the aforementioned passage with the dotted costumes they were handled with an ironic, playful touch by the choreographer and the designer. Rather than displaying their personalities and talents through dance, they were converted into bearers of those funny costumes to produce a visual effect.

While Oldenburg's cooperators in *Massage* — amateurs from the art world such as art critics — assumed the function of stagehands, resembling Rauschenberg's cow, the moving objects and Niki de Saint Phalle's *She* had sensory qualities as objects, but they were never transformed into performers.

The *artistic* level comprises all kinds of expressive modes which "belong to" or constitute the norms of an artistic genre. These genre-specific modes or norms are defined differently in different genres, and there exist several competing sets of norms within the same genre, such as realistic, highly stylized, or abstract modes of expression. At the same time, the artistic norms undergo constant changes, influence each other, and are purposefully violated by artists. It is important that both artists and spectators are familiar with these norms. Therefore, it is quite obvious that the breaking of these norms was at stake in all of the events described here. By breaking the norms — including the performer-spectator relationship — these Happenings moved outside the genres, or at least placed themselves in the interstices between theatre, dance, painting, and sculpture. Two aspects are especially interesting — and again Rauschenberg gives the clearest example. First, the amateur status of the performers reduced art to a common ground with the audience. Here again the "everybody can do it" attitude created not only a sensory close-

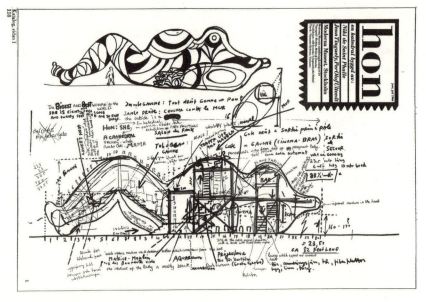

*22. A drawing of Niki de Saint Phalle's and Jean Tinguely's* She — A Cathedral, *Modern Museum, 1966. Courtesy of Moderna Museet, Stockholm.*

ness to the spectators, but also an artistic vacuum, deprived of artistic expectation. At the same time, a second observation can be made: most of these Happenings were only produced a few times or even, like the five New York evenings, reduced to a single performance. No concrete expectations were possible, since no one had seen the event earlier. Those who were among the spectators could feel very privileged — there would not be a second chance to participate in these events. This was as far from commercialism as one can possibly get.

Niki de Saint Phalle's *She* could be visited all summer long, but every visitor necessarily had a personal and incomparable experience due to the complicated structure of the interior of the gigantic sculpture. The objects of the *Movement in Art*, in contrast, were just repeating their own movements. Therefore, these objects did not offer a time dimension which directed the spectators' attention — all observers were free to choose their own time flow.

Although the breaking of norms seemed to deprive the events of all possible expectation, this breaking in itself provoked certain expectations. In this respect, these events are reminiscent of some historical precursors. Most of all I am thinking of the Dadaists in Zurich, Paris, and Berlin during the second decade of this century, but still other parallels outside the early avant-garde could be found. In spite of the fact that they were examples of a very different mode of expression, the *tableaux vivants* and *attitudes* in fashion during the late eighteenth century, in which living persons posed as famous paintings and statues, represented a similar transgression between the genres. Even the medieval *Espositione del Santo Bambino* in Italy, in which the Christ-child was displayed to the public around Christmas, reminds me of such mixed genres as Niki de Saint Phalle's *She — A Cathedral.*

Every time a performer enters, a profound transformation of the artistic code takes place: I cannot consider the performer an artistic object, such as a painting or a sculpture; instead the performer signals an artistic event. The time dimension is radically changed compared to the moving objects or even the hidden objects which the beholder found in *She.* The performer directed the time flow; the spectator could not choose his or her own pace, but was obliged to interpret the action "on the spot," while the event was going on, since there was no "second chance." This is the same situation as in the theatre: nobody can see a performance twice, only another performance (more or less different from yesterday's performance). In this respect, Happenings as events are most similar to theatre, with the performer as the common denominator. This means that the performer changes our interpretative mode from observation to participation.

The *symbolic* level marks the specific ability of theatrical events to indicate an imaginary world, which the performer (re)presents, but which has to be interpreted or decoded by the spectator. Fiction does not have to be narrative or even representative, the imaginary world does not have to be recognizable, but it contains the potential of signifying some "otherness," be it emotional states of mind or fragments of ideologies. Nevertheless, I think that the performing always induces some interpretation beyond the formation itself. As soon as the spectator understands that the performer "performs," the spectator is looking for a symbolic meaning. Under these conditions, such "fiction" will be looked for in the museum just as in the theatre.

From this perspective, one could ask if Rauschenberg's climbing down the rope "means" anything. To answer this question, we need not know what Rauschenberg's intentions were, because they might or might not be relevant to the spectator's interpretation. Performing in itself—

rather than the performer's intentions — constitutes the impetus for fictionalization, independent even of the question of whether the performer pretends these actions or carries out real actions.

When the audience joins the action in *Massage* another complication is added. Here the spectator might pretend or "act out," but the interpretation now includes his or her own doings, thus returning us to the question of intentions. At that point I am no longer speaking of the performer's actions, but of the spectator's own actions and intentions.

In conclusion, I would like to point out what these changes of the art world through the performer have meant to the concept of arts in the 1960s. Obviously all art forms — even musical performances and poetry readings — assumed an intensified degree of theatricality, which might be one explanation why theatre was considered very central to the art scene of that decade. This also brought about a high degree of direct communication between artist/performer and spectator/audience. Most important, perhaps, was the notion that art was transformed from objects to events, which represented a major break with the art world of the 1950s.

For the theatre these changes should serve to remind us that the most essential factor lies in the performer-spectator relationship, an insight of considerable importance in a time when theatre faces a new world of media, in which the "movement in art" still remains a mechanical device. Although film, television, and radio can offer us the simultaneous qualities of sensory, artistic, and fictional impulses, their presentation — even in live programs — cannot include the mutuality of the relationship between performer and spectator which is offered by the theatre. This is why I underline, time and again, the immediate presence of both performer and spectator as one of the basic experiences of theatre.

The interdependence between performer and spectator becomes especially clear when it is carried to extremes. Josette Féral has described an experimental performance in Montreal which allowed for only one spectator at a time.[5] This meant that the actress and the single spectator were the only participants in the performance, which took place in an abandoned tower of a fire brigade. Féral became very much aware of how much she as the spectator contributed to the performance. In a sense, she "acted" as a spectator — and had she stopped acting, the performance would abruptly have come to an end. This extreme case makes clear what actually happens in every theatrical event: without the active participation of the spectators — although hidden in the collective of the audience — no theatrical event takes place. This is, in my view, what makes an event theatrical.

To maintain and to develop this specific quality of the theatrical event is one of the foremost duties of both theatre practitioners and theatre scholars.

# IO | *Theatre Talks*
How to Find Out What
the Spectator Thinks

Late in April 1980 I got a telephone call from the secretary
of a State Commission surveying the future use of the Drottningholm
Court Theatre. This unique eighteenth-century theatre, preserved with
its original wings and Baroque machinery, is used for public performances every summer. Although it is an exciting experience for those
who are lucky enough to get tickets, every performance means attrition
and possible damage to this exquisite building. While working on a balance between the pleasure this theatre can provide and the risks taken,
the State Commission wondered who the members of the audience
were, anyway. That was the reason for contacting me. They wanted me
to carry out some kind of a survey during the summer to find out who
the visitors were, where they came from, why they wanted to see a performance at the Drottningholm Court Theatre, and so forth.

There were at least two more questions to be explored: What were
the expectations of the audience, and what did they actually get out of
their visit? My team of assistants and I had less than one month to pre-
pare this survey because the performances started in May. During the
hectic preparations we came up against a couple of problems. We had
decided to talk to the visitors rather than handing out a sheet of paper
which we might or might not get back, but it would be impossible to
engage people in interviews after the performances. Drottningholm is
situated outside the city of Stockholm, so everybody would be anxious
to get back to town. People normally arrive well before the performance

begins, however, in order to enjoy the beautiful park surrounding the theatre. This hour before they were let into the auditorium would be the only time the spectators would be willing to talk to us.

By the end of the summer of 1980 we had carried out 500 interviews. We knew everything about the expectations and the enthusiasm the audience members brought with them. We were also happy to realize that there were many members of the audience who were not specialists in theatre or music; nor did they represent organizations or companies — they came out of pure curiosity and for the sheer pleasure of experiencing this marvelous milieu.[1]

## In Search of a Method

Still, I did not know what the spectators got out of their visit, other than what I could tell from their happy faces during the intermission. I had no real information about their actual experience. To find out what the spectators feel and think while confronted with the stage images of a performance, I would have to design a project of a different kind. Nevertheless, I was very grateful to have been engaged for the Drottningholm study, which certainly set me to work.

The generous financial funding from the National Board of Research enabled me to carry out a comprehensive study on "The Theatre Audience — The Emotional and Intellectual Experience of Performances." Now I was free to find a method to analyze the whole theatrical experience and nothing but the theatrical experience. I understood that I had to solve a series of problems faced by every researcher in this area: Which audience did I want to study? What exactly did I want to find out? When was the right moment to ask the spectators about their experiences? Under which conditions could I arrive at conclusions of general interest?[2]

I had heard about a few projects under way at some universities around Europe. In one medical instruments were used to measure the heartbeat and breathing of spectators; in another members of the audience were confronted with a videotaped collage of the performance; and in others researchers used conventional questionnaires handed out to the audience after the curtain fell. Each of these methods provided some information, but none of these approaches were really satisfying from my point of view. What I was looking for was a way in which one could learn about the spectators' response to different kinds of performances. My aim was that the "interview situation" should not be too different from what theatregoers normally would do.

## Talking Theatre

The method developed for studying the reactions of an audience at theatrical performances was called "Theatre Talks." Basically this means that about seven people visit a performance as a group and sit down the same evening to talk about their individual experiences. Psychologists claim that seven is an ideal number for such a "talk group," because it is too big to be dominated by a single person and too small to be divided into factions. After having conducted many Theatre Talks during the years, I am prepared to agree. Nevertheless, it was important to me to compose homogeneous groups, so that each one consisted of participants who knew each other quite well beforehand. This was accomplished by engaging people from the same workplaces (e.g., hospitals, schools, companies, and civil authorities). After the performances the groups gathered, preferably in private places, and settled down with cups of tea or coffee.

Every group was accompanied by a group leader. The leaders were graduate and undergraduate students from our department, who were specially prepared and trained for this difficult task. The idea was that the leaders should stimulate a conversation between the participants without engaging themselves in it more than absolutely necessary. Normally they would not ask questions except for reasons of clarity or group dynamic disturbances. It was actually the case that certain persons were too dominant within a group; others were too shy: to balance between different types of personalities was one of the main tasks for the group leaders. Otherwise they were to listen to the more or less spontaneous reactions from the participants. What were the participants talking about? How did they react to opinions from other members of the group? How strongly did they agree or disagree? What alternative interpretations did they offer? We were most interested in seeing which issues were brought up, how these issues were related to the performance they had just seen, and how much these issues differed from individual to individual.

*23. A Theatre Talk group. Courtesy of Sylvia Sauter.*

Of course, there were also risks involved. Lack of balance through group dynamics has already been mentioned. Some people might not easily express their feelings about the performance. The theatrical experience might not be digested directly after the final curtain, although transportation from the theatre to the meeting place allowed for some recovery time. All those disadvantages of Theatre Talks certainly exist, but they did not seem to hamper the progress of the work. The groups obviously succeeded in coping with these types of practical problems. Actually, most groups were very enthusiastic about this form of theatre visit and continued to practice Theatre Talks long after the project had come to an end.

Another problem, which might be considered more serious, is that Theatre Talks take it for granted that the utterances of a participant correspond with the speaker's actual opinion. Of course, people from different strata of society express themselves differently, but we were sure that all of them used words which described their thoughts and feelings. This is both an empirical and an epistemological problem, which we solved simply by assuming that people mean what they say. Any kind of survey which relies on the cooperation of the "observed objects" encounters this problem, be it interviews, questionnaires, or Theatre Talks.

## Organizing Theatre Talks

Once I had decided to use the Theatre Talk as a basic method, I had to manage the operation, which resulted in the following arrangement. Along with some assistants, I organized twenty-five talk groups, most of them consisting of participants from workplaces. Socially and culturally the groups differed greatly, from highly specialized researchers in medicine to young girls working on an assembly line, from 16-year-olds to retired people, from those who live in the suburbs to the inhabitants of fashionable areas within the city. The 180 participants were a good representation of the total theatregoing population, including the habitual visitor as well as those who have not seen a performance for many years.

These 180 participants, forming 25 Theatre Talk groups, and their 25 group leaders were brought to six performances within a period of seven weeks. I thought it was important to bring all groups to the same performance to be sure they really received the same impulses. I also was anxious to have the same spectators at the end of the period as in the beginning. I did not want to lose any considerable number of the participants and also wanted to avoid increasing the "theatre skills" of these spectators by the very project. There are no ways of excluding such effects altogether; one can only minimize them. Therefore, I stopped after six performances, seen in a very short time in the hope that people would not change too much during seven weeks. The performances were very different from each other, not allowing patterns of reactions to reappear at every meeting; thus, all the participants were to see the performances in the same order. I found these restrictions necessary, although they made the practical organization of these visits extremely difficult. During the spring of 1983 exactly 150 Theatre Talks were carried out.

## Analyzing Theatre Talks

Through conventional questionnaires we knew all about our participants' social and cultural background. We had analyzed the performances they had seen, from both an interpretative and a comparative point of view. Now we had more than one thousand individual opinions about six performances. How could we possibly register and report on what all those people thought of all those performances?

In principle there are several ways of analyzing the taped conversations. One approach would have been to simply transcribe the tapes so that we could read exactly what people had said. I still regret that we failed to include at least a few examples of such talks in our final report, which I think would have made illuminating reading. In a later survey on opera and ballet audiences we at least used long quotations from Theatre Talks to illustrate portions of the report.

Another way of reporting (which I applied later on, but not in the project in question) is to ask the group leaders for written summaries of the talks in chronological order or according to headings made up beforehand. The group can be treated as individual members or as a collective. This method allows for an easy overview of the material only as long as the groups are limited in number and the issues of the talks can be restricted, which was not the case in our original project: we had twenty-five groups and wanted to know everything they had been talking about. Thus, we developed an alternative reporting scheme.

## *What and How?*

In an earlier pilot project we had already realized that it is useful to differentiate between what people are talking about and how they express themselves.[3] What is it people talk about? Theatre, of course. What is theatre? This question has both practical and theoretical answers. Surely it includes everything from the theatre building to the makeup of the actors, as well as invisible elements such as the administration, the carpenters, and the hairdressers. I tried to take everything into account. But there is still more to consider. In the analysis of the performances I had already decided to distinguish between the artistic aspects of the performance and the fiction which it produces. At the time when these surveys were carried out, I called the artistic level "formation," meaning everything visible and audible in the theatre (i.e., the actors and their costumes, the lighting, the sounds, etc.). Most of the artistic level is meant to indicate a fictional world on the symbolic level (where we meet characters in a particular guise, light showing the time of day, words making a conversation, etc.). This symbolic level of communication, in turn, can lead to interpretations which give meaning to the whole performance and its significance in the life outside the theatre. Without going into details, I can say that the recording scheme accounted for 89 artistic, symbolic, and interpretative items.

I distinguished the following answers to the question of how people express themselves while talking about almost any of the 89 items. A spectator can describe anything in the performance just by recalling certain moments. The same detail can also be interpreted by the spectator and is more often evaluated. Finally, a person might express feelings and emotions provoked by the performance. Besides these four main categories — describing, interpreting, evaluating, and expressing emotions — I also wanted to register prejudices and other preoccupations as well as expectations and foreknowledge — altogether 21 columns. In combination with the 89 items this results in a cross check pattern containing 1,869 entries. Despite the fact that some combinations proved meaningless, there were still more than 1,400 checks available, where individual utterances on a single item in a performance could be marked. Moreover, most of the registrations also took into account the value and significance of the utterance. Not only did we register that someone had made an evaluation of, say, a costume, but we also marked the "grade" given to that costume, on a scale from 1 to 7. In simpler terms, for any possible utterance during the Theatre Talks there were some 8,900 possible ways of making a note on the registration sheet. Still, many nuances would slip through this net.

On average approximately fifty marks were registered for each individual participant during each talk. To bring this exercise in numbers to an end, let me say that the registered utterances from 180 people on 6 performances amounted to about 30,000 entries. Of course, this mass of information had to be handled by a computer.

## Quality and Quantity

A comment on this transformation of oral statements into figures may be in order. When the computer output produces piles of neatly printed tables with thousands of figures, the whole survey suddenly looks very much like statistics. It is fully possible to calculate average values, standard deviations, index of significance, coefficients, and so forth. This does not mean that we have achieved "hard facts" about the experiences of these spectators. We have to remember how those figures were arrived at: it all started with the relaxed atmosphere of the Theatre

Talks. Here, for example, somebody made a remark on a certain actor: "The actress playing Juliet's role presented this young girl very convincingly as a real teenager." This, no doubt, can be characterized as a real qualitative statement concerning the interpretation of Juliet's part by the young actress. When this utterance is noted on the registration sheet, it is probably placed under the term "actress," where it is marked in both the interpretative and evaluative columns, the latter even registering a positive value. What interests us now is the question: Did this kind of statement occur very often in the Theatre Talks? First, the researcher checks whether the actress was mentioned at all, irrespective of why. In addition, we might want to know the overall judgment not only of this actress, but of all the leading actors in this production — and so on.

There is always a risk that a single number might not fully cover the meaning of a statement. Therefore, we were more interested in general tendencies than in the frequency with which one single check on the registration sheet was used. The difficulties of the transformation itself (i.e., the interpretation of qualitative statements) were balanced by a series of methods to computerize the figures. It was essential for us to preserve the qualitative origin of the material and not to distort its character by statistically overworking it. The team certainly carried out all kinds of statistical calculations, but always bore in mind that we had to deal with sensitive qualitative material. Thus, all conclusions from the tables of figures were concerned with relative values (i.e., compared to other items or other groups of participants or other performances); absolute quantities were of no use for our analysis.

I learned a lot from the computer work. Most significant was the insight that I actually did not have any use for the highly differentiated registration system. More and more, I compiled issues and columns into larger units, which were more relevant for the analysis. Even the method developed considerably: if I were to use the system today, it would be a lot simpler, but nobody could have known this at the time.

## More Theatre Talks

Theatre Talks were later tested under somewhat different circumstances. Soon after the main project had come to an end (when the manuscript of the final report was still to be written) I was engaged in a special study of the audience at the Royal Opera in Stockholm. A general survey of the members of the auditorium was completed with Theatre Talk groups. At this point I thought we had enough knowledge about the influence of demographic and certain sociocultural features of the general experience of theatre. What I assumed to be the main dividing factor with respect to opera and ballet was the earlier experience of these art forms. Therefore, I found six Theatre Talk groups sufficient: three of them were made up of participants who had practically no experience of opera and ballet, while the other three groups consisted of more or less habitual opera visitors.

Theatre Talks were conducted after four operas and three ballets, each representing a different genre and a different time of origin. In many respects the results were quite close to our earlier expectations, but on some crucial points music and dance theatre were experienced differently from spoken drama.[4]

At about the same time I had the opportunity to test Theatre Talks in a very different milieu. During my stay at the University of California in Los Angeles, an Italian director produced the anonymous Renaissance comedy *La Venexiana* at the university theatre. I conducted Theatre Talks partly with students, partly with personal friends. In both cases it proved to be a very adequate method with U.S. theatre audiences as well.[5]

During a teaching session in Utrecht, Holland, in the spring of 1988 I taught and tested Theatre Talks in yet another milieu and also developed variations in the methods of reporting the data. The students proved to be very inventive in finding ways of registering certain aspects of the Theatre Talks according to their own interests, the character of the performance, and the type of group they had to deal with. Of particular interest were some reports in which the students tried to study the talks from the narrative point of view, following the story line of the performance and thus reconstructing the chronological order of the theatrical experience.

These experiments in various surroundings, with quite different purposes, have shown that Theatre Talks are an effective method of investigating spectators' experiences with all kinds of theatrical performances. Not least, this is a very pleasurable way of seeing theatre for those involved — there is no need to fill in forms or set aside time for interviews; instead, they spend an evening with friends talking about a common experience. There are, of course, some problems with this method. One difficulty is that it clearly needs good organization to work smoothly, from booking tickets to finding a nice place to meet after the performance. A methodologically more serious problem is the handling of group dynamics, which presupposes a flexible and inspiring group leader. It is possible to achieve such guidance: none of the groups involved in those projects had to be dismissed due to unsuccessful conduct of the talks.

I also want to stress here the variety of possible ways of evaluating and reporting on Theatre Talks. I think these possibilities are far from exhausted. My experiences with the students in Utrecht in particular showed that there are many more possibilities to be discovered and developed. In the end the success of the investigation seems to depend on the aims and ambitions of the researcher rather than on the limitations of the method.

## What Did We Find Out?

My aim in this chapter has been to describe Theatre Talks as a means of studying the emotional and intellectual understanding of theatre performances. Nevertheless, the reader might wonder what kind of results we arrived at after more than 200 Theatre Talks. Although I have published reports on these on these projects in books and articles,[6] I will try to sum up a few results of more general interest.

In most of our projects Theatre Talks were paralleled by more conventional surveys concerning the general population of the city or the average audience of a particular theatre. I could thus confirm and deepen my knowledge about people's attitudes and preferences, habits, and experiences with respect to theatre. All these factors relate strongly to the sociocultural patterns in a society. Amazingly enough, they do not influence the actual experience of performances to the degree that could be expected, as two short examples show.

It is a well-known fact that women dominate today's theatre auditoriums in the Western world.[7] This suggests not only that women have a different attitude toward theatre than men, but also that women might experience performances in a special way, displaying stronger empathy or using a wider range of their imagination, understanding, and emotions. None of these hypotheses could be proved true. On the contrary: of all the background variables, the difference in gender was the least significant. The difference between men and women, so predominant in their interest in theatre, diminishes to practically nothing as soon as they are seated to watch the performance. Today, a decade later, I believe that more sophisticated methods might bring forward nuances which were not covered in these initial studies in the 1980s.

The theatres in Stockholm are frequented by people of all ages. The younger spectators perhaps represent a slight majority, but no ten-year age group constitutes more than one fifth (20 percent) of an average theatre audience. Despite the even distribution of ages in the auditorium, the experience of theatre performances differs widely. Younger people are more interested in the fictional story presented on stage, whereas the interest in the actors and the staging increases steadily with the age of the spectator; the older the spectators grow, the more they judge what they see. The most noticeable difference, though, is between adolescents and older spectators. The division between youths and grownups is so strongly marked that it almost shocked people who worked professionally with educational theatre. In the case of young people, their evaluation of performances, their feelings of empathy, their interest in the fiction, their rejection of complex characters, and their sense of theatrical qualities were all experienced very differently. The dividing line seems to be around twenty years of age: a seventeen-year-old is more different from a twenty-five-year-old than the twenty-five-year-old is from a fifty-year-old. This obviously is something to bear in mind when school classes are sent to regular performances for educational reasons. A classical drama can become as boring as a lesson in geography, and many of the students will never return to either theatre or geography.

I was especially interested in spectators' judgment of performances. For one thing I tried to find out which background factors were the most influential. There is considerable agreement on the quality of performances within a stratum which could be called the theatre establishment (i.e., all those who attend the theatre at least twice a year). The establishment includes most of the critics in the daily newspapers — their judgment is actually very close to what the majority of the audience thinks. Only very rare theatregoers as well as youngsters display taste of a very different kind.

I also wanted to find out the impact of the theatrical elements on the spectator's judgment of performances. Was a production evaluated with regard to the play, the directing, the set, the costumes, or certain combinations of various elements? The results showed that only one factor is crucial, no matter what performance the spectators saw or what their background was: the quality of the acting. This might not be an altogether new discovery, but the fact that the acting quality is almost entirely responsible for the overall impression of a performance is worth considering. This is also true when the judgment of the acting is negative, although the play or the stage design might have made a positive impression. Last but not least, the evaluation of the actor is always slightly higher than the grade given to the whole performance. Moreover, the appreciation of the acting is also decisive for the spectators' interest in the fiction of the performance: if the actors' quality is considered poor, then the spectators are not prepared to discuss the content of the play; only when they enjoy the acting will there also be an interest in what the performance was all about.

These observations are enlightening from both a theoretical and a practical point of view. The impulses to construct a fictional world come from the theatrical images on the stage, of which the actor seems to be the most dominating. How, then, could the fiction be judged higher than the impulses which give rise to it? Theoretically, it seems quite logical that the acting is given the highest priority. In looking at theatre as a communicative event, the behavior of the spectator deserves a high level of attention when scholars discuss the production of meaning in theatrical productions.

Of course, many theatre directors as well as actors are aware of the strong impact that acting has on an audience. Nevertheless, there are endless discussions on questions of the repertoire in the theatres, as if the plays themselves were the main issue and not the way in which they can be presented. Critics rarely seem to reflect upon the importance of acting when they attribute the success or failure of a production to directors and playwrights. Sometimes the whole theatre business seems to be preoccupied with finding the right play and developing the director's concept; yet the spectators in the auditorium react foremost to what they actually have in front of them: the actors. Of course, I do not want to reduce the importance of drama itself as a foundation on which the work of directors, designers, and actors is built and which gives meaning to what the actors do on stage. I only want to emphasize that the drama means little to the audience unless the actors present it in an adequate manner.

My studies on theatre audiences have eventually led me to the study of acting as one of the major problems in understanding theatre. Of paramount importance is the sensitive act of communication between actor and spectator, taking place over and over in every performance. Here I certainly arrived at the very core of my theatre studies.

# 11 | *Fiction, Mainly Fiction*
## Some Surveys on the Theatrical
## Experience of Young Audiences

At the municipal theatre of Helsingborg in southern Swe-
den, a children's play called *Bunny Brown and Bunny White* was presented
some years ago. In this play, based on a famous Swiss children's book,
the brown rabbit liberates the white rabbit from its cage. Together they
experience a number of adventures, the pleasures of green meadows and
joyful races as well as the dangers of dogs and heavy traffic. Eventually
the white rabbit longs to be back in its cage, where it enjoyed free food
and warm shelter.

In a survey carried out by Karin Andersson, children seven, twelve,
and seventeen years old were interviewed about what they had experienced in this performance.[1] The youngest ones simply retold the story,
literally describing what happened to the white and the brown rabbit.
The seventeen-year-olds related to the story in terms of abstract characteristics such as freedom versus security and responsibility versus
pleasure. The twelve-year-olds dismissed the whole performance as being childish.

Despite the anecdotal character of this survey, at least two features concerning young audiences' reception of theatrical performances
should be pointed out: first and foremost, the all-important difference
between age groups, a well-known fact to all producers of children's
theatre; second, the almost total domination of the fiction on stage,
whereas the way in which it is performed seemed secondary to children.
This latter observation also applies — in my experience — to the genre

of the performance: for children it does not make very much difference if these rabbits were performed by puppets or by adult actors, as a pantomime or as an opera.

## Preferences

The importance of age and the concentration upon fiction were also two of the major results of the extensive survey which we carried out in Stockholm.[2] Of those Theatre Talk groups discussed in the previous chapter, three were composed entirely of teenagers between fifteen and nineteen. These three groups represented youngsters with distinct backgrounds. One group consisted of young people from a municipal home for "difficult" and socially unstable adolescents; another group included students from what could be called a "normal" high school; and a third group was composed of members of an amateur youth theatre group. These social differences had some impact on the ability of the young people to express both intellectual and emotional reactions to the performances in question; but as far as the reactions themselves were concerned, a surprisingly even pattern evolved from the Theatre Talks. It might also be worth mentioning that the gender differences were quite insignificant. As an age group, however, these youngsters showed a completely different pattern of reactions when compared to other age groups: the gap between these young spectators and the older members of the audience was considerable. Obviously, for all young people some far-reaching changes occur during the transition from adolescence to adulthood, including the way they respond to theatrical experiences.

These differences were very clearly observable in their response to the six performances that all three groups attended. To start with, the preferences of the youths were distinct from those of the adult playgoers. The young spectators loved exactly those performances which the adult audiences thought were the least interesting: a musical, *Sound of Music*; a politicized production of a Jacques Offenbach operetta, *La Belle Hélène*, by an independent theatre group; and an energetic juvenile staging of *Romeo and Juliet*. What characterized these performances as a whole? All of them contained a solid, comprehensible plot with many strong actions such as fencing, drinking, playing dice, escapes, love, and death. It is also important to note that all of these productions included a significant number of musical components, from conventional songs in the musical to old-fashioned Renaissance dance music in *Romeo and Juliet*. This mixture of genres seemed to be highly appreciated by the young audience. In this respect, these teenagers reacted very similarly to that part of the audience categorized as "rare theatregoers." This seems reasonable, since neither group had any notable prior experience of theatre.

The performances also had another feature in common, which was very important for the young spectator: the plots of these plays were not only clear-cut and easy to follow, but were also characterized by a certain simplicity as far as the conflicts and interpersonal relations were concerned. In *Romeo and Juliet* there are two rival groups; in *Sound of Music* the Nazi villains are easily depicted; and even in *La Belle Hélène* the conflict between love and power is very obvious. It seems that these clear and strongly outlined constellations are of great importance to young audiences. This also includes the fictional characters: the young spectators need to know the "good guys" from the "bad guys." Their preference for what could be called one-dimensional characters becomes especially convincing when compared to their reactions to other plays, in which more psychologically complicated personalities were dominating. The complicated figures in the Anton Chekhov play *The Seagull* and their no less complicated relations to each other did not impress the young playgoers. They even reacted negatively to a notable psychological play such as *The Smile of the Underworld*, by the modern Swedish playwright Lars Norén, who writes in the tradition of August Strindberg's and Eugene O'Neill's domestic dramas.

This preference for simple, uncomplicated characters also influenced young spectators' choice of identification objects. Two cases are especially enlightening. In the performance of *The Seagull*, the teenagers did not identify with Constantin, the young aspiring writer of plays and poetry, who is confused over his self-identity and his artistic ambitions. Because of his suicide at the end of the play, the young spectators refused to identify with him. Neither did the young actress Nina and her unhappy love relationship with the elderly writer Trigorin serve as an object of identification. Surprisingly, the young spectators identified most strongly with Constantin's mother, the well-established actress Irina. She could be described as a strong and successful woman who achieves what she has determined to achieve. In a similar way, and probably for similar reasons, the object of identification in *Romeo and Juliet* was neither of the title characters, but the earthbound and strongwilled Nurse. To a certain degree, the two violent youngsters Mercutio and Tybalt, who eventually kill each other in a duel, provoked positive responses from young spectators, although these tended toward empathy rather than identification.

## Levels of Communication

While the adult audiences were carefully evaluating both the fictional events and their presentation on stage, the teenage groups of our Theatre Talks rarely bothered to comment upon the artistic values of a performance. Does this mean that young audiences are not affected by the presentation? I do not want to speak about the artistic quality of the performances, since quality proved to be an utterly subjective category, representing the spectators' taste rather than any objective values. The performance in the series of six which has not yet been mentioned was entitled *The Tiger* and consisted of two one-act monologues by Dario Fo. The reactions to this production provide an interesting case in connection with the problem of artistic quality. Whereas all adult groups (at least twenty years old) ranked this performance as the best one, due to the outstanding presentation by the actor Björn Granath, the youngsters put it in third place. This means that they were quite able to appreciate the extraordinary acting in the performance, although they remained less interested in its content. Young audiences are affected by factors other than fictional ones, although it seems less likely that they will speak about artistic means. The question, then, is how a young spectator reacts to theatrical actions.

Since the results from my Theatre Talks project were quite surprising in respect to young audiences, I wanted to pursue this problem further by investigating how children were reacting to theatrical encounters. One of my students offered to study a performance produced for a very young audience in order to survey the relationship between particular theatrical modes of expression and the response she could observe in preschool children.

## A Lonely Ear

At the Marionette Theatre in Stockholm, the artistic and managing director Michael Meschke produced a half-hour program for children three to five years old called *A Lonely Ear*. The production ran from 1990 onward, and Meschke performed himself. I think it is useful for the discussion of theatrical actions and reactions to start with a short description of the performance.

Meschke received the children — thirty to fifty in number — in the entrance hall of the Marionette Theatre, talking to them and showing them around. One was allowed to bang on the big gong to announce the beginning of the performance, while the other children were advised to protect their ears with their hands. Meschke followed them into the auditorium, asking if someone can become invisible. The children usually denied that possibility, but could accept that one can pretend to be invisible, for instance by wearing black clothes and putting on gloves, as Meschke did during the conversation.

Meschke now presented a puppet called Benjamin, representing a child of approximately the same age as the spectators themselves. He demonstrated the mechanics of the marionette, including the threads manipulating the figure. The children especially enjoyed seeing Benjamin creep along the floor, and they were delighted that "he" needed their help to tie his shoelace. This demonstration of Benjamin took place in front of the children, but not on any kind of specific stage. The children responded so far to the puppeteer as a real person, discussing invisibility and puppet mechanics, and at the same time learned something about puppets as artistic devices. Already Benjamin was accepted as a "real" figure. The children seemed to have accepted that a "puppet on a string" could represent a recognizable personality, although they probably knew Benjamin was not "really real."

At this point, about ten minutes after the first meeting in the entrance hall, the house lights were dimmed; the stage was illuminated; soft music was heard. The stage consisted of a table covered by a black cloth that reached the floor, on which some tree-shaped figurines were placed. Behind the table, the face of Meschke was clearly visible, whereas his body and hands were covered in black. In this "forest" a lonely ear became visible. The puppeteer asked the children if they could recognize the little foam rubber piece shaped like an ear. His dialogue with the kids continued until they had agreed "to see" an ear. Other body parts appeared: two legs, a torso, arms. The parts discovered each other, enjoyed the community, and decided to stay together. The children were actively involved in the construction of a body out of these parts. The puppeteer encouraged the children to instruct him on the assembly of the parts; much fun and joy about misfits and misinterpretations were created. Finally a stone was found to serve as a head. Last but not least, a little thing was added which could be either a nose or a penis. Even the placement of this part caused some laughter and giggling.

During the course of the performance, the house lights were lit twice. The first time this happened the puppeteer came forward to show the figure which he and the children had constructed so far: feet, mouth, hands, and the lonely ear. The children were allowed to touch the body parts and to feel how they were connected technically. The second interruption occurred when Meschke showed another figure to the audience, a girl.

The playlet, which also included meetings with some animals in the forest, was brought to an end by the appearance of the girl, who brought a heart to the assembled parts of the body. "She" also told the children that the two figures they saw from now on would be called Adam and Eve. This last step in the performance seemed difficult for the children. They responded by telling the puppeteer of persons they knew by the name of Eve, whereas the name Adam carried no meaning for them. The allusion to the biblical story of the creation of the world reached only the adult members of the audience.

As a communicative act, the development of this performance illustrated for me very clearly how the sensory, artistic, and fictional levels are established and conditioned as parts of an integral process. The sensory contact between the puppeteer and the very young audience was prepared in the entrance hall and was maintained to various degrees during the performance. The interrogation of the spectators always concerned the puppeteer as a person, asking how to proceed, how to handle the puppets, how to build up the incomplete "character." The artistic level of communication was emphasized by various means: the demonstration of the marionette Benjamin, the discussion about invisibility, the presentation of the foam rubber figures, and also the use of music and light. All these elements were, one by one, made very clear to the spectators.

What concerns me especially in this context is the question of how the fictional level was created. The children saw a piece of foam rubber shaped like an ear. This shape was obviously recognizable from their own experience, a theatrical condition which is very common — something which appears on stage is recognizable from everyday life experiences. When the ear started to speak and told the audience how lonely it felt, the children understood the words and their meaning, but the context was not recognizable: ears and other body parts do not speak, wander in the woods, or operate on their own (though Nikolai Gogol thought otherwise in his famous story "The Nose"). Nevertheless, the children had no difficulties in accepting the theatrical situation. But the children also knew that the piece of rubber foam was not a real ear, that it was the puppeteer who spoke, and that the forest consisted of some other pieces of foam rubber. In other words, the situation was totally artificial. Having learned how such an artificial situation can be created was probably a great help for the three-year-old children who had not been to puppet shows before. The dominating personality of the puppeteer on the sensory level and the obvious artificiality of the artistic level conditioned the spectators to accept the embodied actions on the fictional level: a soft piece of rubber foam, moving about artificially and equipped with the puppeteer's voice, became the fantasy image of a lonely ear. It did not resemble anything "real," but supported by the sensory and artistic levels it became performative in this particular situation.

An embodied action is, as stated earlier, only embodied for someone else. But it is also linked to the artificiality of the situation for both the performer and the spectator. One could say, perhaps, that it is the artistic level of communication which triggers the impersonation of certain actions. When the performativity of an action is perceived as such by someone else, this person — the spectator — refers this action to his or her own experiences: the embodied action becomes referential. The referentiality relates the action to two sets of references: experiences outside of the theatre (everyday life, historical, technical, psychological knowledge, ideological, and political ideas, etc.) or experiences of theatrical modes of expressions (conventions, stylistic features, genres in

24. *A child's drawing based on attendance at the play,* A Lonely Ear.
*Courtesy of Teatervetenskapliga institutionen, Stockholm University.*

prior performances or during the course of the present performance). A character, then, emanates from somewhere between the embodied actions and the intra- or extratheatrical references of the spectator.

Could the very small children in the audience of the Marionette Theatre in Stockholm follow this complicated interaction among sensory, artistic, and symbolic levels of communication and fulfill the demanding task of constructing references in relation to what they perceived as embodied actions? They certainly could. One of my students, An van Kiel, carried out an audience survey during six of these performances.[3] In addition to noting the level of concentration during the half-hour performance, the laughter, and the question-and-answer interplay between puppeteer and children, she also accompanied the groups to their day care centers and asked them to make drawings about their experience. Those drawings demonstrate very clearly that the kids had "understood" the theatrical presentation, although interesting differences between the age groups could be observed.

The youngest, being only three years old, concentrated mainly on the body parts, drawing them one at a time to cover the whole sheet of paper. Those who were a little older drew simultaneously the separate parts and the finished figures of the boy and the girl. Only those who were five years and older also registered some details of the theatre, such as the small proscenium arch or a spotlight above the stage. In their perception of the performance, most children neglected the reality of the theatre — the puppeteer, the technique, the props — and concentrated literally on the "building of the character." Despite their consciousness of the theatrical process during the performance, they felt free to transpose the embodied into the referential.

## School Theatre

Are children and youngsters at all interested in theatre? What does theatre mean to them in their own lives? What position does children's theatre have in a society? In this connection — and not only here — it might be useful to distinguish between children's theatre and theatre for teenagers. For smaller children, theatre is probably a means of psychic and social development (i.e., part of their socialization), a term also used in Gunborg Carlsson's dissertation on ten-year-old theatregoers.[4]

Theatregoing as a habit is not developed during this early stage of childhood, whereas the teenage years become decisive in this respect. Different groups of young audiences have to be distinguished. How are habits of theatregoing developed?

A general survey was carried out when the first Theatre Talks were conducted, on the annual frequency of theatre visits of youngsters fifteen to nineteen (see table 1).

TABLE 1. *Children's Attendance at Theatres*

| Visits/year | 15–19-year-olds | Total population of Stockholm |
|---|---|---|
| 0 | 38% | 35% |
| 1 | 14% | 22% |
| 2–5 | 48% | 38% |
| 6 or more | 0% | 5% |

Table 1 indicates the tremendous effect that school theatre has had in the Stockholm area. Every second teenager visits a theatrical performance at least twice a year, some even more often. Most of the rest of the youngsters never go to the theatre; only a few undertake occasional theatre visits, while approximately one third of the young population never attends a theatrical performance. These figures must be compared with other figures. Even the age group following the youngest one has about one-third nontheatregoers; but the number of occasional visitors increases, the group attending of two to five performances a year diminishes, and a few percent are attending six or more performances. This trend runs through a turning point at about the age of fifty, when the tendency shows a growing group of nontheatregoers and a minor group of regular visitors.[5]

The extremely high number of youths in Stockholm attending two to five theatre performances might very well be explained by the then still very active school theatre policy in this city. The school theatre authorities attempted to provide two performances a year for each student, although this ambition sometimes was not achieved.[6] Nevertheless, it seems as if the overall goal of presenting theatre to schoolchildren was very successful. Since this school theatre project had been going on for several decades — although in various forms — it is likely that the generally high interest in theatre shown by the population in Stockholm, when compared to other cities, can be seen as a partial result of these high ambitions. Two out of three inhabitants of Stockholm visit the theatre at least once a year, which means that most of these people were introduced to this art form at an early age, probably through school theatre. Thus, school theatre has become part of the conceptional context of Swedish theatre.

## Hollywood Next?

Seen from a conventional perspective, school theatre includes a number of different activities: the school invites students to visit a certain theatre for free; a theatre offers special performances as school theatre; a free group comes to the school to perform; a certain teacher invites the class to go to a performance together. Some of these forms offer the possibility of visits to theatre performances without the interference of a teacher. This remark is not meant to denigrate teachers' ambitions to instruct their students, but doubts do exist as to what extent pre-information concerning theatre performances is very helpful for young audiences.

The real problems are the prefabricated interpretations of plays, which are supposed to be supportive for students' understanding of theatre. But such interpretations are more likely to reduce the theatre visit to something that equals a math lecture: of no great value at the time, but possibly something one might need later in life. When confronted with an acknowledged interpretation, the students realize how little they understand of the play and how irrelevant their own ideas are. One can tell a student that *The Seagull* depicts the prerevolutionary society in Russia, in which the wealthy owners of estates live their useless lives. For a seventeen-year-old such an interpretation probably only impairs the opportunities to develop a reasonable view of the play. The subjects which more urgently appeal to a young person are probably related to the generation gap and the struggle for individual independence.

School systems have provided explanatory introductions to theatre performances for a long time. Of course, these were informed by an endeavor to teach a student the great achievements of human culture. To a young man of seventeen this means nothing; the clever interpretations of others make a young woman of seventeen feel inferior: neither of them will ever return to a theatre. The experience of theatre must rely on their own reactions, emotionally and intellectually; they must themselves find the "Pleasure of Sorrow," to quote Henri Schoenmakers.[7] Otherwise, they will be a lost generation for the theatre.

Here a contradiction obviously arises between the structural context of school theatre and its official ambitions, on the one hand, and the attitudes toward the individual production, on the other hand. The accessibility of theatre can be undermined by traditional educational goals. Teachers often do not dare to let students have their own experience. There is a clear risk that young people prefer other forms of entertainment such as movies and concerts to "educational" theatre. I can point out at least two immediate reasons for that. Youngsters visit movie theatres and rock concerts without the company of parents and teachers, thus avoiding "good advice" and prefabricated interpretations. Furthermore, these art forms appeal directly to young people's emotions, while they perceive too many theatre performances as something intellectual. A teenager is probably more greedy to delve into feelings than to expand into intellectual adventures.

By what means will the theatre reach out to young audiences? Do theatre productions for youngsters have to look like Hollywood films, with one-dimensional, stereotyped characters, action-dominated stories, black-and-white morals, occasional songs, and a happy ending? Basically it is true that young audiences respond positively to these features, in the theatre as well as in the cinema. Of course, a theatre performance for youngsters does not have to imitate the film industry or the rock music business, but it certainly will have to learn from them. How such conclusions can be made productive for tomorrow's youth theatre is no longer a scholarly question, but a challenge to theatre artists.

# 12 | Strindberg's Words versus the Actor's Actions

The Success of the Actresses at
the Intimate Theatre in Stockholm
(1907–1910)

Strindberg's relationship with actors was always peculiar. Rather than seeing them on stage he imagined them in his bed, at least if they were female, while he regarded male actors as potential rivals, like Viggo Schiwe, or as real usurpers, like Gunnar Wingård.[1] Strindberg scholars have often been fascinated by these biographical factors; indeed, these factors until recently have dominated the study of his plays. As intriguing as his sexual behavior was, I am not much interested in Strindberg's private life; nor am I interested in his sexual preferences and fears. Here I focus on his professional interest in the art of acting.

Strindberg's preoccupation with acting was especially significant in the years 1907 to 1908, when he had access to a whole ensemble of young actors at the Intimate Theatre in Stockholm. In the "Memorandum to the Members of the Intimate Theatre from the Director," written in July 1908, the subsequent "Open Letters" that he addressed to the same general readership, and the numerous personal letters and notes to the same actors, Strindberg came as close as he could to what might be considered his "Theory of Acting."

## Strindberg's Theories

As was the case with most of Strindberg's views on artistic matters, his approach to the art of acting was complicated and ambiguous. In the opening pages of the "Memorandum" he attempts a definition of the actor's profession: "The art of acting is the hardest and the easiest of all arts. But like beauty it is almost impossible to define. . . . In aesthetics the art of acting is not considered one of the independent arts but rather one of the dependent ones. It cannot exist, of course, without the author's text. An actor cannot do without an author, but, if necessary an author can do without the actor" (p. 21).[2]

Here Strindberg poses the question of who takes precedence in the theatre. As an artist and a writer for the stage, it was his privilege and his moral right to claim that the dramatist is the most necessary element in any theatrical enterprise. Many people certainly share his view — even some readers of this book — but do we really have to believe in what Strindberg states so frankly in the paragraph just quoted, as if it were a matter of fact? The question is more complicated than he implies, of course, and my approach to it follows several stages: I start with Strindberg's own views, most notably those concerning the spoken word, and then go on to a theoretical critique of his standpoint by way of some historical examples of the acting style of the Intimate Theatre.

Strindberg's knowledge of the practical business of acting seems to have been quite limited. His own experience as an extra at the Royal Dramatic Theatre dated back to a period some forty years before he wrote the "Memorandum." In the meantime he had been married to two actresses, Siri von Essen and Harriet Bosse, who might have taught him a fair amount, but it is questionable to what extent they could have influenced his ideas about acting. It is also clear that he did not approve of most of the acting that he saw while he remained an active playgoer; under the heading "The Audience's Favorite" (p. 40), he gives a vivid description of the faults and shortcomings of those stars who occupy the attention of the spectators and the press.

For Strindberg, the actor is the medium of the theatre, through whom the dramatist articulates his ideas on stage. His view of the actor can be compared to the composer's view of the musician: the musician executes the score that the composer has written. Strindberg himself had frequent recourse to musical terms such as "legato" and "ritardando" when writing about a dramatic text and sometimes called a play a "score." And just as a composer is assumed to know how the composition should sound, Strindberg claimed to know how his plays should be performed. His personal credo was articulated in a letter to his co-director at the Intimate Theatre, August Falck, following the premiere of *Queen Christina*, which had been performed upon an almost entirely bare stage: "'In the beginning was the word!' Yes, the spoken word is all."[3] In the "Memorandum," he points out that since the writer knows his own text better than anyone else he consequently knows what his intentions were in writing it. Thus, in order to execute their task well, he instructs his actors to begin by learning their parts: "If the actor has a thoroughly vivid concept of the character and the scene he is to play, the next thing he must do is to memorize the role. That begins with the spoken word, and I believe the spoken word is the major fact about the art of acting. If the utterance is right, gestures, play of features, bearing, and stance follow of themselves if the actor has a strong imagination" (pp. 23–24).

Strindberg's "Memorandum" is a well-known text, and there is no need to quote extensively from his instructions to young actors to speak "well" and extremely slowly in order to create the required tone in the larynx and to let the tongue, lips, and teeth take care of the articulation. All vowels and all consonants are equally important. Strindberg never tires of collecting examples of mistakes in the pronunciation of Swedish. He emphasizes the importance of speaking "legato," which means "that all the words in the phrase steal after each other in rhythmic movement in keeping with one's breathing" (p. 20). Strindberg's conception of theatrical performance was linear. The line starts with the writer, who writes words which are embodied by the actor to become a fictional role, which will eventually be perceived by the spectator. At the end of the line we find the audience, which is supposed to appreciate a dramatic work by way of the actors, who are looked upon as a kind of intermediary.

Strindberg's linear conception neglects the fact that theatre always and only exists in the form of performances. A performance presupposes two partners or, rather, two participants: a performer who acts and a spectator who reacts. Presentation and perception coincide temporally and spatially. These statements sound trivial, but the problem is that such a view of the theatrical event does not automatically make room for Strindberg as dramatist or as theoretician of theatre.

Furthermore, my model of theatrical communication does not even establish a clear distinction between the performer and the fictional character. If we are honest, none of us has ever seen Miss Julie on stage. What we see are only images which we, the spectators, translate into our own fictional fantasy world.

The three categories of actions prove to be quite a useful instrument in analyzing the performances which took place at the Intimate Theatre almost a century ago. What aroused my curiosity about these performances in the first place was the popularity of certain productions at this theatre, while other plays presented there, including *The Ghost Sonata* and *The Pelican*, were critical and popular disasters.

### Strindberg's Actresses

During the three years of its existence, the Intimate Theatre put on twenty-four of Strindberg's plays. Six of these productions were performed so frequently that they featured in 60 percent of the theatre's programs. Moreover, two productions were each presented more than 150 times. Which were these two plays, and why were they so popular?

The most frequently performed play by Strindberg at the Intimate Theatre was *Easter*, with 182 performances. Is it such an outstanding play? In *Strindbergs dramatik*, Grunnar Ollén observes that *Easter* has been produced frequently all over Europe, but generally because it has few characters and requires only a single set. At the same time, he maintains that "few plays by Strindberg appear to have received such unsatisfactory performances as this one."[4] The second most popular production was *Swanwhite*, with 152 performances. This play is certainly not among Strindberg's most successful. After its long run at the Intimate Theatre it has hardly been performed at all, apart from a few occasions when an exceptional actress was available, like Max Reinhardt's wife, Helene Thimig, in Berlin in 1913, Tora Teje at the Svenska Teatern in 1914, and the young Inga Tidblad at the Vasateatern in Stockholm in 1926.

*Easter* and *Swanwhite*: what, if anything, are we to conclude from their conjunction in this respect? The public response to these productions at the Intimate Theatre may, of course, be deduced, at least in part, from contemporary reviews. To what, in particular, were the critics reacting? Concerning *Easter*, one critic praised Anna Flygare in the role of Eleonora as follows: "Flygare won a splendid new success in this part, to be added to her previous triumph in *The Bond*. She has a winning directness, she is wholeheartedly devoted to her task, and she immediately takes a firm grip upon the audience's imagination."[5]

One year later, another critic summed up the success of the production thus: "The drama succeeded in spellbinding its audience to an exceptional degree, not least because of the artistic presentation bestowed upon one of the central figures in the drama, the psychologically suffering Eleonora."[6] Both critics admit that Flygare's performance exceeded their expectations. Set against the prevailing model of theatrical actions, the result was stunning. In this case, the exhibitory actions of the young Anna Flygare joined with her encoded actions and together the sensory and artistic communication fused with the fictional communication, so that the embodied actions were no longer understood as such, but amounted to the illusion of an illusion. Anna Flygare was perceived as being one with her role, a performance in which no cracks or gaps were noticeable. Every playgoer knows how rare such moments are in the theatre, and so did spectators between 1908 and 1910. Where *Swanwhite* is concerned, the critical response was as follows:

> The young Miss Falkner, who is a pupil at the theatre, presented in her delicate virginity an indescribably delightful image of the Swanwhite of the saga, and her understanding was natural and right. But so far, her voice and face are not fully at her disposal, for both need a great deal of work to serve as a really sensitive means of expression. On the other hand, there are moments when her movement exerts an unconscious power of speech, which transfigures the spectator.[7]

> Swanwhite was the young Miss Falkner, whose soulful face and tender appearance afforded a rich illusion of the dream princess, especially the mellow and melancholy sides of this creature. Maybe she was a little too modest and this impaired her performance, but nevertheless, her acting won both hearts and minds, and here certainly lies a promise stored up for the future.[8]

Compared to their comments on Anna Flygare, the critics' attitude to Fanny Falkner is more divided: they appreciate her frail appearance and consider it princesslike or simply perfect for this type of role. But her encoded actions are not sufficiently developed. While the exhibitory and the embodied actions can be apprehended as one and the same, the lack of appropriate artistic means proved to be fatal in certain other roles. In this part, as Swanwhite, she was obviously living up to the expectations of the critics.

What were the expectations of these critics? Most of the time, the same critics were utterly critical of Strindberg's theatrical enterprise. Their initial enthusiasm over the opening of an intimate theatre in Stockholm one year earlier had quickly changed into a very detached and

*25. Fanny Falkner as Swanwhite in Strindberg's Intimate Theatre, 1908.*
*Courtesy of Strindbergsmuseet, Stockholm.*

reserved attitude. Most of them disliked Strindberg's chamber plays, partly because of their unusual dramatic structure, partly because they recognized too much of Strindberg's private life in them. Stockholm was then a city of only 300,000 inhabitants, where gossip certainly spread very easily. They disliked *Queen Christina* because of its poor stage design, of which Strindberg was so proud, and they disliked the actors, who were accused of being amateurs. Against this background it is astonishing to read the above-quoted reviews, expressing so much appreciation and enthusiasm.

Part of the explanation for this exceptional esteem for the two actresses can be found in the critics' background. First of all, they were all relatively young and new as critics. Around the turn of the century, there was a change of generation at most Stockholm newspapers, bringing in young journalists who were educated during the 1890s. To be educated during that decade meant turning away from the naturalism of the 1880s and developing an aesthetic of beauty and fantasy. Internationally, the most well-known of this Swedish generation of writers and critics is certainly Selma Lagerlöf, Nobel laureate and author of books like *Gösta Berlings Saga* and *Nils Holgersson*. For this generation, beauty meant more than reality.

For the theatre this change of aesthetic preferences brought a reevaluation of older acting traditions, where style and beauty, but also fantasy and exoticism, were the dominating ideals. A Swedish actor — typically, his most successful part was the title role in *Cyrano de Bergerac* — taught his acting students: "What is right in life is not necessarily right in the theatre. The natural way to behave on stage is a mixture of truth and convention."[9] Some of Strindberg's actors certainly had already heard this kind of advice during their theatrical education.

This is also the time of great success for dancers like Loïe Fuller and Isadora Duncan and actresses like Eleonora Duse. They represented a new emphasis on physical appearance — the sensory communication — and at the same time an ephemeral view of the body. It is from this perspective that we can understand expressions like "dream princess," "tender appearance," "delightful image," and even "delicate virginity" that were bestowed on Fanny Falkner's Swanwhite. This also makes me think of all the photographs of young, beautiful, more or less draped women which were printed and distributed around the turn of the century.

What distinguished the two most successful productions at the Intimate Theatre were two leading ladies, each of whom was able to combine her personality with the role she was performing to create something quite exceptional. But they accomplished their success in different ways. While Anna Flygare transformed herself, Fanny Falkner remained herself. Comparing photographs of Anna Flygare in the role of Eleonora with her private picture made me aware of how well she used her encoded actions to create a fictional character on stage: she looks like two completely different persons.[10] In Fanny Falkner's case, the encoded actions instead impaired the process of impersonation: the critics wanted her just the way she was. Her exhibitory actions coincided with their image of Swanwhite. Even Strindberg shared this view: he had convinced the director of the Intimate Theatre to cast Fanny Falkner in that role, while he himself developed a close private relationship with her, addressing her as his last fiancée.

### Words versus Actions

Was Strindberg mistaken when he thought that the word meant everything in the art of acting? According to him, once the actor had understood the meaning of the writer's text, the role would emerge automatically from the actor's actions. But this was obviously not the case.

Strindberg's linear conception of the actor's function in theatrical communication prevented him from seeing the effect of the actor's exhibitory and encoded actions — not that Strindberg was unaware of them, but to him, as the writer, they were of no real importance. The short history of the Intimate Theatre showed that the combination of these actions made *all* the difference.

Theatre is primarily a communicative event, the encounter between the actor and the spectator. In this encounter the exhibitory, encoded, and embodied actions contribute equally to the act of communication with the audience. In this situation, contact is achieved primarily through the performer, whereas the writer and the text are merely one of the sources which the actor utilizes. Rather than being the writer's servant, the actor produces his or her own images, thus making the writer the servant of the actor.

# 13 | *How Long Is a Jewish Nose on Stage?*
### Ethnicity and Nationality in the 1930s

As we all know, ethnicity and nationality make major contributions to a sense of identity for both individuals and groups. And ethnic and national categories also contribute to how we perceive other individuals and groups. As we also know, in matters of ethnicity and nationality, prejudices and stereotypes are plentiful. In almost all regional conflicts in different parts of the world throughout history, ethnic and national identities often serve not only to separate one's own group from one's neighbors but also to denigrate, even demonize, one's neighbors.

Often the artistic production of an individual or group reflects the prejudices and stereotypes that operate in the cultural field at large. But sometimes the arts, especially theatre, are not mere mirrors of the beliefs and attitudes of the individuals within society. Sometimes a cultural artifact or event, in its politics and ideology, serves to question the received opinions and values.

I would like to discuss some aspects of these complicated matters by looking at a few productions in which Jews played a prominent part. The region I have chosen is Sweden and the time the 1930s. I think Sweden constitutes a good case for such a discussion. It was a democratic country in the 1930s, one of the few still left in Europe, and therefore had a free press and guaranteed freedom of speech. This implied a relatively good flow of information, even about events in Nazi Germany. Swedes can be considered to have been aware of what was going on in Germany itself as well as in the occupied regions. A fascist movement existed even in Sweden, but it was not very strong and never dominating. There was, however, a "Jewish question," even if it did not have the same implication as among Nazis. In Sweden the "Jewish question" concerned the admittance of Jewish refugees.

Sweden was not very receptive to Jewish refugees. Many Jews, especially from Germany, would have liked to come to this remote Nordic country, but they were not welcomed. When an increasing number of refugees knocked at Sweden's doors in the late 1930s, the reactions were strongly negative. Students protested, doctors worried about the "import" of Jewish medical experts, and politicians created committees. In 1937 a new law concerning the legal rights of refugees was introduced by the Swedish parliament. As the crisis intensified for German Jews who tried to escape Nazism, Sweden imposed harsh restrictions. The authorities were very effective in turning away the Jews. Together with Switzerland, Sweden urged the German authorities to print a red "J" on Jewish passports to make them identifiable at the border. No more than 2,600 Jews were allowed into Sweden before the war. After the war had started and Germany was confronted with millions of Jews in Poland, other, "final" solutions were invented. No more Jews were allowed to leave Germany, and thus they constituted no more problems for the Swedish authorities.

My concern is the reactions of the Swedish theatre during this period. When I started to investigate this topic, I assumed that I would find productions that were sympathetic to Jews and productions with more or less anti-Semitic tendencies. I thought it would be easy to distinguish between them according to the content of the plays and in the ways in which Jews were portrayed on stage. My task proved to be much more complicated. I soon discovered that I could not limit myself to a survey of the performances and their political motifs and themes. The contexts of theatrical life, its place in society, its structure, and its conventions were obviously of major importance for the interpretation and effects of a performance. Therefore I find it necessary to start with a short overview of the conceptual, structural, and conventional contexts of theatre in Sweden during the 1930s.

## Contexts

On the level of the *conceptual* context, I want to indicate how theatre was looked upon in general and especially by politicians, who were responsible for the overall cultural politics. These conceptions or attitudes are especially important during periods of change such as Sweden experienced during the 1930s. The social-democratic government, which took power in 1932, considerably advanced the state's involvement in culture, especially the support to state-run theatres. In addition to the Royal Theatre (the opera) and the Royal Dramatic Theatre/Dramaten, the government had created a new national theatre in 1933, the National Theatre Center, which consisted of a network of theatre organizations that took responsibility for arranging local theatre performances all over the country. Within a few years, the Swedish National Theatre Center was able to produce most of its performances with its own actors and staff. Parallel to this development, the Gothenburg City Theatre was formed in 1934. It became the second municipal theatre in Sweden, soon to be followed by others.

Despite the financial and organizational support of the state and the cities, every theatre was supposed to be free in artistic matters. The managing director of these theatres was economically responsible to the board, which consisted mainly of politicians and other representatives of the "public will"; but in artistic questions, the managing director was principally free to do whatever he or she liked to do until the appointment ran out. This freedom in principle had its practical restrictions, especially when it came to politically controversial issues.

One such issue was whether the theatres were obliged to follow the general Swedish policy of remaining neutral toward the politics of other countries, in this case Germany's legitimization of anti-Semitism. Was the situation in Germany only a matter of German interest? If so, was Swedish concern only a form of interference? Was there a humanitarian interest in the maltreatment of Jews in Germany? There were different opinions in Sweden on these matters, both in general and in relation to various theatres. The question of political neutrality was not only a conceptual question, but also a structural one.

I am defining the *structural* context as the organizational forms of the theatre world, including both the production side and the audiences, critics, newspapers, festivals, and so forth. The structural context of the Swedish theatre is mainly characterized by the various forms of public subsidies, which also lend different status to the theatre companies. There were the three state-financed theatres, two of which are so-called royal theatres; this epithet means that the Opera and Dramaten were almost 200-year-old royal institutions with the status of national theatres. This was especially important to the German Embassy, as the frequent notes from the embassy to the Foreign Ministry clearly indicate. The municipal theatre in Gothenburg was largely supported by the city, but a considerable part of the budget had to be brought in through the box office. All other theatres were private theatres, maintaining their existence through their box office income only. In the 1930s there were no alternative, politically oriented groups of the type which were established in the 1960s and 1970s. On the other hand, most of the private theatres had stable ensembles and a year-round repertoire of considerable variety. Revues including political matters and documentary plays engaged in the social or political issues of the time, light farces, and family comedies were all mixed in an attractive menu for the Stockholm theatre audiences. In such a way, they combined the ambitions of the free groups and the private theatres of later periods.

The *conventional* context — referring to the means of theatrical expressions typical of certain genres, times, and places — constitutes a special problem. The theatrical conventions not only governed the artistic expressions of the time, but also constituted a link between inherited clichés and the perception of reality. Theatre has a long-established tradition of stereotyped portrayals of ethnic features, which have been maintained and passed from generation to generation. I am reminded of such typical images as "the gypsy" or "the Indian." Such stereotypes are also related to class — the worker, the capitalist — or religion, sexuality, and regionality. Older traditions also include the villain, the heroine, and so on. The mixture of theatrical clichés — as an established convention — and what can be assumed to be pictures of reality is complicated. Most workers do not look like capitalists, and every ambitious actor tries to capture typical features of the fictional character. In other words, theatrical conventions might very well include a grain of reality. This statement might be reversed: the picture of reality also contains a grain of (theatrical) clichés! If that is true, it would mean that the presentation of a Jew on stage also influences our perception of Jews in society. Any "typical" feature of a theatre Jew thus underlines the "otherness" of Jews in general.

## *Shylock, Twice*

Shylock has become an impossible stage figure for most Europeans after the Second World War. In the 1930s he was still a popular character, either an unreasonable moneylender who deserved his fate or a deplorable representative of a people about to face problems. Looking back from our post-Holocaust perspective and understanding, it is difficult to imagine how this Shakespearean comedy was perceived at a time when nobody could even imagine the Holocaust to come. The very notion of *The Merchant of Venice* as a comedy seems alien to the postwar generation — or at least did so for a while. More than sixty years ago, the situation was different.

In April 1936 a production of *The Merchant of Venice* premiered at the City Theatre of Gothenburg. The director Knut Ström, who was also a well-known stage designer, had produced this play in the light and sunny atmosphere of an imaginary Venice. In this friendly city the audience met singing gondoliers and happy groups of people wearing carnival masks. The production was favorably received by the press and was performed ten times before the theatre closed for the summer. Being successful, the production was revived and performed another fifteen times after October 1936, the only difference being that a large part of the cast had been replaced by other actors. The role of Shylock was alternately performed by John Ekman, who was cast in the original production, and by Sture Baude, who could be seen in the revival premiere. Both were widely reviewed in the press, and there exist a number of photographs — a record which clearly indicates the differences in interpretation.

These differences were considerable and, I think, significant. John Ekman was a physically heavy man, who used his huge body as an integrated part of his modeling of Shylock. His Shylock was firmly rooted in the world. With his slow and distinctive movements and his strong voice — at times of excitement going up to a falsetto — he clearly dominated the stage. He showed fatherly concern for his daughter Jessica, but also a friendly openness toward the lad Bassanio, who is the person who actually needs Shylock's money. We have a picture of John Ekman in act 1, scene 3, when Georg Rydeberg's Bassanio approaches him to ask for a loan and Shylock keeps calculating. John Ekman, with his knees far apart, turns his body and the sheet of paper toward Bassanio, to show him what the costs would be. He turns his face openly toward the young man and waits for his reaction.

Sture Baude, in a photograph taken at the same moment of the stage action, wears the same costume as John Ekman — except for his hat — but one realizes immediately that his Shylock is a different one. Sture Baude is a small, thin man; but it is not the difference in stature itself which is significant, but the use of it. Baude turns his body away from Kotti Chave's Bassanio, glances at the young man from the corner of his eye, presses his knees together, and keeps the paper with his calculations tightly to himself. From the newspaper critics, we know that the translation was altered toward a more pronounced everyday language; furthermore, Sture Baude chose to have his Shylock speak in a clearly foreign accent. Other photographs as well as written documents emphasize these differences.

Despite the fact that they both were wearing the yellow-black caftan typical of Venetian Renaissance Jews, the obligatory Jewish headwear, and the orthodox Jew's curls, they constituted very different Jews. Ekman represents the patriarch, the just but renounced Jew, who tries to get along, but once provoked overreacts in his revenge. Baude, in contrast, does not wear a patriarchal beard, but sports extremely bushy eyebrows, which draw attention to the playing of his eyes and signal to the spectator a dishonest, threatening, and generally negative hustler.

My interpretation can easily be supported by various reviews from the newspapers. After John Ekman's presentation, several critics made remarks concerning the contemporary situation of European Jewry, despite the fact that Nazi Germany had slowed down its anti-Semitic actions due to the Olympic Games to be held in Berlin during the summer of 1936. Martin Strömberg writes about Ekman's interpretation: "[Shakespeare's] England did not have a Jewish question, and the audiences were hardly so open-minded as to understand the writer's sympathies with the poor, fate-stricken moneylender. Only much later events have created the background which illuminates the new and deeper significance of the drama."[1] This production, claims another critic, has given the play "an actuality for our time, fatal as well as horrifying — the position of the Jews in the Western world."[2]

While Ekman's presentation of Shylock led the critics' reflections toward the general situation of the Jews in Europe, Baude's interpretation

*26. Shylock twice: John Ekman and Sture Baude respectively in the Gothenburg production of* The Merchant of Venice *in 1936. Courtesy of Göteborgs Teater Museum.*

of Shylock provoked no such reactions. The critics showed respect for Baude's acting skill, but remained silent about its significance, despite Germany's post-Olympic efforts in the autumn of 1936 to expel its Jewry.

In my view the critics' silence reflected the admiration for Sture Baude's eminently convincing presentation. What he presented came close to a caricature of the Jewish hustler, comparable to the drawings in *Der Stürmer* or its Swedish equivalent, *Den svenska nationalsocialisten*. Whatever the critics thought about this picture of a Jew, the only protest I could find was expressed ambiguously: "Mr. Baude underlined and maybe overemphasized some racial characteristics, in the way they are traditionally perceived."[3]

Instead of noting or protesting the anti-Semitic tendency in Baude's interpretation, the critics remained indifferent or silent, praising the professional achievements of the actor. What conclusions could be drawn from the critical reactions to these two versions of Shylock? It is certainly inappropriate to arrive at any general conclusions from this single example, but one might feel challenged to ask: Do critics reflect on the political implication of a role/play only when the role gives them a "good reason"?

## Mamlock

In February 1938 a play was presented to the audiences of the Blanch Theatre in Stockholm, which in the most outspoken way presented the beginning of the story of Nazis and Jews in Germany. The play was called *Professor Mamlock* and was written by the German playwright Friedrich Wolf, active in the Communist movement during the Weimar Republic. It had earlier been performed in other countries, including Norway, where it had been presented at the National Theatre in 1936. The play addressed very directly the treatment of Jews during the period 1932–1933, from the unofficial maltreatment of Jews to the official legislation which eventually excluded Jews from all professions in Nazi Germany.

Professor Mamlock is a doctor who has created his own clinic, where the first as well as the last act of the drama are set. Acts 1 and 2 show the situation in Germany just before the Nazi takeover. Anti-Semitic attitudes have spread to medical clinics as well as the school in which

Mamlock's daughter is exposed to fascist classmates. In acts 3 and 4 the effects of the new legislation both for the private life of the Mamlock family and for its Jewish friends and the likewise disastrous consequences for the hospital are demonstrated. Some critics doubted if this play was a dramatic masterpiece, but no one questioned that it most effectively exposed a central issue of contemporary politics and social questions; "nobody can avoid the thought that these events, which occur only a day's journey from our border, tomorrow could happen in our own country."[4]

In Per Lindberg's and Harald Garmland's staging, the play was set in a very realistic environment. Despite the minimal size of the Blanch Theatre's stage, designer Garmland created not only a copy of a dining room, but also the interior of a clinic — the equipment was supervised by a nurse to ensure the documentary accuracy of the stage. This was of major importance for the production: the believable set, authentic in its smallest details, was supposed to help the spectator to see the truth of the unbelievable story told in the play.

This realism was also applied to the costumes, which can be easily studied in the preserved photographs. But these photographs also reveal the Jewish "mask" that defines Professor Mamlock on stage. This clichéd image becomes even more obvious when one compares the stage photo with a private photo of the actor, Harry Roeck Hansen, who also happened to be the managing director of the theatre. His makeup as Mamlock consisted of bushy eyebrows, a mustache, and curly hair. In a little drawing preserved at the Drottningholm Theatre Museum the characteristics of the Jewish mask have been slightly exaggerated. It is not farfetched to interpret it as a caricature of the Jew: the curly hair, the small glasses, the tiny mustache, the scared face. The artist Annie Bergman probably did not intend an anti-Semitic portrayal, but this drawing — which was only meant to entertain — nevertheless comes close to being an anti-Semitic comment.

In an interview Harry Roeck Hansen remarked that for this role he had "no direct model, but various studies of cultivated and educated Jews. I could mention the names of maybe ten persons, who all in a way contributed to this character role."[5] The actor also tried to imitate the characteristics of Jewish behavior: he found the shifts between emotional outbursts and utmost self-control most typical. All this was included in the use of his voice and his facial and gestural expressions.

The critics praised Roeck Hansen's competence in creating a believable character.

In the case of Professor Mamlock I also had to consider the affinity between recognizable features which we think of as existing in reality, the realism of the stage, and, last but not least, the stage conventions as signifiers of a recognizable reality. Those who produced the play in Stockholm were no doubt eager to create the most realistic stage images possible. Roeck Hansen's makeup must be understood in this framework, although it turns out that despite his intentions to draw upon his own observations of real Jews in the Stockholm community he produced many of the stereotyped traits of the stage Jew.

This mixture of realistic approach and theatrical conventions was not only pursued by the actor (and obviously accepted by the director, Per Lindberg), but also accepted by the audience. Of course, most of the spectators had met Jews and had some idea of what Jews look like "in general." Even the customs officers at the Swedish borders claimed that they could easily recognize Jews just by their looks and behavior. This generalizing attitude has its equivalent in the cliché of the "theatre Jew," which had gradually changed during the centuries since Shylock first saw the theatrical light of the world. Despite the best intentions of the producers, the stereotype contaminates the mask, confirms the prejudices, and becomes political.

## Zunder

"Indications of Jewishness" have functioned in opposite ways in the examples mentioned so far.[6] I want to add one more example from Swedish theatre life during the end of the 1930s. Again, the issue is the appearance of an actor and the question of how to interpret a face — in this case the face of Gottlieb Zunder.

For a long time, the German Embassy in Stockholm had urged Dramaten to stage a German play written during the "new era." After some reluctance, the director of Dramaten, Pauline Brunius, agreed to have such a play produced at her theatre. The play was called *The Little Court Concert*, written by two German actors of the time. The operettalike play is based upon the romantic paintings of the Biedermeier painter Carl Spitzweg, including such works as *The Poor Poet*, *The Librarian*, and *The*

*Love Letter.* These paintings were used as backdrops for the ten tableaux on stage.

This play presents a dealer in ladies' underwear who arrives with his suitcases in a ninteenth-century German town. His name is Gottlieb Zunder, and in the first scene we see him in a hotel lobby. To bystanders and the hotel manager he complains about his late arrival, because he was delayed at the gate. A female singer, with whom he had to share the carriage, flirted with an officer at the gate in such a way that Zunder lost time. The townspeople sense an erotic affair, an immoral act, and demand that this lady be thrown out of town. Going to the Duke to maintain moral order, they learn that this same lady has been invited by the Duke to sing at a court concert. Now the citizens of the town rapidly turn against Zunder. He is accused of being a simple salesman — he has never claimed anything else — and even a smuggler of coffee and tobacco, who is no longer protected by the Duke. After making him a watcher of public morals, they easily change their minds and accuse Zunder of having cheated them. Having found a scapegoat for their own embarrassing behavior, they physically drive him out of town. The rest of the plot is of no interest here.

Even such a sketchy description of the play makes it clear that Zunder is the villain, who is needed for a while to keep the play going, but whom the dramatists have to get rid of later in the plot. The change of attitude toward Zunder by the citizens is a very important scene, because it touched on one of the open questions of the play. Since it was a "new" German play, the critics and probably even the rest of the audience expected some references to Jews. For some critics there was no doubt that Zunder was portrayed as a Jew: "There is also a 'modern' tendency in this play . . . The clearly indicated racial character which the director has made the actor Ivar Kåge imply in this figure [Zunder] was unnecessary from the textual point of view, although intended by the dramatists. It would have been more desirable if this anti-Semitic point had been less carefully developed at the Swedish National Theatre."[7]

The particular feature which this critic and others were referring to was the nose which the actor Ivar Kåge used: it was not a "typical" hooked, Jewish nose, but rather a pointed, "Nordic" nose. But the very fact that this character in a German play of the period displayed an abnormal nose was obviously enough to ensure far-reaching interpretations.

In this case, the aim was not to present some kind of reality, but to construct a villain in an otherwise trivial play. But in 1940, the second year of the Second World War, no German play could be considered a triviality. Even the critics who refused to see that nose as Jewish or who explicitly interpreted it as an Aryan nose — "we cannot start to discuss the length of noses in the theatre!"[8] — were alert to the fact that a nose always meant something special on the stage of that time.

Zunder's long, pointed nose was replaced by a flat, broad nose a few days after the premiere — one of the rare instances when the reactions in the newspapers actually had some effect on the production. The motive of the stranger as villain and the idea of the scapegoat remained, of course, thus still supporting a possible anti-Semitic interpretation of Zunder.

### Interpreting Stereotypes

Two Shylocks, Mamlock, and Zunder provide four examples of Jews on the Swedish stage of the 1930s. In two instances the actors' presentations of Jews were perceived in a clearly positive way — John Ekman and Harry Roeck Hansen — and also gave support to the critics' comments on the situation of the Jews in Germany. Two other actors — Sture Baude and Ivar Kåge — used similar clichés, yet their roles tended toward anti-Semitic caricatures. Obviously, the differences in the response cannot be sufficiently understood by the relationship between the theatre cliché of an ethnic group and the reality of this group.

Were it only Professor Mamlock and Zunder — both of German origin, by the way — one could claim that it is the difference between the ideologies of the plays which is responsible for the opposing interpretations. As the two Gothenburg Shylocks indicate, however, the political inclinations of a play are not sufficient to explain the effect of a Jewish nose on stage. It seems important to emphasize once more the central position of the performer, not only in principle, but also for the very interpretation of a role. Through the use of extratheatrical role models as well as the use of theatrical clichés the outcome might be a willfully distorted picture, on the one hand, and an easily recognizable theatrical figure, on the other hand. The borderline between them is very thin and certainly not distinguishable at first sight. Some contribution to a role, probably very significant, comes from the actor's own attitude. The way in which a performer interprets a fictional character probably creates the difference between a sympathetic and a repelling character. I have to express myself in terms like "probably," because I have not seen any proof of this connection between private attitude and fictional character. The two Shylocks, however, are worth at least a hypothesis.

The information about the private attitudes of the actors and directors involved in these productions is limited. Roeck Hansen produced a number of other anti-Nazi plays during the end of the 1930s in his little Blanch Theatre in central Stockholm. The director Per Lindberg also worked with a number of antifascist pieces until his death in 1944. Knut Ström in Gothenburg was mostly known as a set designer, and I assume that as a director he did not have very much influence on the actors' interpretation of the roles. Ivar Kåge had appeared in other "dubious" roles earlier — for instance, as a Jewish banker in 1938, equipped with all the possible stereotypes.[9] Similar references could be made to the director Rune Carlsten, who came to guide Dramaten's guest performance in Berlin in 1941. On a personal level Carlsten found the trip very rewarding.

Although the performers were largely responsible for the images produced on stage, the spectators' interpretations are greatly influenced by other factors, which are to be found in the conventional, structural, and conceptual contexts of theatre. The life situation in the 1930s — well known as it is for us — must also be seen as an integral part of the interpretation of symbolic communication.

Much has already been said about relevant theatrical conventions of the time. So far, these conventions have mainly been related to the actors. Of course, such stereotypes were also accepted by the spectators. As usual, there is a correspondence between the images produced on stage and the willingness to appreciate and to interpret these images. Today explicit or conventional makeup and other artificial aids are used with great restriction by most performers. The link between exhibitory and encoded actions is obviously considered strong. In the 1930s the distinction between exhibitory and encoded actions was seen as important. Through the mask the performer had the opportunity to "become" another personality, and the audience could expect to see the same actor in almost "unrecognizable" disguises. This trend was especially noticeable in minor roles, in which the performer did not have the time to develop his or her character on stage. In Europe there was the generally used French term *charge* for actors specializing in small, but distinctive parts. The audiences seemed to appreciate these small artistic solo actions: an actor comes on stage, and within a very short time the character is fully established. In theatre reviews, these acts are regularly mentioned and highly appreciated. The Jew is very often no more than a *charge* role in the dramaturgy of European drama; but even when fully developed like Shakespeare's Shylock, G. E. Lessing's Nathan, Richard Cumberland's Scheva, Eugène Scribe's Rachel, Arthur Schnitzler's Professor Bernhardi, or Wolf's Professor Mamlock, the Jew is a stock character with particular makeup, costumes, movements, and grimaces. This was the way in which the stage Jew was seen both by performers and by spectators.

The significance of Shylock, Mamlock, and Zunder also has to be considered within the structural context — where and when these characters meet the public. The two Shylocks stepped onto the stage of the Gothenburg City Theatre at a time when this institution still was very young — the end of the second season. The City Theatre had a history as a private theatre in Gothenburg; nevertheless, the new director Torsten Hammarén had hardly had a chance to show his qualities yet. The ambiguity of the production — leaving enough room for one actor to alter the whole ideological tendency of the production — was a "failure," which would not occur often in the years to come. On the contrary, toward the end of the 1930s and especially during the war, the Gothenburg City Theatre won fame in Sweden as one of the most outspoken anti-Nazi theatres in the country.

Mamlock appeared on a very different kind of stage. Harry Roeck Hansen and his wife Esther had run the Blanch Theatre in the center of Stockholm since 1927. Being an excellent pair of comedians themselves, they produced many entertaining plays, but they were also keen on inviting directors and fellow actors for more ambitious projects. The production of *Professor Mamlock* was no exception — or rather it was the normal exception. The same pattern is true for other private theatres in Stockholm, where, for example, Kaj Munk's *He Is Sitting at the Melting Pot* and Maxwell Anderson's *Winterset* — both very strong anti-fascist plays — were presented. A number of private theatres in Stockholm had strong and respected artistic directors. These men and women were actors and directors as well as managing directors with full economic responsibility, and they were part of the theatrical establishment in terms of their artistic commitment. Nobody questioned their feeling of political responsibility and their honest engagement in socially important matters. The need to make money with certain productions was not seen as interfering with the political and humanitarian issues that were brought up in others. The picture of Mamlock on the stage was no doubt trustworthy on the stage of the Blanch Theatre.

If the Stockholm audiences wanted to see a politically engaged theatre in those days, they had to turn to the private theatres, not to the national theatre. Dramaten was altogether a different case. Because it was the national theatre of Sweden, several groups were very carefully watching what was going on there: the German Embassy, the Foreign Ministry, the critics, as well as other theatre people. In 1939, during a guest performance of the Schiller Theater with Heinrich George from Berlin, the Nazi-German flags were blowing in the wind outside the Dramaten, a sight which some thought was a disgrace to the entire city. Berlin urged Dramaten to "repay" the visit of the Schiller Theater, a wish which was eventually followed by a guest performance of Dramaten's production of Strindberg's *Gustaf Wasa* in Berlin in 1941. The director of the production of *Gustaf Wasa* in 1939 was the same person who directed *The Little Court Concert* in 1940. The Germans were pleased, the critics reported the success in Berlin, and managing director Pauline Brunius had done what was expected of her. Within the theatrical structure, Dramaten lost its position as the leading stage in Sweden. Due to the political weakness of the leadership of the national theatre, the productions of Dramaten, including Jewish stereotypes on stage, could be criticized openly in political terms. The political and artistic evaluations of productions were seen as a whole.

In the public debate of the time (i.e., the late 1930s and even more so in the early 1940s) the politically low profile of Dramaten was blamed on its managing director, Pauline Brunius. Earlier in her life she had been a big star in popular drama; being a woman, she was accused of not being strong enough to stand up for political ideals. I think this picture is misleading. The position of Dramaten was not decided by its leadership alone and not by the ambitions of its artistic staff. The political correctness of Dramaten was questioned by the Swedish government, especially the Foreign Ministry, and by the German Embassy. There is a heavy dossier in the archives of the Foreign Ministry with numerous letters and notes from the German Embassy. These letters went much further than the critics and the public could possibly understand at the time. One example might illustrate this engagement on the side of the Germans. The managing director of the Swedish National Theatre Center was asked by the Foreign Ministry if a controversial play which the theatre intended to produce in the early 1940s was also planned to be produced by Dramaten. Since this was not the case, it was all right for his theatre to continue with the production. The reason for the inquiry of the Foreign Ministry was an inquiry from the German Embassy. The cultural attaché had found out that the play in question was critical of the Nazi regime in Germany and therefore wanted to know if it would be shown on the stage of the national theatre, Dramaten. Since this was not the case, the German Embassy did not care if it was shown elsewhere.

## Political Theatre

I think it is reasonable — for my purposes here — to designate a production a case of political theatre only when there is a real political issue at stake. By this I mean something quite simple. First, the political issue is something which can be decided politically — there is platform, a parliament, or an authority which has the political power to make certain decisions. These decisions, of course, have consequences for certain people. Second, it must be possible for people outside the political authority to act in relation to the political issue in question. In other words, it is appropriate to think that political theatre deals with issues which really are decided on a political level and that it is possible to act in relation to these issues in order to affect the political decision. I am aware that these limitations narrow the topic of political theatre; there are, of course, other situations in history when political theatre has no chance to appeal to any parliamentary system or other "liberal" authorities. To debate the function of theatre in totalitarian political systems or to analyze the effects of ideologically nonconformist productions is not my purpose in this chapter. My topic is the effect of a theatre of resistance within the framework of a still-functioning democratic society.

The four performances used as examples in this essay all fall into the frame I have set up for political theatre. There was a "real, political issue": the admission of Jewish refugees to Sweden. This political question could be affected through public debates, demonstrations, committees, and theatre performances. These performances were not taking place in a vacuum — on the contrary, they could contribute directly to these public debates. I hope to have shown that some of them did so; others did not. More surprisingly, even a negatively evaluated stage character like Zunder could add something to the controversy. The conditions for Jews in Germany as well as the Swedish refugee policy were highly politicized issues. Every theatre production bringing a Jew on stage risked becoming part of the debate, whether it was a classical play or an old German play or a new German play. To deny the political implications of the stage Jew would, at the time, have been a political statement in itself.

The political effect of Jews on stage cannot be measured or understood by these stereotyped masks. The examples demonstrate that such masks can be used with sympathy or with antipathy, thus contributing negatively or positively to the political debate outside the theatre. In other words, the effects cannot be judged by the length of the nose alone — the entire conventional, structural, and conceptual context as well as the political implications of this issue have to be taken into consideration. This does not mean that the actor presenting a stage Jew does not have any responsibility for the interpretation and the political relevance of this figure. The actor assumes a great deal of responsibility for how the figure is perceived by the spectator.

For the Jewish refugees, indirect protagonists of these plays, their theatrical image was a matter of life and death. For the actors, as the exponents of a humanitarian theatre, performing a Jew on stage became a matter that went far beyond aesthetics and relied upon profound ethical decisions. For the spectators, political actions were possible and necessary. For the politicians, decisions could have been changed, but Sweden remained closed for refugees until April 1940, when the "brothers and sisters from the Nordic countries under German occupation" were seen as "natural" refugees with a "natural" right to stay in Sweden.

# 14 | *Text, Performance, Event, 1611*
## A Historical Play by a Catholic Protestant

In the first book of Moses we are told about the Great Deluge and how Noah saved himself and his sons. The tenth chapter continues the story of Noah's sons Shem, Ham, and Japheth. The sons of Japheth, in turn, were Gomer, Magog, Madal, Jovan, Tubal, Masek, and Tiras. About them it is said, in verse 5, that they spread out into pagan countries with their people. Magog was the one who came to Sweden to establish the Swedish kingdom. His son Ubbo founded the city of Uppsala, later the site of the first university in Sweden. About 400 years after Magog's arrival in Sweden, people left their original religion to worship new gods: Thor, Odin, Frigga, and others. About 2,000 years later the Swedes obviously did not serve their gods sufficiently, so their own gods decided to punish them. They spread starvation and death over the country. In the year 2758 after the Creation of the World the catastrophe had reached devastating proportions, so the king of the period, Sigtrud, had to take measures to prevent the extinction of his people. He decided to kill half the population, especially those who were old, disabled, or useless to society. A young lady by the name of Disa received this message and protested against the king's decision. When the king heard about Disa, she was ordered to come to court under the following conditions: Neither by day nor by night, neither walking, riding, nor sailing, neither in clothes nor naked . . . Disa succeeded in doing so and advised the king not to kill the people but to send them to northern areas to colonize new lands for the kingdom. King Sigtrud was very impressed, followed her advice, and made Disa his queen.

## A Lousy Play

The play in which we learn about these ancient stories, called *Disa*, was performed in Uppsala in 1611. It does not end with the royal wedding. In the fifth and last act the queen of the Amazons, Pentesilea, appears. She is coming back from the Trojan War and wants to retire to her original home in Uppsala.

This fantastic play had a lasting success. In the year of its first production it was printed twice, and in the following decades it was reprinted again and again, although with some cuts and some additions. *Disa* was also staged by many theatrical companies and even produced as an opera. This success lasted for almost 200 years: there is an unbroken tradition of theatrical productions until the end of the eighteenth century. After that period only a few experimental productions have taken place; otherwise the play is considered "dead," according to Sweden's leading literary experts.

This negative reevaluation of *Disa* started in the middle of the nineteenth century, when literary historians were writing the first overviews of Swedish drama. The play was regarded as an example of the unskilled beginnings of the yet undeveloped art of drama in the cold North. As a drama it had no literary merits at all: it was considered clumsy and dull both in its language and in its plot construction. The author of the play, Johannes Messenius, had no skills and no natural feeling of how to write a dramatic text.[1] However it might have fascinated audiences in earlier centuries, the play no longer warranted literary study or theatre productions. This negative judgment of Messenius and his dramas has prevailed in successive literary histories to the present. Even in the most recent Swedish literary handbooks Messenius' only merit is that he introduced national history in Swedish drama; otherwise, the scholars would rather not recommend these dreadfully composed and poorly written texts to anybody.

In my view, these almost scornful presentations of Messenius and his drama reflect less a shift or change in taste between his time and the modern age than a profound difference in the concept of what a

# En lustig Commœdia,

### Om then Förständige och Högtberömde

## Sweriges Drottning

# Fru DISA,

### Hwilken sanfärdeligen på rim utsatt, och hållen i Upsala Marknad den 17 och 18 Februarii, Ahr efter Guds Börd 1611.

### Af
# JOHANNE MESSENIO,
### Professore thersammastädes.

## Tryckt Ahr 1727.

dramatic text is. For literary researchers Messenius' dramas are primary literary works, in which the structure of the text is the prime interest. From this perspective they compare the text to other literary works of the same time. In 1611 Shakespeare wrote *The Tempest* and Ben Johnson his *Alchemist*; and in Spain Lope de Vega certainly wrote a few dozen autos and comedies. What is Messenius compared to them? What they neglect completely is the fact that *Disa* is a text which has been performed: it was part of the theatrical event which took place at a certain place and a certain time.

The theatrical event contains not only a dramatic text but also the actors — in this case Messenius' students — a stage, and not least an audience. Because I am aware of the theatrical event, my attitude to Messenius' text is completely different. I do not consider it as a "work of art," but as the prime source of an event that took place in Uppsala on seventeenth and eighteenth February 1611. Before going into the analysis of the text as play-script, I want to extend my polemic examination of literary history, because I also sense a concept of literary development which does not favor old dramatic texts.

## The Paradigm of Development

The writings of literary historians show a clear tendency to position Messenius' dramas in a historical chain of development. This is especially clear with older historians, but the paradigm of literary development is firmly rooted even in contemporary historical discourse. These scholars are very eager to place *Disa* in the environment of dramatic works of the time. Since there were very few dramas written in Sweden prior to Messenius, they connect his writings to the medieval practices — which he hardly has departed from, according to their view — and analyze the text itself to show how underdeveloped it is in relation to the demands of dramatic art.

Theatre scholars also have been placing Messenius in this chain of development. They usually ask two questions. First, they look for influences and models that Messenius could have been exposed to. Not very much is known about early Renaissance drama in Sweden, and there certainly was not an abundance of dramatic writing in Swedish. Consequently, Messenius could not work in a rich tradition; there were no theatrical models available to him, and therefore his theatrical techniques must have been poor. Second, scholars examine the text itself to see what staging devices are absolutely necessary. Since they already have decided that the practical possibilities were limited, they claim that these texts did not need anything more than a primitive podium.

The same tendency can also be observed in international research, and I would like to note just one example. Around 1950 two books were published about the reconstruction of Shakespeare's Globe Theatre in London.[2] John Crawford Adams departed from the assumption of the "absolutely necessary" for the staging of Shakespeare's plays. His suggestion for the Globe Theatre was a simple half-timbered building and minimal equipment for the stage. His reconstructed Globe had hardly any decorative elements at all. Adams was using the same source material as C. Walter Hodges, but they arrived at completely different conclusions. Hodges' reconstruction almost reminds me of a Renaissance palace, with rich decorations, tasteful details, and elaborate stage facilities. While Adams was looking for the "necessary minimum," Hodges searched for the "possible maximum."

It is easy to understand that Swedish drama and theatre historians were inscribing Messenius into the "necessary minimum." The reason for this attitude is undoubtedly the paradigm of development: in accordance with natural sciences, even scholars in the humanities wanted to see the growth of culture from embryonic beginnings through early adolescence to a mature, fully developed period, from which decline and dissolution follow. If I were to believe in this kind of historiography in the case of Disa, the "development" had not even reached the adolescent stage.

I have reasons to believe that the contrary was the case. I asked myself if I could find circumstances which would allow me to look for a "possible maximum" instead of an embryonic beginning. Is it possible to assume that Messenius' drama was well adopted to the situation in which it was performed? Did Messenius have reasons to present a performance which surmounted everything that Sweden had seen on stage so far? There are at least two strong arguments for such a view: the personal and the political circumstances in which the original production was mounted in 1611. In other words: the biography of the author and the context of the performance.

## *Messenius and Sweden*

At the beginning of the seventeenth century Sweden aspired to become an empire. In the same year in which *Disa* was performed for the first time, a new king ascended the throne, Gustaf II Adolf, who was only seventeen. He had inherited three wars: one against Denmark, which he settled in 1613; one against Russia, which ended in 1617; and one against Poland, which eventually involved Sweden in the Thirty Years' War. While military strength brought Sweden to the forefront of the European power play, the country's cultural development was rather backward. The political liberation from Denmark, economic hardship, and the need to feed its people left no room for a substantial cultural engagement. The royal princes were, according to the ideals of the Renaissance, well educated in letters, arts, and politics, but they were almost the only ones in the country. The University of Uppsala, founded in 1477 and later famous for such teachers as Anders Celsius and Carl von Linné, had disintegrated totally during the sixteenth century. It served only as a small seminar for priests.

Therefore, the Swedish government employed an utterly suspect but highly educated humanist, a doctor of philosophy and *poeta Caesareus*, Johannes Messenius. The university badly needed his learning, but did not want the man. After all, he was a native Swede, born in 1579 not far from the shores of Lake Vättern in southern Sweden. He went to school in Vadstena, famous for its convent, where once the holy Birgitta lived. At the end of the sixteenth century Vadstena was still the last outpost for the Catholic congregations in this Protestant country. Sweden has been and still is a Protestant nation, ever since Gustaf Wasa's acceptance of the Reformation in 1527. The Catholics were able to regain some of their rights during the reign of Johan III, the second son of Gustaf Wasa, who was king of Sweden from 1568 to 1592. This monarch was married to a Polish princess, Katarina Jagellonica, who convinced her husband that Catholicism was the right faith. Their son, Sigismund, was to become king of both Catholic Poland and Protestant Sweden, but was finally dethroned in Sweden, which led to the previously mentioned war with Poland.

After Johan's death, Duke Karl, later the king of Sweden as Karl IX, reinstated the Protestant faith in all of Sweden. At the Assembly of the

Estates in Uppsala in 1595 Catholic services were declared illegal, which also meant the final closing down of the convent in Vadstena. Young Messenius, who had already been involved in Catholic circles in Vadstena, was brought to safety in Poland.

Messenius, being sixteen years of age at the time, was enrolled at the Jesuit college of Braunsberg (Braniewo) near Danzig (Gdansk). He became an educated humanist and, it was thought, also a member of the Societas Jesu. After eight years, in 1603, he was sent to Rome to complete his studies at the Collegium Germanicum, which served as the final educational step toward higher priesthood. In a way this shows how highly the Jesuit fathers valued his capabilities.

Messenius stayed in Rome for only a few weeks and never entered the famous college. Instead he returned to Germany, more precisely, to Ingolstadt in southern Germany, where he achieved the degree of a doctor of philosophy. During his extensive traveling in the area he was also pronounced poet of the empire by the Habsburg emperor in Prague. Later, around 1607, Messenius returned to Danzig and tried to gain a position at the court of Sigismund of Poland. For that purpose he had compiled a *Genealogia Sigismundi*, a genealogical table of the Swedish-born king. Since he did not receive the desired reaction from the Polish court, he reworked his *genealogica* to suit the Swedish king Karl IX, who actually was the uncle of Sigismund. He sent his treatise to Stockholm and, at the same time, offered his services to Sweden. He was successful in that Karl actually invited him to come to Stockholm. After fourteen years abroad Messenius returned to Sweden, assuring the king of his faithfulness to Protestantism and immediately proving his loyalty by writing an anti-Jesuit pamphlet. After some deliberations Messenius was appointed *professor juris utriusque* at the University of Uppsala.

Messenius is said to have been a fierce man, full of energy and temperament, a fighter — one might even call him a "choleric." Soon after his arrival in Uppsala he was engaged in several serious controversies with the other professors and the head of the university. Some of these controversies stemmed from the application of strict Jesuit methods in his teaching. These less learned debates at the University of Uppsala are the clue, for they point to the engagement with theatre. Since some other professors trained their students in performing antique comedies, Messenius had to enter the competition even in this area — and he had to do better: he wrote his own play in Swedish and, furthermore, treated a

Swedish historical subject. *Disa* (1611) was his first dramatic work. Messenius intended — as Strindberg did 300 years later — to display all of Swedish history on stage, in a total of fifty plays.

Even this short account of Messenius' life up to 1611 and the circumstances around his engagement in Uppsala suggests that he had every reason to produce the most spectacular and lavish performance possible. But we must wonder what the theatrical possibilities were at the time.

## The Performance in 1611

One of the main criticisms of *Disa* was the clumsy and dull exposition in the first act. In the Prologus (all stage directions are written in Latin) the story is explained according to the dramatic rules of the time. The gods are tired of their disobedient servants and therefore have sent starvation throughout the country, but Disa will save the country and become queen. In the first scene the head of the gods, Thor, complains about his people. In the following two scenes Odin, god of war and wisdom, and Frigga, goddess of fertility, confirm what the first god already has told the audience. The fourth scene is a little comedy about a man who has had a bad dream and wants the Astrologer to explain it. A little masked figure, called *larvator*, makes fun of the learned man, who explains the dream in the same terms in which the gods have spoken. The fifth and last scene of the act involves a peasant family (wife, husband, and son) who have already experienced starvation; the son dies on stage from hunger. After having buried him, they proceed to the temple in Uppsala to ask the advice of Frigga, who sends them to the king. Act 2 opens with the peasants coming to the king's palace.

It is true that all of these scenes, including the prologue, tell basically the same story — the plot is not moving forward. To understand this "awkward" structure, one has to imagine the context of the performance. First, *Disa* was presented on an open-air stage. There was nothing exceptional about giving an outdoor performance in February. The crowning of King Karl IX had taken place in winter just a few years earlier, with many outdoor activities; besides, any large indoor facility would have been as cold as outside. Second, the performance took place in an open market square, not in a secluded precinct, during the yearly winter market called Disting, after Queen Disa. A large number of people would have been walking and talking, buying and selling, all over the place. I imagine a scene similar to the Breughel painting of the Kirmes market, well known to most theatre historians. In this environment it seems quite natural that some spectators came in time to watch the performance, whereas others observed a little later that something extraordinary was going on. Messenius obviously wanted to make sure that the latecomers had a chance to catch up with the ongoing play. Meanwhile, he entertained those who came in time by offering them a rich variation of the same story. First, the spectators could watch the pomp of the gods with their typical props, then the cheerful little comedy about the astrologer, while the last scene showed how serious the starvation had become. What may seem a clumsy product of an unskilled dramatist was in reality a clever and effective strategy when seen in the concrete circumstances in which the performance was presented.

The costumes are an example of the "possible maximum." The title heroine uses at least three different costumes. At first she is wearing some kind of everyday dress, but we do not know how it looked. When she is ordered to appear before the king "neither naked nor in clothes," she has put a net over her body. After the king decides to marry her, he asks a servant to bring out the "yellow wedding gown" for his new queen. In the last act Pentesilea wakes up Disa; she might come on stage still wearing the wedding gown or a nightgown of some sort.

The rest of the characters also offered a great variety of costumes from all ranks of society: gods, a king and courtiers, the nobility, servants, peasants, maids. A dedication in the printed version of the text from 1611 indicates that Messenius' theatrical enterprise was supported by some rich families, whose sons were his students (i.e., the performers of this production). The entire cast list is also included in the printed text. These families may well have contributed costumes and props for the production.

Messenius was familiar with Jesuit stage practices after all his years in central Europe, so he was probably capable of constructing an extraordinary stage by contemporary Swedish standards. Since the plot moves from location to location — the heaven of the gods, an open field, Disa's home, the palace in Uppsala — he probably used a number of *mansiones* as background to the podium. Disclosing these houses with curtains, as the Jesuits did, gave him the opportunity for surprising entrances and quick exits. Due to the competitive situation at the univer-

*28. The artist Ove Ström's sketch of the original staging of* Disa *in 1611.*

sity, Messenius certainly spared no expense to produce a spectacular show. Other possibilities in the text could also be exploited.

In addition to wearing a net when she enters the king's court, Disa uses other tricks to live up to the king's demand. She arrives at dawn, which is neither day nor night, and she has eaten an onion to be neither hungry nor full. These effects are hardly visible on stage; but how was she moving (since she was not allowed to walk, to ride, to sail, etc.)? The equipage in which she was brought on stage, or possibly in front of the podium, must have been spectacular. Disa arrives with one leg on the back of a goat and the other on a sled pulled by two servants. She can be seen in this fashion in many drawings and paintings during the following centuries, when Messenius' play was still performed by amateurs and professionals.

All thirty-nine speaking parts in Messenius' original production were played by male students. Girls were of course not allowed to attend the university. There are numerous female characters in the cast list — the title role, Frigga, Pentesilea, the king's servants, Disa's maid, and others. This theatrical convention of the time might have several possible effects. The female parts may become a parody when they are performed by male actors. But there is no reason to assume that this was the case in this performance. Messenius was much too serious about creating his history lecture to spoil it by ridiculing the women of the story. There might, however, have been other effects. The sight of Disa wearing just a net was probably only acceptable when it was performed by a boy. A more or less naked woman on stage belonged to the realm of fantasy, which could be created by a boy actor. Such a "transsexual" approach need not lack erotic undertones. The sensory level of communication seems to oppose the symbolic level, but it might be exactly this double exposure which lends the scene its effect, in the spectators' minds rather than on stage.

I think that Messenius was very much aware that most of his audience were peasants, selling their rural products and buying whatever they could not produce themselves. I find it remarkable how seriously the peasants are treated in his play. The common approach was to make fun of peasants on stage, a practice which reached far into our own century. In the first-act scene with the peasant family, there is absolutely nothing to laugh at. The peasants sent to colonize northern Sweden are also portrayed with care. Messenius yielded to the temptation to conclude his play with a good fistfight among the peasants, however, probably to cheer up the crowd after a long performance of five acts with five scenes in each act.

The success was apparently immediate, although we do not have any direct documents about the audience's response. The number of printings and productions indicates *Disa*'s broad popularity. There were also other reasons for lasting appreciation of Messenius' first play.

## History and Identity

Messenius' ideas coincided perfectly with the needs of his time. Sweden, just about to conquer Europe — or rather the northern part of it — was in need of a national identity and a history comparable to those of other civilizations such as the Romans, the Greeks, or the Jews. Messenius did not even have to invent this genealogy, since Swedish historiographers during the sixteenth century were already very keen on introducing these ideas, which later developed into what was called "Gothicism." As early as 1434, at the Concilium in Basel, Bishop Nicolaus Ragvaldis informed his European colleagues of the true origin of the Swedish nation. The brothers Johannes and Olaus Magnus treated early Swedish history in a similar way in their *Historia de Gentibus Septentrionalibus* (1554), in which they also provided a complete list of all the Swedish kings from Magog to Gustaf Wasa. Despite later historical research — to which Messenius made considerable contributions himself later in his life — the idea of the Swedish kingdom as one of the ancient civilizations prevailed over the centuries and actually reached its peak during the Romantic era in the early nineteenth century. At that time Gothicism developed into a national movement, led by some well-known Swedish poets who had founded the Gothic Society in 1811. Messenius only needed to combine those elements in *Disa* and to transform them into a popular political tableau.

The play starts with the Nordic god Thor, who tells the audience the mythical background of Sweden. He claims that the Swedes are descendants of a Jewish tribe, described in the Torah. Four hundred years later, we are told, the pagan gods took over — Thor himself, Odin, Frigga, and all the others from Aasgard. Thus, Swedish ancient history was firmly rooted in both the Old Testament and Nordic mythology. Historians could count the kings generation by generation: King Sigtrud is said to have been the eighteenth Swedish king. Adding the biblical years since the Great Deluge, they stated that the beginning of his reign was in the year 2758 after the Creation of the World. All this made perfect sense for a sixteenth-century historian. There had been endless theological discussions concerning the counting of the generations of the Bible, including the 950-year-old Noah. Accepting Jewish as well as Christian theology on that matter, the remaining mathematical calculation is simple. In the Jewish calendar the Christian year 2000 equals the year 5760. This means that the Creation of the World occurred in 3760 B.C. and the reign of Sigtrud was established in the year 1002 B.C.:

$$
\begin{array}{rl}
5760 & \text{Jewish year} \\
-\,2000 & \text{Christian year} \\
\hline
3760 & \text{B.C. (Creation of World)} \\
+\,2758 & \text{Sigtrud king} \\
\hline
1002 & \text{B.C.}
\end{array}
$$

This is an epoch close to the time of the Trojan War. After having used the Books of Moses and the Nordic gods, Messenius certainly wanted to bring in Greek mythology too. When act 5 opens, the queen of the Amazons, Pentesilea, arrives in Uppsala in order to retire in her home town. When asked why she chose Uppsala, she readily explains her own genealogy. Once upon a time she left Sweden in the company of her uncle Berik, the fourteenth king of Sweden, who sought to expand his country by conquering other nations. This Gothic tribe eventually settled in the land of the Scythians in the south of Russia. The word "Scythians" resembles the Swedish word for archer or marksman, *skytte* (German *Schütze*). Herodotus, however, said that the Amazons came from Skythia, so they must originally have been Swedes. This is the historical logic of the Renaissance. To Messenius it must have seemed quite natural that Pentesilea came back home to Sweden. Anyway, it was his very own idea.

When all these myths were well established as parts of Swedish history, the play could end with fancy *larvatores* and a traditional fight among the farmers who had come back from their northern provinces to pay tribute to the wise Queen Disa.

## Performances — Conventions — Contexts

*Disa* is not a play I would recommend for the repertoire of a theatre today. Nor am I suggesting that it should be preserved and performed. To find out what can be learned about a historical text without relying on the assumptions of traditional literary historiography, it was necessary to explore *Disa* as theatrical event.

The concept of the theatrical event brings together performance, conventions, and contexts. The performance, as always in my writings, includes the presentation on stage and the perception by the audience. In the case of *Disa*, it is obvious that very few accurate observations are possible. The only available source is the printed text of the drama. Although the little book is unusually rich in information — including the performance dates, the place, the cast list, and a dedication and preface by the author — it does not contain evidence of the stage, the acting style, the blocking, and other details of interest to the theatre historian that would provide a description of the stage actions scene by scene. Nevertheless, it is amazing to see how much information about the presentation can be retrieved from the text. While it is very helpful to try to distinguish between the communicative levels, it is also advisable to relate these levels to the theatrical conventions of the time.

These conventions include not only the artistic traditions dominating theatrical productions at a certain time and place, but also how this artistic work is organized and how theatre life is structured. The competitive situation in Uppsala after the arrival of Messenius, when the professors tried to overshadow their colleagues through theatrical productions, is an interesting and important aspect of Swedish theatre history. The different backgrounds and pedagogical ideals of the dominating professors can also be seen as part of theatrical conventions. It is not surprising that these background features point to influences outside of Sweden. Swedish culture has always depended on impulses from abroad, which are eventually absorbed and transformed.

Sometimes information about a performance permits certain conclusions concerning important conventions. More often scholars use their knowledge of the conventions to illustrate possible practices in a performance. Such conclusions are not without risks. Conventions, especially artistic ones, often do not exist in manifest forms but are invented or imagined by critics and scholars. In historical cases, I advocate the liberty of breaking conventions for artists and audiences. The alternative of the "possible maximum" should never be ruled out beforehand.

The contexts of Messenius' *Disa* are manifold, and this essay attempts to illuminate only a few of them. The choice of which contexts are worth discussing is ultimately made by the scholar, although all serious researchers try to find the most appropriate aspects. Even in the choice of context "unconventional" approaches might be rewarding. There are no given contexts of a theatrical event, just more or less interesting ones. For example, I might pay more attention to the class structure in the play; I have mentioned Messenius' fair treatment of peasants, but there is certainly more to say. The gender aspects also deserve more attention; I noted the all-male cast, but other gender issues in the play might be discussed. Cultural politics could also be considered; *Disa* was not only a market play, but also a political play both in Uppsala and at the royal court in Stockholm.

My point of departure was the maltreatment of Messenius' drama in literary history. This essay gives an alternative view by bringing together a few performances, the major conventions, and some contexts to draw a historical picture of the theatrical event which *Disa* constituted in Uppsala in February 1611.

## 15

# *Beyond the Director's Images*
## Reviews and Views of Robert Lepage's Production of *A Dream Play* at the Royal Dramatic Theatre

In [Robert Lepage's] production of *A Dream Play*, which has now had its premiere at Dramaten, the actors never touch the floor. The scenic space consists instead of a seemingly free hovering cube with three walls, of which the floor — or the wall which is at the bottom — slopes toward the audience.

The cube is not very big, maybe a room of 4 x 4 meters. The cube has a number of square openings which serve as doors, windows, or other passages. The cube can rotate. On these 16 square meters the whole Dream Play is acted out. Through sounds and light, projections, and this rotating cube, Lepage executes Strindberg's stage directions.[1]

The performance of *A Dream Play* starts by transforming the bright albedo-sphere of heaven into the heavier and tighter atmosphere of the earth. The performance demonstrates a transformation from the prima materia of the unconsciousness of childhood, via the painful depressions of nigredo, to the communal initiation, during which all characters throw their old identities into the fire to purify them. When the old ego dies, a psychological rebirth can take place, after which they may possibly enter the albedo phase.[2]

These two statements obviously refer to the same production, Robert Lepage's staging of August Strindberg's *A Dream Play* at the Royal Dramatic Theatre in Stockholm in November 1994. The first statement appeared in a review published in a Stockholm evening newspaper the day after the premiere; the second is from a master's thesis in theatre studies, presented in the spring of 1996. The considerable differences between these two statements might just reflect my random choice, but they might also indicate the profound differences between reviews printed in the daily press, on the one hand, and analytical essays written by scholars in theatre journals or as academic dissertations, on the other hand.

Assuming that there are major divergences between these two types of essays, my interest here is to explore what distinguishes a review from a scholarly analysis of a performance. On what levels can these differences be noted? Are these texts on theatrical performances to be compared at all? I can see various reasons for these differences:

pragmatic factors such as different working conditions for critics
and scholars;
conventions such as long-standing traditions of newspaper criticism
vs. the fairly new discipline of performance analysis;
methodological differences, which derive in part from journalistic
and scholarly practices;
theoretical considerations, in the sense that critics and scholars
address distinctly different readers.

Before I consider these possible explanations, I must show where the differences lie and to what extent they go beyond more obviously practical variations in styles, tastes, and ambitions among critics and scholars.

The materials for this explorative study are half a dozen randomly chosen newspaper reviews of the production from 13 to 16 November 1994 (at most four days after the first night) and an article in a theatre journal from the fall of 1995 as well as the master's thesis already quoted.

## Theatre Critics

All of the newspaper critics struggled to describe the revolving, hanging, tipped, and perforated cube which Lepage had mounted in the former painters' workshop under the roof of Dramaten. It is impossible to

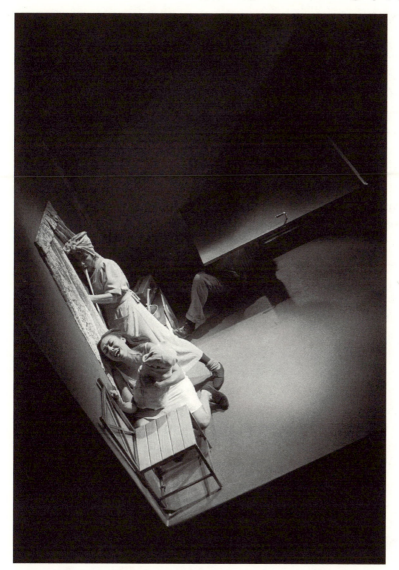

*29. Robert Lepage's production of* A Dream Play *at the Royal Dramatic Theatre in Stockholm in 1994. Courtesy of Bengt Wanselius.*

know whether any reader who had not seen the elaborate construction could properly picture the cube and its workings. Because it was the centerpiece of the whole construction, all critics had to take its measure, first and foremost by trying to find an appropriate description of how it looked and how it operated.

Despite the limited space a critic is allowed in a daily newspaper, almost all of them felt that they had to spend quite a few lines on this cube. As the dominating stage device of Lepage's *Dream Play* the cube deserved a thorough description, but I can also see a more external reason for all the labor expended on finding adequate descriptions of the "thing." Robert Lepage is well known as an *enfant terrible* among theatre directors, especially concerning his stage designs, and the upcoming premiere was anticipated by interviews in which Lepage talked about his fascination with virtual realities, videos, and electronic music. Furthermore, he had performed his one-man show *Needles and Opium* in Stockholm just a few month before. In other words, Lepage's stage devices are news, and in this connection even theatre critics take on the function of reporting journalists. The readers had a "right" to be informed about Lepage's latest inventions.

Apart from being news, the cube also had to be evaluated in relation to Strindberg's play. Since the program for the performance had Strindberg's short *Preamble to A Dream Play* reprinted on the first page, some passages from the author's idea of dreaming were frequently quoted as a reference to Lepage's stage. Imitating the "incoherent but seemingly logic form of dreams," says Strindberg, "everything can happen, everything is possible and probable. Time and space do not exist." Did Lepage create a world in which time and space no longer existed? Did his cube dissolve reality? Did the characters of this production "split, double, multiply, evaporate, condensate, scatter, and converge"?[3] The critics do not agree, of course. Some found the cube a perfect tool to erase any sense of time, logic, and space, thereby forcing the performers into unconventional actions; while others found the endless climbing of the actors along the oblique walls tiresome and the turning cube a monotonous use of an initially cute toy. These differences in taste are usually not argued very well in the critiques — the reviewer naturally has the right to express an opinion. A closer look reveals that those differences also disclose more profound conceptions of normative aesthetics.

One way of stating such aesthetic convictions is to refer to Strindberg himself. According to some critics, since it is his play any kind of production should be measured by the demands of the text. These references to the play's author do not solve the problem, because they are used by both sides — those in favor of Lepage's cube as well as those who oppose the director's "machinery" find confirmation in Strindberg's writing. The aesthetic ground for the evaluation of the production is rather to be found in insignificant statements which are not supposed to be read as aesthetic principles. Two short examples provide evidence for this observation.

Hans Ingvar Hanson praises one of the actors for his "natural sharpness in details, which make him a living character every moment he is on stage." When Hanson later remarks that in this confined space of the cube "no entrance or exit could be done in a natural way,"[4] we start to realize that this critic has problems in appreciating an acting style that does not emphasize the psychologically realistic presentation of characters. Therefore he also has difficulties in seeing advantages in placing the actions within an eternally revolving box. For him Lepage's production does not create a dream, but only monotonous melancholy and "simple boredom." This critic's concept of theatre is firmly rooted in realist traditions, and he is not prepared to change his mind.

Ulrika Milles, by contrast, praises Lepage for his faithful interpretation of Strindberg's text as compared to other Strindberg productions she has seen. According to her, Lepage "plants a mixture of avant-garde circus and postmodern concepts of style right into the heart of a classical play of our cultural heritage." From this perspective, she is able to appreciate Francesca Quartey's Indira's Daughter as a "white Modesty Blaise figure combined with an Indian goddess." Agnes becomes a "knight in female shape about to save her prince who is locked up in the castle."[5] These interpretations are quite personal, but clearly inspired by the dominating features of the production.

The reviews also demonstrate some recurring patterns in the ways spectators responded to the performance. When spectators have a negative response to a production, they usually are not willing to analyze its thematic and symbolic meanings. There is, however, a significant deviation from the standard behavior of audiences.[6] While a spectator normally would judge a performance by the standards of the acting, especially by the principal performers, most of the critics here make the peculiar cube the focus of their evaluation. This stage device occupies such a dominant place in the reviews that several critics did not even include the name of the main actress. Even in the most positive reviews the actors are barely mentioned — and if so, it is mostly in terms of the unusual movements the performance required or the unconventional costumes. This neglect of actors and their contribution to the performance seems to be a direct consequence of the domination of the stage equipment. Instead of observing the actors, the critics concentrated upon the director and his devices.

Lepage's cubic box was described, evaluated, and related to Strindberg's technique of dream plays, but there are hardly any interpretations going beyond the director's images. Is this lack of interpretation a special case, an exception to the norm? Or is it characteristic of theatre reviews, which must be written quickly for newspaper publication and tend toward the journalistic convention of providing facts, not analysis? Was it possible to transgress the dominating effect of the cube to advance to the deeper meaning of the characters, the circular narrative, and the significance of style and acting?

## Scholars

As a contrast to the critics, I want to present the views of two young scholars on Lepage's *A Dream Play*, whose contributions to this discussion are very different in approach and format.

Ola Johansson's article is entitled "Completeness Passing By — Three Guest Appearances in Stockholm 1994–95." After some general remarks on the aesthetic ideal of turn-of-the-century theatre artists — to unite all artistic means into what Charles Baudelaire called "divine unity art" — Johansson turned to the question of how the modern theatre fulfills its role as "performative art" in relation to other art forms. "The theatrical performance consists of the three dimensions of space, irreversible presence, and authentic human interaction."[7] Although such a statement seems to be commonplace, these basic characteristics of theatre are, according to Johansson, not always so fully realized in production. He notes that during the last two years three guest artists in Stockholm have emphasized the importance of presence, space, and interaction.

Johansson's first example is Lepage's *A Dream Play*. Like the critics, he describes the hanging cube as a kind of vertical revolving stage turned toward the auditorium. He interprets the anachronistic costumes — ranging from the fashion of Strindberg's times to T-shirts and jeans — as a sign that no single narrative code of time and place dominated the dramatic action. The performance does nothing to conceal the reality of the stage in order to pretend a dreamlike world; on the contrary, the very physicality of the set and the laborious movements of the actors create a distance between the performance and reality outside the theatre.

> Both regarding the verbal and the visual, theatre is a plastic phenomenon, a space in which attention is directed toward the performative conditions of presence. Accordingly, Lepage has omitted illusions and foregrounds instead a materialized interpretation of the dream of suffering mankind. In Lepage's version of the dream, the physical presence of actors and spectators materializes the theatre's own reality, a concrete, physical reality in its own right, capable of expressing abstract ideas.[8]

Johansson reminds us that the "the boards, which signify the world," not only are used on the stage floor, but also serve as the material of the benches on which the audience members sit. The unity of stage and audience, actions and reactions, materialized world and a world materialized, was the core experience of Lepage's *A Dream Play* as well as Christoph Marthaler's *Murx den Europäer . . .* from the Volksbühne in Berlin and Theatre de Complicité's performance of *The Three Lives of Lucie Cabrol.* They are all "in a consistent way making physical presence," which created holistic unities of the kind which Johansson wishes to see more of on the Swedish stage.

Katarina Thorell approached Lepage's production from a very different angle. Her point of departure can only be described in theoretical terms, which in her case means a special frame in which she places the performance, involving both alchemy and the Buddhist interpretation of the Hindu gods and goddesses. This last view, which is of course close to the theme of the play, enables Thorell to see the relationships between the three worlds of the Hindu gods: The third world of the earth, the second world of the not yet perfected souls, and the first world of the Nirvana. The god Indra, certainly a member of that first world, sends his daughter, who still has to be perfected, into the third world to be purified through learning. Indra does not send her down to earth simply to check out the conditions of humankind — as the three gods do in Brecht's *Good Woman of Sezuan* — but instead to bring about the purification and transformation of the daughter. Such purification processes are also described in alchemy, especially in the Eastern traditions of alchemy.

The dramaturgy of the play is then seen not only as a skillfully composed plot, but as a description of the alchemical operations. This process starts in the "prima materia" of the stable, goes through "seperatio" and "coagulatio" to "mortificatio" in the scenes with the lawyer, advances to "solutio," and finally reaches the "sublimatio" in the state of the albedo, the whiteness of the Nirvana. Looking at this production of Lepage as a movement through the alchemist's phases of the process of purification, Thorell gives many of the scenes a surprising interpretation, such as the pains and tribulations people are suffering in the Foul Beach scene: the pain is a mortification, the deadly state of transition, necessary to be able to proceed to the pleasures of the Fingal Grotto. But the analysis also shows an overall understanding of the "female power which is needed to transform society."[9] The three men surrounding Indra's daughter — the Officer, the Lawyer, and the Poet — symbolize the basic elements. The Officer is earthbound, representing our physical development — he is played by three actors, a boy, a young man, and an old man; the Lawyer has reached the water element, during which our emotional life develops; the Poet has already jumped to the fire-element, representing inspiration and mental power, but he has neglected the air-element, through which our intellect is trained. This is the reason why all these men are immature and incapable of reaching the same high level as the daughter herself.

This interpretation is not based on Strindberg's text alone; it includes the scenic elements, like the water on the stage floor, the firelike projections, the naive movements and gestures of the actress playing the daughter, and the three actors creating the role of the Officer mentioned above. This last observation is interesting in principle. Katarina Thorell states frankly that she will not evaluate the actors in terms of their skills and performing power, but she wants to see their acting characteristics as parts of the fictional characters. "Evaluations are not meaningful for this analysis, since I only interpret what I see on stage and not what I wanted to see on stage," she says.[10] Thus, she interprets both the positive and negative aspects of the acting as features of the role, nevertheless including the acting style of each actor as well as the style of the ensemble.

## Reviews vs. Essays

The characteristics of these two essays can be summarized in a few points. Both develop within a distinct frame of interpretation, one drawing upon aesthetic theory, the other developing a concept of alchemical processes. Most of the reviews lack this interpretative quality. Only one of the critics made an attempt to see Lepage as part of the avant-garde tradition. This lack of aesthetic theory does not prevent the critics from expressing aesthetically based judgments, however, as we have seen.

The two scholars show very limited interest in the director and his intentions, which was a major interest of most critics. The same is true of the actors, whose stage personalities did not attract any comments in these two essays. The performance as such is the main focus of the scholars, while the text and Strindberg himself receive less attention.

In order to observe differences between the reviews and essays, I identify four different levels of writing: the pragmatic, the conventional, the methodological, and the theoretical. Here I would like to offer some tentative conclusions, partly derived from the material presented here, partly based on my own professional experience as a reader of daily reviews and scholarly essays.

The *pragmatic* factors in writing about performances are quite obvious. The critic has to write quickly, often within one day, and the space allowed in the newspaper is limited. These limitations do not apply to scholarly work. In addition, it is important to realize that the critic as journalist also has to consider the news value of the story, while scholarly publications often appear when the production already has been removed from the repertoire.

I think there are considerable *conventional* differences between critics and scholars, especially concerning the attitudes toward the dramatic text, its author, and not least the director. The reviewer is very often strongly attached to the text and considers the dramatist a key figure of the theatrical event. In performance analysis, the drama text is just one of the elements to be analyzed, less important than the acting. Another difference concerns the director. Over time, it is striking that the director has become increasingly important to critics, who consider the director the central creator of the performance.[11] Scholarly analysts of performance also recognize the director as a unifying principle, but other production factors often serve as the main point of interest. I think the importance of the director has been decreasing over the years during which performance analyses have been published.[12]

From a *methodological* point of view, it is obvious that the different working conditions have resulted in different approaches to the writing of analytical texts. The critics usually only see one dress rehearsal, and their writing has to be relatively spontaneous. Therein lies a special value, both for the reader of newspapers and for the researcher of theatre history. Very often these are the only traces of audience reactions to be found. The scholar is sometimes able to see a number of performances of the same production and can compare the effects on different audiences and the variations in each presentation. The scholar also has the time to develop an argumentative discourse and is expected to relate the analysis to the whole of the performance. A critic almost of necessity has to choose certain moments of the performance to demonstrate opinions, while the scholar carefully selects dominant aspects which are significant to the overall interpretation.

There are also *theoretical* reasons for the differences between reviews and essays. I think it is reasonable to assume that critics are mostly engaged in *searching for the meaning* of a performance, an intended or at least possible meaning primarily related to the director as the creator of the event. Scholars, in contrast, *construct meanings* by giving their interpretations a clearly established frame. The differences between seeking and constructing the meaning of a performance are considerable.

In conclusion, I would like to give my personal view on what I think critics and scholars could learn from each other. Critics might be advised to make more use of explicit aesthetic and theoretical points of references and to focus more attention on the actual performance rather than speculating about the intentions of dramatists and directors. The scholars could learn to trust their spontaneous personal experiences and to discover the value of evaluations. I wish that both critics and scholars would be more attentive to the actor as the "real creator" of the theatrical event and would realize the impact of the actor upon the primary theatrical experience and its interpretation. This might promote an adequate understanding of the art of theatre in the terms that Ola Johansson was suggesting: as a specific space, as irreversible presence, and as authentic human interaction.

# To Be Continued

My ideas about the theatrical event as a scholarly paradigm for theatre studies have always influenced my discussions of the objectives of the discipline. A decade of administrative duties and academic tasks passed while I was working on these essays, leaving limited time for scholarly curiosity and ambitious projects. This book gives me an opportunity to summarize some of the aspects which I personally have found to be of special importance for my own writings as well as for future applications of the theatrical event.

## Performance and Perception

The need to create closer ties between performance analysis and reception theory has been one of the guidelines in constructing the concept of the theatrical event. The analysis of live theatrical performances has been one of the priorities of theatre studies. Many colleagues have contributed to a wider understanding of stage performances, but I also saw certain problems which I considered essential.

First, it was not clear to me what position the scholar was taking while writing a performance analysis. Was the researcher a kind of "all-knowing" observer, standing outside of the performance event, or was the scholar to be considered a spectator — one of the spectators in a specific audience attending a particular performance? For me the answer to this question — once it was raised — was very obvious. I could not even imagine that any methodology could account for an omnipotent scholar who would be able to describe and analyze a performance in "objective" terms, discovering or constructing its underlying meanings. For me even the scholar was part of the theatrical event and part of the context in which it took place. Starting from this assumption — which was a lot more controversial ten or fifteen years ago than it is today — my scholarly task was to find a way to analyze the relationship between the performance on stage and the response to it in the auditorium.

Through the model of theatrical communication, I have attempted to locate the spectator within the theatrical event. This ambition is most obvious when I describe performances which I attended myself, such as *Miss Julie* in Copenhagen or *Mistero Buffo* in a park in Stockholm. My prior knowledge of writers and artists naturally colored my perception of these performances. I agree with Gadamer when he states that no researcher can step outside his or her own horizon of understanding, but that it is possible to widen this horizon through learning and experience. To account for the type of learning and experience which might have influenced the process of understanding is not only the scholar's task but also a key for the reader's understanding of the scholar's understanding.

Time and again I have underlined the aspect of pleasure in theatrical communication, but maybe I should have offered a more differentiated view of pleasure in the theatre. First, I do not think that only the spectators enjoy a theatre event — the pleasure also includes the performers. Every performance aims at success in terms of being appreciated by an audience. To sense the positive response from the audience is the most profound desire in every performer, and the satisfaction when it actually happens is perhaps the foremost motivation for performers to exhibit themselves on stage, evening after evening, despite stage fright, nervous tensions, stress, and fear of blackouts. The reward of a successful performance for the actors goes far beyond the bow after the curtain falls. Considering the spectators' pleasure in the theatre, one could speak about a whole range of "pleasures": aesthetic pleasure, the pleasure of recognition — be it of the play, the performer, the style, the theatre building, the company — the pleasure of understanding in the sense in which Brecht speaks about "Vergnügen," the delight of intellectual insight. Sometimes I wonder if it is not this basic experience of pleasure which brings us back to theatrical events again and again. In my view, any theory of theatrical communication must take into account the whole breadth of communicative features — from the simplest satisfaction of recognizing an actor's face to the deepest appreciation of the intellectual complexity of the performance.

It is one thing to claim that every theatrical event is part of various theatrical and nontheatrical contexts, but it is quite an intricate task actually to show the connections between events and contexts. The aspect of playing culture, for example, changed my perception of early Nordic theatre, from the rock carvings of the Bronze Age to medieval palimpsests; *Disa* in the market place became different from *Disa* on a printed page; stars like Sarah Bernhardt, Eleonora Duse, Clara Ziegler, Ellen Terry, and their contemporaries depended on means of transportation and publicity as much as on their own capacity to touch an audience; Shylock was not just another ethnic figure when the persecution of Jews had become official politics in a neighboring country; Dario Fo builds on Italian stereotypes, but his ideas travel interculturally to northern Europe to be transformed into a tight encounter between a Swedish actor and Swedish audiences.

The awareness of the significance of contextual perspectives has been rapidly growing during recent years and now far exceeds traditional "background" of a topic. The context is not only a background; on the contrary, contexts are integral to the understanding of the event itself. The scholar decides which contexts — theatrical as well as nontheatrical — are most relevant for a discussion. A theatrical event might "offer" certain perspectives as especially attractive and fruitful, but it is always up to the researcher to relate the event to one context or another. The only justification for the researcher's choice is the result: if a certain aspect offers interesting insights, this is the best argument for the application of such a perspective.

## Present and Past

Out of the approximately twenty productions analyzed in the second part of this book, I have personally only seen about ten. What difference does this make? Are my analyses of the performances I have seen "truer" or better verified than my analyses of those I have not seen? What are the differences in writing about contemporary and historical productions, and how significant are these differences?

The major difference between theatrical events in which I have participated and those which I have not seen is of course my own experience. Having been there, I responded to the activities on stage as well as to the audience around me. But exactly what do my experiences contribute to the analysis of the event? This is a central but complex question in relation to performance analysis. My experience of the performance is like any other experience, limited in time and place. When I am writing about the performance, my experience of it has been transformed to a memory of an experience (which, in turn, is a new kind of experience). Analyzing the performance, I actually use my memories — of the stage activities, of the behavior of other spectators, and of my own experiences (i.e., emotional and intellectual reactions toward the theatrical event). In written form, accounts of my memories are just like any other document related to the performance, be it a video or a review or the notes of the director. In other words, my own experiences are transformed into "material" — documents of extraordinarily high value and flexibility, but also of some uncertainty as time passes after the event itself.

At what point does a performance that I have seen personally become a historical performance? The next day or ten years later or when the next generation does not have any memories of the persons involved? Answers can only be given in practice, just as by our first professor in theatre history at Stockholm University, Agne Beijer. He was a theatre critic for thirty years, but as a scholar he would never have written about any performance he had seen. Today's theatre scholars like Erika Fischer-Lichte or Jacqueline Martin hardly hesitate to analyze Robert Wilson or Ingmar Bergman or *The Phantom of the Opera* or any other theatre event they have attended. But Fischer-Lichte has also been writing about *Untitled Event*, a Happening which Cage, Cunningham, Rauschenberg, and others produced at the Black Mountain College as long ago as 1952. At that time both Fischer-Lichte and RoseLee Goldberg were very young, and even Marvin Carlson was still in his teens. Today they are all relating to the *Untitled Event* as if it were part of our common experiences. Here an interesting reversion of the process described above takes place. On the one hand, events become memories for those who participated; on the other hand, memories also become a kind of "experience" or collective awareness for those who have only heard or read about them. The performance has become part of what can be called the discourse of theatre events.

The discourse of theatre events transgresses the artificial distinction between contemporary and historical performances. Here both theatre historiography and performance analysis are integrated into a historiography of the past and the present. The perspective of the historiographer is directed backward as much as forward: what will come is always related to what has been.

This process of historification becomes especially manifest in the moment of writing. Every event — experienced by ourselves or told by others — becomes a narrative of history. My model of theatrical communication has been helpful in locating a number of important ingredients in the relationship between performer and spectator, between the event and the context, between the past and the present, as well as between theatre and life.

## Theatre and Life

In chapters 3 and 5, I have attempted to leave the restricted area of traditional theatrical activities and to look at some agents who appear in more or less theatrical events: political orators, circus artists, goalkeepers, parish priests, and also a "Turkish Tailor." A number of other "actors" of this kind could be mentioned: news anchors on television, rock artists, public relation officers at press conferences, terrorists hijacking an airplane. Similar situations would include stock markets, board meetings, fashion shows, political rallies, Olympic games, carnivals, and graduation days. It is not my intention to define these activities as "theatre" — nor do I wish to extend theatre studies to cover all kinds of public events — but I can observe that the interactions between public agents and their "audiences" bear a number of similarities to theatrical communication. There are "actors" making use of their exhibitory actions; there are more or less clearly encoded modes of communication; and there are symbolic functions in these public appearances. At least two major points can be made about these observations of the life-world around us.

First, these "theatrical" modes of communication are assuming a prominent place in today's Western civilization, especially through the mediatization of public life. Whatever happens around the world is almost simultaneously brought to our living rooms, where we are confronted with continuous role-playing, extravagant costume design, delicate lighting effects, and an efficient dramaturgy in the presentation of public events. There is also a growing awareness of the importance of the communicative aspects when public events are "staged." The spoken word — purposefully and effectively presented — replaces written information more and more. To get a scholarly grip on these public events, numerous theories have been developed in media studies and psychology, and old theories like rhetoric and hermeneutics have been revived, but there is still room for other theoretical perspectives.

Theatre studies can contribute to these necessary theoretical extensions by applying its own experiences to areas which do not belong to its ordinary objectives. Theatre has always implied an opening to the public sphere; I might mention Cicero's recommendation to the public orator to watch professional actors and Goethe's advice to actors to study clergymen in the church closely. There are more recent examples in the history of political "actors" such as Benito Mussolini, Adolf Hitler, Charles de Gaulle, and Ronald Reagan. But also in less obvious cases the theories of theatrical communication are illuminating and instructive when used outside theatrical situations. The point in this application of theatrical theory to nontheatrical events is that such a procedure can add substantially to the understanding of public life, in today's world as well as in history.

This brings me to my second point. The application of theatre theory — or at least of theatre as theoretical model — is of course not new. I need only mention Erving Goffman's attempts to use theatre as a metaphor for public and private life to make clear what kinds of applications I have in mind. I have described some of these "theatricalities" in chapter 3. In Goffman's terms, theatre symbolizes the interaction between different agents or actors whose motives are more or less openly presented on stage or hidden in the wings, who act out scenes, follow the script or improvise, cooperate with the director, and so forth. Goffman's idea of theatre was very traditional: a proscenium stage on which a family drama is enacted in a psychological style in a recognizable living room. Goffman's famous book *The Presentation of Self in Everyday Life* (1959) had so many followers using the theatrical metaphor that in his later work Goffman issued a warning against stretching this metaphor too far. He was certainly right, since he never pretended to develop a theoretical model out of this metaphor.

In various chapters I have tried to demonstrate that, for instance, role-playing is a far more complicated issue than "someone pretending to be someone else." In most social theorizing in which theatre is used as a metaphor, this step from private person to pretended figure is described as an act of will and perhaps also of skill. Did Hitler take lessons from an actor, train his skills in front of a mirror, and thus deceive the German masses? Such a description would be the result of a simplified use of theatre as a model for social actions. The interaction between performer and spectator, the interplay between exhibitory, encoded, and embodied actions, the significance of sensory communication, the mass audiences and their influence on the spectator — all these ideas could be useful theoretical tools to take a closer look at Hitler's interactions with his German audiences. Such an investigation would definitely not "reduce" or "elevate" Hitler's speeches to theatre, but it would point toward some communicative problems which go far beyond mere technical analyzes of rhetorical techniques.

There are, of course, many examples of the increasing interest in theatre studies as a reservoir of possible theoretical ideas which help us to understand today's and yesterday's world. I see this curiosity as a positive sign of self-consciousness and self-esteem within a discipline which finally has outgrown its initial preoccupation with its own existence. Instead of desperately developing its own methods and borrowing from neighboring theories, theatre studies has reached a stage of theoretical maturity and interdisciplinary significance.

# Notes

## 1. Approaching the Theatrical Event

1. Max Herrmann, *Die Entstehung der berufsmässigen Schauspielkunst im Altertum und in der Neuzeit*, p. 7 (my translation).

2. Eric Bentley, *The Life of Drama*, p. 150.

3. Marvin Carlson, *Theories of the Theatre*, p. 10.

4. Ibid., p. 10.

5. In this chapter I am only dealing with scholarly approaches to theatre, whereas aesthetic-normative debates on how theatre ought to be understood and classified are a different matter. Josette Féral makes a very clear distinction between analytical theory and theories of production, which seems necessary in the discourse on theatre theory, although the distinction might be difficult to maintain at times. See Josette Féral, "Towards a Theory of Fluid Groupings," *Theaterschrift* 5–6 (1994). Marvin Carlson does not reflect on this in *Theories of the Theater*; but ten years later, he discusses this item very extensively in his book *Performance*.

6. Max Herrmann, *Forschungen zur deutschen Theatergeschichte des Mittelalters und der Renaissance*, p. 7 (my translation).

7. Such an overview (including references to central works in this field) can be found in Jacqueline Martin and Willmar Sauter, *Understanding Theatre*, chap. 4

8. Erika Fischer-Lichte, *Semiotik des Theaters*, vol. 1, p. 202, note 24 (published in English as *The Semiotics of Theatre*).

9. Tadeusz Kowzan, "Le signe au théâtre: Introduction à la sémiologie de l'art du spectacle," *Diogène* 61 (1968). See also his *Littérature et spectacle*. In his recently published summary of theatre semiology, even Kowzan has included the spectator. See his *Sémiologie du théâtre*.

10. I readily admit that there are exceptions, such as Jean Marie Pradier, Andre Helbo, Patrice Pavis, Marco de Marinis, and Anne Ubersfeld.

11. I deliberately disregard the huge body of research on dramatic texts, both theoretical (such as those by Pfister, Elam, Styan, and others) and devoted to dramatists (such as Brecht, Shakespeare, etc.).

12. This quotation form Zagorsky I owe to Lars Kleberg, who found it in the Russian journal *Art of the Theatre*, where a survey by Meyerhold, registering audience response during performances in 1924, provoked fierce debate. See Willmar Sauter, "The Eye of the Theatre: The Audience Meets the Performance — Experience, Repertoire, Habits," in *Advances in Reception and Audience Research*, vol. 2.

13. Henri Schoenmakers, "The Spectator in the Leading Role," *Nordic Theatre Studies* (Special International Issue: New Directions in Theatre Research). The FIRT Congress in Stockholm in 1989 opened with a visit to *Don Giovanni* at the Royal Opera.

14. Hans-Georg Gadamer, *Wahrheit und Methode* (English translation: *Truth and Method*; 1979).

15. Martin and Sauter, *Understanding Theatre*, chaps. 6, 7, 11, and 16.

16. Quoted in "Theatre History vs. Theatre Today: Introductory Notes by the Editor," *Nordic Theatre Studies* (Special International Issue).

17. Erika Fischer-Lichte, *Kurze Geschichte des deutschen Theaters*, p. 7 (my translation).

18. See Guido Hiss, "Zur Aufführungsanalyze," in *Theaterwissenschaft Heute*, ed. Renate Möhrmann. See also Martin and Sauter, *Understanding Theatre*, especially chap. 10, "Theoretical Pluralism."

19. This question was raised in an interesting discussion, chaired by Erika Fischer-Lichte, during the Twelfth World Congress of the International Federation for Theatre Research (IFTR/FIRT) in Moscow in June 1994.

20. Martin and Sauter, *Understanding Theatre*, chap. 8, gives a more explicit account of the communication model (see the introduction, above).

21. Phenomenology's basic work is Edmund Husserl, "Ideen zu einer Phänomenologie und einer phänomenologischen Philosophie," in *Husserliana*, vol. 3. A preliminary study first appeared in his *Logische Untersuchungen* in 1900–1901. In the field of literature and art, see Roman Ingarden's *Das literarische Kunstwerk*. An essential contribution to the field is Dietrich Steinbeck's *Einleitung in die Theorie und Systematik der Theaterwissenschaft* (1970). My use of the term "level" derives from these phenomenological approaches (Steinbeck: "Schichten"), but could usually be replaced by synonymous terms such as "aspect," "mode," and at times even "means."

22. Martin and Sauter, *Understanding Theatre*, chap. 12.

23. "The Analysis of Acting — La voix d'or of Sarah Bernhardt," Unpublished paper given at the FIRT/IFTR Congress in Montreal, 1995.

## 2. Theatre or Performance or Untitled Event?

1. Worthen, "Disciplines of the Text/Sites of Performance," *TDR* 39/1 (1995): p. 13–28. Subsequent quotations are cited in the text.

2. Pierre Bourdieu, *Homo academicus*.

3. Milton Singer, *Traditional India*; Victor Turner, *The Anthropology of Performance*; Richard Schechner, *Performance Theory*.

4. Turner, *Anthropology of Performance*, p. 21.

5. Schechner, "A New Paradigm for 'Performance' in the Academy," *TDR* 36/4 (1992).

6. Warman, "Theatre Not Dead," *TDR* 39/2 (1995): 7–10.

7. Dolan, "Geographies of Learning," *Theatre Journal* 45/4 (1993).

8. Macgowan and Melnitz: *The Living Stage* (1955), p. 54. I am aware that this now historical book does not cover today's attitudes in the United States, but I see its significance from a historical perspective, not least in comparison with Herrmann.

9. Herrmann, *Forschungen zur deutschen Theatergeschichte*, p. 7 (cf. note 6 in chapter 1).

10. Richard Hornby, "Letter to the Editor," *TDR* 39/3 (1995): 11.

11. See chap. 10 for more about Theatre Talks.

12. Steinbeck, *Einleitung*.

13. Féral, "La théâtralité"; and Watson, "Naming the Frame," *New Theatre Quarterly* 13/50 (1997).

## 3. Reacting to Actions

1. Erika Fischer-Lichte, "Theatricality," *Theatre Research International (TRI)* 20/2 (1995).

2. Roland Barthes, *Essais critiques*, p. 41.

3. Féral, "La théâtralité."

4. Martin and Sauter, *Understanding Theatre*, p. 99.

5. Sarah Bernhardt, *The Art of the Theatre*, p. 42.

6. Watson, "Naming the Frame."

7. Gadamer, *Truth and Method.*

8. W. Sauter, "Who Is Who and What Is What? Introductory Notes," in *Advances in Reception and Audience Research*, vol. 2, pp. 5–16.

9. Nicola Frijda, *The Emotions.*

10. Schoenmakers, "Aesthetic Emotions and Aestheticised Emotions in Theatrical Situations," in *Advances in Reception and Audience Research*, vol. 3.

11. Josette Féral, "The Theatrical Event as Space," in "The Theatrical Event as Scholarly Paradigm."

12. Erland Josephson, *Rollen*, pp. 110f.

13. Kurt Johannesson, *Svensk retorik.*

14. Well described by Bernard Beckerman, *Theatrical Presentation.*

## 4. Theatrical Events Revisited

1. This paragraph is translated from a modern Swedish transcript, published in the catalogue *Med allranådigaste tillstånd — en utställning om teaterns framväxt i svensk landsort* (With most gracious permission — an exhibition of the evolution of theatre in the Swedish countryside), edited by Peter Gripewall (Eskilstuna: Konstmuseum, 1993), p. 36. On page 37 there is a color print of the Three Marys in the chruch of Fornåsa, mentioned earlier in the article.

2. *Nordic Theatre Studies*, 7 (1994), ed. Kacke Götrick. The articles I refer to here and in the following are Sveinn Einarsson, "How Old Is the Theatre in the Nordic Region?" and Terry Gunnell, "The Play of Skírnir." Cf. also Gunnell's unpublished dissertation, "The Concept of Ancient Scandinavian Drama: A Re-evaluation," University of Leeds, 1991.

3. Gustaf Ljunggren, *Svenska dramat*, p. 3. Ljunggren, the first professor of aesthetics at the University of Lund, mentions a number of countries and regions from which the news of indigenous rites has come to Sweden.

4. *Nordic Theatre Studies* 7: 17.

5. *The Past Is a Foreign Country* (Cambridge: Cambridge University Press, 1985).

6. I am particularly indebted to Tiina Rosenberg, who brought the aspect of playing culture to our attention during a discussion of the project "Theatre in Sweden — From the Middle Ages to Our Times." An early contribution to this topic, although not explicitly discussed here, is of course Joh. Huizinga's *Homo Ludens* (1938); the relationship between playing and theatre has recently been discussed by Wilfried Passow, for example in "Esperienze preverbali del bambino come base della creazione e comprensione dell teatro," in *Quindi* (Bologna, 1994).

7. Ljunggren, *Svenska dramat*, p. 9.

8. Hans-Georg Gadamer, *Wahrheit und Methode*. p. 101. In this essay, I use my own translation (Gadamer's emphasis).

9. Ibid., p. 103.

10. Ibid.

11. Ibid., p. 104.

12. Ibid., pp. 104f.

13. A theoretical discussion of this model can be found in "New Beginnings." above.

14. Gadamer, *Wahrheit und Methode*, p. 289 (Gadamer's emphasis).

15. Gianni Vattimo, *The Adventures of Difference*, p. 24.

## 5. Culture as Human Encounter

1. Milton Singer, *Traditional India*.

2. Kazimierz Kowalewicz, "Small Steps towards the Spectator," in *Advances in Reception and Audience Research*, vol. 2.

3. Pierre Bourdieu, *La distinction*.

4. H. Van Maanen and S. E. Wilmer (eds.), *Theatre Worlds in Motion*.

5. W. Sauter, *Braaavo!*; and Kai Lahtinen, *Vem tillhör teatern?*

## 6. Sarah Bernhardt in Phenomenological Perspective

1. The English translations of most quotations are from the biographies by Cornelia Otis Skinner and by Arthur Gold and Robert Fizdale. References in the text are cited as Otis Skinner or Gold.

2. Sarah Bernhardt, *The Art of the Theatre*. The following quotations refer to this English edition.

3. Claudia Balk, *Theatergöttinnen*, p. 237.

4. Bert O. States, *Great Reckonings in Little Rooms*.

## 8. Reflections on *Miss Julie*, 1992

1. Jacqueline Martin, "A Midsummer Night's Ritual: The Director's Concept," *NTS* 18, supplementary issue (1993): 7–9.

2. Program brochure to *Miss Julie* by Staffan Valdemar Holm (1992); my translation.

## 9. Museum-Stage

1. Janna Olzon, "60-talets Happenings."

2. See Kathryn Boyer, "Political Promotion and Institutional Patronage." Cf. also Serge Guilbaut, *How New York Stole the Idea of Modern Art*.

3. Basic information on these events can be found in Olle Granath (ed.), *Moderna Museet 1958–1983*.

4. See Goldberg, *Performance Art*.

5. Féral, "The Theatrical Event as Space."

## 10. Theatre Talks

1. Willmar Sauter, *Publiken på Drottningholm.*
2. Sauter, "Who Is Who and What Is What?"
3. Sauter, "Das Publikum — Verständnis und Erlebnis von Theateraufführungen," in *Advances in Reception and Audience Research*, vol. 1.
4. Sauter, *Braaavo!*
5. Willmar Sauter, "La Venexiana — A Short Report on the Audience."
6. In addition to the publications mentioned in the notes above, I also refer to Sauter, Isaksson, and Jansson, *Teaterögon.*
7. Willmar Sauter and Curt Isaksson, *Vem går på teater?*

## 11. Fiction, Mainly Fiction

1. Karin Andersson's report for the university in Lund has not been published.
2. Sauter, Isaksson, and Jansson, *Teaterögon.*
3. "Ett ensamt öra." An Van Kiel.
4. Gunborg Carlsson, *Teater för barn.*
5. Sauter, Isaksson, and Jansson, *Teaterögon*, p. 493, table 23 h.
6. Margareta Clemensson, "Stockholms kommunala skolteaterverksamhet."
7. Henri Schoenmakers, "The Pleasure of Sorrow," in *"Performance Theory"*: Advances in Reception and Audience Research 1, ed. H. Schoenmakers (Utrecht, 1986).

## 12. Strindberg's Words versus the Actor's Actions

1. The Danish actor Viggo Schiwe appeared as Jean opposite Strindberg's first wife, Siri von Essen, who played Julie when *Miss Julie* premiered in a private performance at the Copenhagen University Student Union, in March 1889. Strindberg flirted with the idea that Siri had an affair with Schiwe off stage as well as on. His third wife, Harriet Bosse, later married the actor Gunnar Wingård, after she had appeared with him in the premiere of Strindberg's play *The Crown Bride* at the Svenska Teatern in Helsinki, in April 1906.
2. The translations are from Walter Johnson's edition of *Open Letters to the Intimate Theatre.* Page references follow this edition.
3. Strindberg, *Brev* (Letters), vol. 16, p. 783.
4. Gunnar Ollén, *Strindbergs dramatik*, p. 342.
5. *Svenska Dagbladet*, 18 April 1908.
6. *Svenska Dagbladet*, 11 April 1909.
7. *Stockholms Dagblad*, 31 October 1908.
8. *Svenska Dagbladet*, 31 October 1908.
9. Nils Personne is quoted in Inga Lewenhaupt, *Signe Hebbe*, p. 236.
10. These two photographs were published in *TheaterAvantgarde*, ed. Erika Fischer-Lichte, as figs. 56 and 57. They accompany my essay in this book, called "Eine verschrumpfte Avantgarde — Das Intima Teaterns des August Strindberg," pp. 291–323.

## 13. How Long Is a Jewish Nose on Stage?

1. *Göteborgs Tidning*, 22 April 1936.
2. *Göteborgs Posten*, 22 April 1936.
3. *Ny Tidningen*, 2 November 1936.
4. *Morgontidningen*, 12 February 1938.
5. *Svenska Dagbladet*, 11 February 1938.
6. My terminology. The quotation marks are supposed to indicate the deliberate choice of words.
7. *Socialdemokraten*, 2 November 1940.
8. *Svenska Dagbladet*, 11 February 1938.
9. Sauter, *Theater als Widerstand*.

## 14. Text, Performance, Event, 1611

1. The material concerning Messenius' *Disa* has been presented in my introduction to the latest edition of the play in 1989. All conclusions are based on the sources registered there, but these are entirely in Swedish. Readers of the Swedish language are therefore referred to Messenius, *Disa*.
2. John Adams' book is entitled *The Globe Playhouse*, and C. Walter Hodges' title is *The Globe Restored*.

## 15. Beyond the Director's Images

1. Claes Wahlin in *Aftonbladet*, 13 November 1994.
2. Katarina Thorell, "En alkemisk dröm" (An alchemical dream), p. 35.
3. "Ett drömspel" (program notes of Kungl. Dramatiska Teatern, 1994), p. 2.
4. Hans Ingvar Hansson in *Svenska Dagbladet*, 14 November 1994. The actor he is refering to is Björn Granath — cf. chap. 7 on *Mistero Buffo*.
5. Ulrika Milles in *Expressen*, 13 November 1994.
6. Cf. chap. 10.
7. *Teatertidningen* 75 (1995): 11.
8. Ibid., p. 12.
9. Thorell, "En alkemisk dröm," p. 35.
10. Ibid., p. 2.
11. See Curt Isaksson, *Pressen på teater: Teaterkritik i Stockholms dagspress*.
12. This is probably more "wishful thinking" than reality. Most performance analyses are still written about the productions of major directors like Lepage, Wilson, Stein, Brook, and Mnouchkine.

# Bibliography

*NTS Nordic Theatre Studies*
*TDR The Drama Review*
*TRI Theatre Research International*

Adams, John C. *The Globe Playhouse: Its Design and Equipment.* 2nd ed. Cambridge, Mass: Harvard University Press, 1961 (1942).

Adorno, Theordor W. *Ästhetische Theorie.* Gesammelte Schriften 17. Frankfurt/M: Suhrkamp, 1970.

Aston, Elaine. *Sarah Bernhardt: A French Actress on the English Stage.* Oxford: Berg, 1989.

Bakhtin, Mikhail. *Rabelais och skrattets historia: Francois Rabelais' verk och den folkliga kulturen under medeltiden och renässansen.* Göteborg: Anthropos, 1986 (Russian original 1965).

Balk, Claudia. *Theatergöttinnen. Inszenierte Weiblichkeit: Clara Ziegler — Sarah Bernhardt — Eleonora Duse.* Berlin: Gesellschaft für Theatergeschichte, 1994.

Barthes, Roland. *Essais critiques.* Paris: Editions du Seuil, 1964.

Beckerman, Bernard. *Theatrical Presentation: Performer, Audience and Act.* New York and London: Routledge, 1990.

Bentley, Eric. *The Life of Drama.* London: Methuen & Co, 1966.

Bernhardt, Sarah. *The Art of the Theatre.* Trans. by H. J. Stenning (1924). New York and London: Benjamin Blom, 1969.

Bourdieu, Pierre. *La distinction: Critique sociale du jugement.* Paris: Editions de Minuit, 1979.

———. *Homo academicus.* Paris: Editions de Minuit, 1984.

Boyer, Kathryn. "Political Promotion and Institutional Patronage: How New York Displaced Paris as the Centre for Contemporary Art, ca. 1955–1968." Dissertation, University of Kansas, 1996.

Brecht, Stefan. *The Theatre of Visions: Robert Wilson.* Frankfurt/M: Suhrkamp, 1979.

Butler, Judith. *Bodies That Matter: On the Discursive Limits of Sex.* London and New York: Routledge, 1993.

Carlson, Marvin. *Performance: A Critical Introduction.* London: Routledge, 1996.

———. *Theories of the Theatre: A Historical and Critical Survey from the Greeks to the Present.* Ithaca and London: Cornell University Press, 1984 (2nd ed. 1993).

Carlsson, Gunborg. *Teater för barn: Tre åldersgruppers upplevelser av professionell teater* (Theatre for children). Malmö: Gleerups, 1984.

Case, Sue-Ellen, Philip Brett, and Susan L. Foster (eds.). *Cruising the Performative: Interventions into the Representation of Ethnicity, Nationality, and Sexuality.* Bloomington: Indiana University Press, 1995.

Cixous, Hélène. "The Laugh of the Medusa," In *New French Feminisms,* ed. E. Marks and I. de Courtivron. New York: Schocken, 1984.

Clemensson, Margareta. "Stockholms kommunala skolteaterverksamhet" (Municipal school theatre in Stockholm). Unpublished. Stockholm University, 1985.

Derrida, Jacques. *Writing and Difference.* London: Routledge & Kegan Paul, 1978.

Diamond, Elin. *Unmaking Mimesis: Essays on Feminism and Theatre*. London and New York: Routledge, 1997.

Dolan, Jill. "Geographies of Learning: Theatre Studies, Performance, and the Performative." *Theatre Journal* 45/4 (1993).

———. "Responses to W. B. Worthen's 'Disciplines of the Text/Sites of Performance.'" *TDR* 39/1 (1995).

Einarsson, Sveinn. "How Old Is the Theatre in the Nordic Region?" *NTS* 7 (1994).

Elam, Keir. *The Semiotics of Theatre and Drama*. London and New York: Methuen, 1980.

Esslin, Martin. *The Field of Drama: How the Signs of Drama Create Meaning on Stage and Screen*. London: Methuen Drama, 1987.

Febvre, Michèle. *Danse contemporaine et théâtralité*. Paris: Editions Chiron, 1995.

Féral, Josette. *Rencontres avec Ariane Mnouchkine: Dresser un monument à l'éphémère*. Montreal: XYZ, 1995.

———. "La théâtralité: Recherche sur la spécificité du language théâtral." *Poétique* 75 (1988).

———. "The Theatrical Event as Space: La Tour (The Tower) by Anne Marie Provencher." In "The Theatrical Event as Scholarly Paradigm." International Colloquium of Theatre Studies, 1996, Stockholm. Unpublished.

———. "Towards a Theory of Fluid Groupings." *Theaterschrift* 5–6 (1994).

Fischer-Lichte, Erika. *Die Entdeckung des Zuschauers: Paradigmenwechsel auf dem Theater des 20. Jahrhunderts*. Tübingen and Basel: A. Francke Verlag, 1997.

———. *Kurze Geschichte des deutschen Theaters*. Tübingen and Basel: A. Francke Verlag, 1993.

———. "Performance, Art and Ritual: Bodies in Performance." *TRI* 22/1 (1997 Supplement).

———. *Semiotik des Theaters*, vols. 1–3. Tübingen: Narr, 1983. Published in English: *The Semiotics of Theatre*. Bloomington: Indiana University Press, 1992.

——— (ed.). *Theater Avantgarde: Wahrnehmung — Körper — Sprache*. Tübingen and Basel: A. Francke Verlag, 1995.

———. "Theatricality: A Key Concept in Theatre and Cultural Studies." *TRI*, 20/2 (1995).

Fitzpatrick, Tim (ed.). *Altro Polo. Performance: From Product to Process*. Sydney: Frederick May Foundation for Italian Studies, 1989.

Foucault, Michel. *The History of Sexuality*. New York: Vintage, 1980.

Frijda, Nicola. *The Emotions: Studies in Emotions and Social Interaction*. Cambridge: Cambridge University Press, 1986.

Gadamer, Hans-Georg. *Wahrheit und Methode: Grundzüge einer philosophischen Hermeneutik*. Tübingen: J. C. B. Mohr (Paul Siebeck), 1960. English translation: *Truth and Method*. London: Sheed and Ward, 1979.

Goffman, Erving. *Frame Analysis: An Essay on the Organisation of Experience*. Cambridge, Mass.: Harvard University Press, 1974.

———. *The Presentation of Self in Everyday Life*. Harmondsworth: Penguin, 1971 (1959).

Gold, Arthur, and Robert Fizdale. *Divine Sarah: A Life of Sarah Bernhardt*. New York: Vintage Books, 1992.

Goldberg, RoseLee. *Performance Art: From Futurism to the Present*. London: Thames & Hudson, 1988.

Granath, Olle (ed.). *Moderna Museet 1958–1983.* Stockholm: Moderna Museet, 1983.

Guilbaut, Serge. *How New York Stole the Idea of Modern Art: Abstract Expressionism, Freedom and the Cold War.* Chicago: University of Chicago Press, 1983.

Gunnell, Terry. "The Play of Skírnir," *NTS* 7 (1994).

Habermas, Jürgen. *Theorie des kommunikativen Handelns.* Vols. 1–2, Frankfurt/M: Suhrkamp,1981.

Harbage, Alfred. *Shakespeare's Audience.* New York and London: Columbia University Press, 1941.

Helbo, André, et al. (eds). *Théâtre: Modes d'approche.* Brussels: Editions Labor, 1987.

Herrmann, Max. *Die Entstehung der berufsmässigen Schauspielkunst im Altertum und in der Neuzeit.* Ed. Ruth Mövius. Berlin: Henschel, 1962.

———. *Forschungen zur deutschen Theatergeschichte des Mittalters und der Renaissance.* Berlin: Weichmann, 1914.

Herzel, Roger W. "Molière's Audience: New Light from the Registre d'Hubert 1672–1673." In *Advances in Reception and Audience Research*, vol. 3. Amsterdam: ECRAR Publications, 1992.

Hiss, Guido. "Zur Aufführungsanalyse." In *Theaterwissenschaft heute: Eine Einführung,* Renate Möhrmann. ed. Berlin: Reiner, 1990.

Hodges, C. Walter. *The Globe Restored: A Study of the Elizabethan Theatre.* 2nd ed. London: Oxford University Press, 1968 (Ernest Benn Ltd, 1953).

Hornby, Richard. "Letter to the Editor." *TDR* 39/3 (1995).

Huizinga, Johannes. *Homo Ludens.* The Hague: Vanderbelt, 1938.

Husserl, Edmund. "Ideen zu einer Phänomenologie und einer phänomenologischen Philosophie." In *Husserliana*, vol. 3. The Hague: Martinus Nijhoff, 1950.

Ingarden, Roman. *Das literarische Kunstwerk.* Tübingen: Niemeyer 1931. English translation: *The Literary Work of Art.* Evanston, Ill., 1973.

Isaksson, Curt. *Pressen på teater: Teaterkritik i Stockholms dagspress.* (The press on theatre). Theatron-serien, Stockholm: STUTS, 1987.

Iser, Wolfgang. *Der implizierte Leser.* Munich: Hanser, 1972. English translation: *The Act of Reading: A Theory of Aesthetic Response.* Baltimore: Johns Hopkins University Press, 1978.

Jauss, Hans Robert. *Ästhetische Erfahrung und literarische Hermeneutik.* Frankfurt/M: Suhrkamp, 1982. English translation: *Toward an Aesthetic of Reception.* Minneapolis: University of Minnesota Press, 1982.

———. *Literaturgeschichte als Provokation.* Frankfurt/M: Suhrkamp, 1970.

Johannesson, Kurt. *Svensk retorik från Stockholms blodbad till Almedalen* (Swedish rhetoric). Stockholm: Norstedts, 1983.

Johansson, Ola. "Passerande helheter — tre gästföreställningar i Stockholm 1994–95" (Completeness passing by — three guest performances). *Teatertidningen* 75 (1995).

Josephson, Erland. *Rollen* (The role). Stockholm: Brombergs, 1991.

Kindermann, Heinz. *Theaterpublikum der Antike.* Salzburg: Otto Müller Verlag, 1979.

———. *Theaterpublikum des Mittelalters.* Salzburg: Otto Müller Verlag, 1979.

Kirshenblatt-Gimblett, Barbara. *Destination Culture: Tourism, Museums, and Heritage.* Berkeley, Los Angeles, and London: University of California Press, 1998.

Kleberg, Lars. *Teatern som handling: Sovjetisk avantgarde-estetik 1917–1927* (Theatre as action: Soviet avant-garde aesthetics 1917–1927). Stockholm: Norstedts, 1980.

Kowalewicz, Kazimierz. "Small Steps towards the Spectator." In *Advances in Reception and Audience Research*, vol. 2, ed. Willmar Sauter. Utrecht: ECRAR Publications, 1988.

Kowzan, Tadeusz. *Littérature et spectacle*. The Hague and Paris: Monton, 1975.

———. *Sémiologie du théâtre*. Tours: Nathan, 1992.

———. "Le signe au théâtre: Introduction à la sémiologie de l'art du spectacle." *Diogène* 61 (1968).

Kristeva, Julia. *Powers of Horror: An Essay on Abjection*. New York: Columbia University Press, 1982.

Lacan, Jacques. *Ecrits: A Selection*. Trans. Alan Sheridan. New York: Norton, 1977.

———. *The Four Fundamental Concepts of Psycho-analysis*. New York: Norton, 1978.

Lahtinen, Kai. *Vem tillhör teatern? Åbo teatrars publik och dess smakuppfattningar 1990–1994: En historisk och kulturpolitisk exkurs* (To whom does the theatre belong? Theatre audiences and their taste in Turku City 1990–1994: A historical and cultural excursus in politics). Unpublished dissertation, Turku University, 1996.

Lehmann, Hans-Thies. "Theatralität." In *Theaterlexikon: Begriffe und Epochen, Bühnen und Ensembles*, ed. M. Brauneck and G. Schneilin. Reinbeck bei Hamburg: Rowohlts Enzyklopädie, 1988.

Lewenhaupt, Inga. *Signe Hebbe, skådespelerska, operasångerska, pedagog* (Signe Hebbe, acresss, opera singer, teacher). Theatron-serien, Stockholm: STUTS, 1988.

Ljunggren, Gustaf. *Svenska dramat intill slutet af sjuttonde århundradet*. (Swedish drama to the end of the seventeenth century). Lund and Copenhagen: Gleerups, 1864.

Lough, John. *Seventeenth-Century French Drama: The Background*. Oxford: Clarendon Press, 1979.

Macgowan, Kenneth, and William Melnitz. *The Living Stage: A History of World Theatre*. Englewood Cliffs, N.J.: Prentice-Hall, 1955.

Martin, Jacqueline. "A Midsummer Night's Ritual: The Director's Concept." *TRI* 18, supplementary issue (1993).

Martin, Jacqueline, and Willmar Sauter. *Understanding Theatre: Performance Analysis in Theory and Practice*. Stockholm: Acta Universitatis Stockholmiensis, Almqvist & Wiksell International, 1995.

Messenius, Johannes. *Disa*. Introduction and commentary by Willmar Sauter. Stockholm: STUTS, 1989.

Ollén, Gunnar. *Strindbergs dramatik*. Stockholm: Sveriges Radios förlag, 1948 (4th ed. 1982).

Olzon, Janna. "60-talets Happenings." Unpublished seminar essay. Stockholm University, 1991.

Otis Skinner, Cornelia. *Madame Sarah*. New York: Paragon House Publishers, 1988.

Pavis, Patrice. *Dictionaire du théâtre: Termes et concepts de l'analyze théâtrale*. Paris: Editions Sociales, 1980.

Pfister, Manfred. *The Theory and Analysis of Drama*. Cambridge: Cambridge University Press, 1988.

Postlewait, Thomas. "A Concept of 'Period Style' in Cultural History: A Problem in Historisation." *NTS*, Special International Issue: New Directions in Theatre Research. Proceedings of the Eleventh World Congress of the FIRT/IFTR (1990).

———. "Historiography and the Theatrical Event: A Primer with Twelve Cruxes." *Theatre Journal* 43 (1991).

Pradier, Jean-Marie. "Ethnoscénologie: La profondeur des émergences." In *La scène et la terre: Questions d'ethnoscénologie,* ed. C. Khaznadar and J. Duvignaud. Arles: Actes Sud, 1996.

Ricoeur, Paul. *De l'interprétation: Essai sur Freud.* Paris: Editions du Seuil, 1977.

Sauter, Willmar. *Braaavo! En studie över publiken på Operan i Stockholm.* (A study of the audience of the Royal Opera in Stockholm). Stockholm: Kungliga Teatern, 1987 (English and German summaries).

———. "The Eye of the Theatre: The Audience Meets the Performance — Experience, Repertoire, Habits." In *Advances in Reception and Audience Research,* vol. 2, ed. Willmar Sauter. Utrecht: ECRAR Publications, 1988.

———. *Publiken på Drottningholm: Rapport från publikundersökningen sommaren 1980* (The audience at the Drottningholm Court Theatre). Teatervetenskapliga småskrifter 13, Stockholm: STUTS, 1981.

———. "Das Publikum — Verständnis und Erlebnis von Theateraufführungen: Projektbericht über eine Erhebung anhand von Studentenaufsätzen zu 7 Aufführungen." In *Advances in Reception and Audience Research,* vol. 1, ed. Henri Schoenmakers. Utrecht: ICRAR Publications, 1986.

———. *Theater als Widerstand: Wirkung und Wirkungsweise eines politischen Theaters, Juden und Judendarstellung auf der schwedischen Bühne 1936–1941.* Stockholm: Akademilitteratur, 1979.

———. "Theatre History vs. Theatre Today: Introductory Notes by the Editor." *NTS,* Special International Issue: New Directions in Theatre Research. Proceedings of the Eleventh World Congress of the FIRT/IFTR (1990).

———. "La Venexiana — A Short Report on the Audience." (UCLA) Arbetsrapport no. 16 of the project "Teaterpubliken." Unpublished. 1985.

———. "Who Is Who and What Is What? Introductory Notes." In *Advances in Reception and Audience Research,* vol. 2. ed. Willmar Sauter. Utrecht: ICRAR Publications, 1988.

Sauter, Willmar, and Curt Isaksson. *Vem går på teater? En inventering av publikundersökningar 1924–1981.* (Who visits the theatre? An inventory), Teatervetenskapliga småskrifter 14, Stockholm: STUTS, 1982.

Sauter, Willmar, Curt Isaksson, and Lisbeth Jansson. *Teaterögon: Publiken möter föreställningen — upplevelse, utbud, vanor* (The eye of the theatre: The audience meets the performance — experience, repertoire, habits). Stockholmsmonografier 68, Stockholm: Liber förlag, 1986.

Schechner, Richard. "A New Paradigm for 'Performance' in the Academy." *TDR* 36/4 (1992).

Schechner, Richard. *Performance Theory.* Rev. and expanded ed. New York and London: Routledge, 1988.

Schoenmakers, Henri. "Aesthetic Emotions and Aestheticised Emotions in Theatrical Situations." In *Advances in Reception and Audience Research,* vol. 3. Amsterdam: ICRAR Publications, 1992.

———. "The Spectator in the Leading Role." *NTS,* Special International Issue: New Directions in Theatre Research. Proceedings of the Eleventh World Congress of the FIRT/IFTR (1990).

Singer, Milton. *Traditional India: Structure and Change.* Philadelphia: American Folklore Society, 1959.

———. *When a Great Tradition Modernizes: An Anthropological Approach to Indian Civilization.* New York: Praeger, 1972.

Somi, Leone di. "Four Dialogues on the Theatre." In *The Development of the Theatre*, by A. Nicoll. London: Harper Co., 1927 (4th ed. 1958).

States, Bert O. *Great Reckonings in Little Rooms: On the Phenomenology of Theatre.* Berkeley, Los Angeles, and London: University of California Press, 1987.

Steinbeck, Dietrich. *Einleitung in die Theorie und Systematik der Theaterwissenschaft.* Berlin: De Gruyter, 1970.

Strindberg, August. *Brev* (Letters). Ed. Björn Meidal. Vol. 16. Stockholm: Bonniers, 1989.

———. *Open Letters to the Intimate Theatre.* Trans. and ed. Walter Johnson. Seattle: University of Washington Press, 1968.

Styan, J. L. *Drama, Stage and Audience.* Cambridge: Cambridge University Press, 1975.

Taranow, Gerda. *Sarah Bernhardt: The Art within the Legend.* Princeton, N.J.: Princeton University Press, 1972.

Thorell, Katarina. "En alkemisk dröm: Alkemisk analys av Robert Lepages uppsättning av Ett Drömspel på Dramaten 1994–95" (An alchemical dream: Alchemical analysis of Robert Lepage's production of *A Dream Play* at Dramaten, 1994–95). Master's thesis, Stockholm University, 1996.

Turner, Victor. *The Anthropology of Performance.* New York: PAJ Publications, 1987.

———. *From Ritual to Theatre: The Human Seriousness of Play.* New York: PAJ Publications, 1982.

Ubersfeld, Anne. *L'école du spectateur.* Lire le théâtre 2. Paris: Editions sociales, 1981.

Van Kiel, An. "Ett ensamt öra: En studie i Marionetteaterns föreställning och dess publik" (One lonely ear: A study of the Marionette Theatre's performance and its audience). Unpublished. Stockholm University, 1990.

Van Maanen, H., and S. E. Wilmer. (eds.). *Theatre Worlds in Motion: Structures, Politics and Developments in the Countries of Western Europe.* Amsterdam and Atlanta: Rodopi, 1998.

Vattimo, Gianni. *The Adventures of Difference: Philosophy after Nietzsche and Heidegger.* Baltimore: Johns Hopkins University Press, 1980.

Warman, Jonathan. "Theatre Not Dead," *TDR* 39/2 (1995).

Watson, Ian. "Naming the Frame: The Role of the Pre-interpretative in Theatrical Reception," *New Theatre Quarterly.* 13/50 (1997): 161–170.

Wittgenstein, Ludwig. *Philosophische Untersuchungen.* London: Blackwell, 1953. (German and English ed.).

Worthen, William B. "Disciplines of the Text/Sites of Performance." *TDR* 39/1 (1995).

# Index